CUSTOMERS
.COM

CUSTOMERS
.COM

How to Create a
Profitable Business
Strategy for the
Internet and Beyond

PATRICIA B. SEYBOLD

with Ronni T. Marshak

RANDOM HOUSE

BUSINESS BOOKS

First published in the United States by Times Business,
Random House, New York

Simultaneously published in the UK by Random House Business Books,
Random House, 20 Vauxhall Bridge Road, London SW1V 2SA

Third Impression 1999

Random House Australia (Pty) Limited
20 Alfred Street, Milsons Point, Sydney,
New South Wales 2061, Australia

Random House New Zealand Limited
18 Poland Road, Glenfield
Auckland 10, New Zealand

Random House South Africa (Pty) Limited
Endulini, 5a Jubilee Road, Parktown 2193, South Africa

Random House UK Limited Reg. No. 954009

Papers used by Random House UK Limited are natural, recyclable
products made from wood grown in sustainable forests. The
manufacturing processes conform to the environmental
regulations of the country of origin

ISBN 0 7126 8071 3

Companies, institutions and other organizations wishing to make
bulk purchases of any business books published by Random House
should contact their local bookseller or Random House direct:

Special Sales Director
Random House, 20 Vauxhall Bridge Road, London SW1V 2SA
Tel 0171 840 8470   Fax 0171 828 6681

www.randomhouse.co.uk
businessbooks@randomhouse.co.uk

Printed and bound in Great Britain by Redwood Books, Trowbridge, Wiltshire

My father, John W. Seybold, the wisest man I know

My son, Jesse James Breuer, the bravest man I know

My husband, Thomas G. Hagan, the smartest man I know

ACKNOWLEDGMENTS

This book could never have been written without the major contributions of several people and the unstinting support of my entire company, the Patricia Seybold Group.

Special thanks go to:

- *Ronni Marshak, for her many contributions—most particularly the Babson College case study—her support, her encouragement, and her ability to lighten up what would otherwise have been a very dull read indeed!*

- *Michael Goulde, for writing and researching most of the Dell OnLine case study.*

- *Geoffrey Bock, for writing and researching most of The Wall Street Journal Interactive Edition case study.*

- *Sue Aldrich, for contributing most of the chapter on fostering customer loyalty.*

- *Pamela Berry and Jeffrey Perfect, my assistants, for helping me connect with all the people I had to interview over and over again!*

- *And thanks, most of all, to the heroes and heroines described in this book—the Customers.com visionaries—who have grasped the import of what today's electronic business technologies now make possible and have used those technologies to make it easy for their customers to do business with them!*

CONTENTS

Setting the Stage

HERE'S A SIMPLE TEST: Have you ever used an automated teller machine? Of course you have. Have you ever ordered theater or movie tickets using an automated phone system? Have you ever signed your name on a handheld computer to accept delivery of a package? Have you ever received stock quotes or news updates on your pager or other handheld device? Do you ever receive electronic mail from your customers? Do you receive e-mails or faxes from your suppliers with quotes, product information, delivery status updates? Have you ever gone onto the World Wide Web to get more information about a type of product you're interested in buying? Have you ever used a Web site to get technical support information to solve a problem you're having with a product that isn't working quite right? Have you ever purchased anything over the Internet? Does your company's Web site let customers order products, check delivery status, get a list of all the products they've ordered from you in the past, or correct their mailing address? If you answered "yes" to any of these questions, then you have engaged in electronic commerce.

Would you like to know how *your organization* can benefit the most from electronic commerce? Would you like to know how your *customers* can benefit from your electronic business initiatives? That's what this book is about. This book summarizes the best practices for electronic commerce and electronic business today on the Internet and beyond. Within these pages you'll walk behind the scenes at more than a dozen pioneering companies—companies that have committed themselves to doing what it takes to make it easier for their customers to do business with them. These companies are reaping the rewards of their efforts today and will continue to do so in the future.

What will happen to your company if you can create a successful e-business strategy? First and foremost, you'll get to stay in business—no mean feat in today's fast-paced global information economy! Second, you'll reap rewards. You'll be able to:

- Increase customer loyalty
- Increase profitability
- Decrease time-to-market for new products

- Reach your customers in the most cost-effective way with targeted offers
- Reduce your costs per transaction substantially
- Reduce your customer service costs dramatically
- Reduce customer service time appreciably

Going Beyond the Web

ONE OF THE most significant advances in technology today is the combination of the Internet and the World Wide Web. The ubiquitous nature of the Internet, with its inexpensive Web browser clients and universal access, makes it an excellent platform for communicating more effectively with customers. New companies are springing up whose only presence—at least to customers—is via the Web. These "virtual" companies, such as Amazon.com, Security First Network Bank, and Virtual Vineyards, have had the luxury of designing their businesses from scratch, using the latest Internet technology.

But they have also faced new challenges. They've had to figure out how to lure customers and how to keep them without relying on face-to-face interactions. Many people think of the Internet as impersonal. Yet these virtual companies have created very close bonds with their customers without ever meeting them or, in many cases, talking with them.

How do these on-line businesses create fanatical customer loyalty? They carefully streamline every aspect of the customer's interaction with them. They ensure that nothing ever falls into a "black hole." And they reassure the customer at every step of the way. Before the customer has time to wonder whether something's been taken care of properly, he receives notification that it has.

Of course, we don't all have the luxury of starting from scratch. Most of us have brick-and-mortar companies with people, and sales forces, and distributors, and call centers. Yet we're also trying to leverage the Web to make it easier for prospects to find out about our companies and products and easier for customers to transact business with us electronically, twenty-four hours a day, seven days a week.

One of the things I learned in doing the research for this book is that you cannot do business on the Internet in a vacuum. Instead, Internet commerce needs to be part of a broader electronic business strategy—a strategy that embraces all the ways that you let your customers do business with you electronically: by Touch-Tone phone, by fax, by e-mail, by kiosk, via handhelds, and via the Web. If you don't coordinate your Web initiatives with the rest of the ways you do business electronically, you'll probably waste a lot of time and money! For most companies, their Web presence is a logical extension of their existing business model. It's a new distribution channel and a new marketing medium. Ideally, Internet commerce builds on efforts you're already making in other areas of your business, initiatives such as customer loyalty programs, one-stop shopping, and customized manufacturing.

Like the companies profiled in these pages, you'll probably discover that, in order to really use the Internet and the Web effectively, you're going to need to redesign a number of fundamental, customer-impacting business processes. Then you'll want those streamlined processes to flow through your preexisting business systems. You'll also need to consolidate all the disparate pieces of customer-related information you have floating around in your different departments and applications. You'll want to develop comprehensive customer profiles. As you embark on these rather profound initiatives, you'll realize that you can leverage the investments you're making by not limiting their scope to the Web but rather by using the same streamlined processes and information to make it easier for customers to do business with you by telephone, fax, e-mail, or face-to-face. The impetus to make these fundamental changes may arise from your desire to do business over the Internet. But, if you do it right, the changes you'll make will pay off every time you touch the customer in any way.

It's the Customer, Stupid!

WHAT'S THE SECRET of a successful e-business initiative? Why have many Internet-based businesses crashed and burned? Who's really making or saving money on the Internet, and what have they done differently from those who have failed? I stumbled upon the answers to these questions in 1995, when I began researching the best practices in electronic commerce. Once I saw the simple truth that was staring me in the face, I expanded my research. I began to look beyond the Internet and the Web. I found that there were a number of complementary customer-facing technology initiatives—using telephones, kiosks, smart cards, and even "smart cars"—that shared the same properties I had discovered among the successful Internet players.

What's the winning formula? You guessed it! It starts by focusing on your existing customers, figuring out what they want and need and how you can make life easier for them. Then you can expand your efforts to reel in prospective customers. Once you lure prospects to you, closing the sale and cementing a profitable, long-term relationship becomes a snap, because you've already made it easy for customers to do business with you!

Sound easy? Well, it's not! The idea of focusing on making it easy for customers to do business with you is simple. But implementing this vision is difficult. As you'll see from skimming the sixteen case studies that follow, each of these organizations has been hard at work for more than twenty-four months. This work requires a visionary leader, typically someone with a marketing bent and background. It requires a lot of perseverance. It requires a good deal of investment. It requires a unique partnership between business pragmatists and information technology visionaries. And it requires buy-in by and participation of the entire organization.

Preparing the Ground for Electronic Business

I'M A GARDENER. I love to add mulch and compost to the soil each spring and fall and see the results pay off in the lush blooms I enjoy all summer at my home in Maine. Preparing your organization for e-business takes the same care and premeditation. Yes, you can just get started: plant a few bulbs, throw in some seeds. But if you want to really enjoy the rewards, you'll need to put in the necessary time, effort, and money. In the first few chapters, I'll lay out a blueprint for you: the five strategic steps you'll want to take so that your e-business initiatives will really blossom.

Looking Behind the Scenes at Sixteen Companies

WHAT DO THE sixteen organizations profiled in these pages have in common? They've all spent the last two to four years investing in initiatives that let their customers do business with them electronically—quickly, easily, and cost-effectively. What can you learn from walking with me behind the scenes at each of these organizations?

- You'll learn how they've shifted their corporate cultures from product-centric to customer-centric.
- You'll learn how they've moved from mass marketing to targeting markets of one.
- You'll learn how they've redesigned their core business processes from the outside in, starting from the customer's perspective.

- You'll learn who led the charge, what organizational challenges they overcame, and how they did it.
- You'll learn what information technology infrastructures they used and how they evolved that infrastructure over time.
- You'll learn what paybacks they've seen and why they're so bullish about their electronic business initiatives.

In researching this book, I've had the good fortune to work with and interview scores of visionary business people. Each of them told me a fascinating story—a story about how they thought about the issues confronting their business, what they understood about what their customers wanted and needed, and what they had done to respond to those customers' needs, both spoken and unspoken.

As you'll soon see, all of the organizations described in this book have made innovative use of today's information technology. Yet their stories don't begin and end with technology. Equally important were the business process changes and organizational changes they implemented to make it easy for their customers to do business with them.

Business Executives and Technology Planners Need to Work Together

THERE'S A NEW breed of executive in ascendancy in today's organizations: the technology-literate executive. These are the people I talk with every day. They're not afraid of technology. Nor are they enamored by it. They're not early adopters of hot new gadgets. They're pragmatists: they wait for proven, reliable solutions that will enhance their quality of life and help them run their businesses better. What they want is for their organizations to run better, faster, and smoother and to be much more proactively responsive to their customers. They're frustrated by antiquated information systems and organizational silos that get in the way of streamlining customer-facing business processes.

Moreover, there's a hardy group of information technology pioneers in business today. These are the people who embraced the PC revolution, flocked to the Internet, and understand and value object-oriented software design and networked, distributed computing. They can be powerful and important allies for the savvy business executive, for they bring years of experience combined with a vision of what's really possible. These are the people I spend the most time with. I understand and empathize with their hopes and dreams and their frustrations as they struggle through organizational inertia to try to make things happen.

My goal for this book is to bring these two groups of people together: business executives who want progressive, customer-focused organizations, and the technology visionaries and implementers who can deliver on that promise. My hope is that by telling the stories from many organizations that have used electronic commerce technologies cost-effectively to improve their relationships with their customers, I will spark a healthy dialogue among these two very different kinds of movers and shakers.

I've worked with hundreds of organizations over the past twenty-some years, helping them select and implement information technology. I've witnessed firsthand the schism between information technology professionals and business executives, managers, and frontline personnel. I've seen a lot of pain, recrimination, and finger-pointing, as well as a fair amount of satisfaction, delight, and excitement as teams of business people and IT professionals plan and work together.

What I've discovered is that there is one common cause that galvanizes these often-opposing camps into excited camaraderie and teamwork. That cause is the customer. No one argues about whether or not we should make it easier for our customers to do business with us. The only arguments have to do with "What shall we do?," "How shall we do it?," "How soon can we do it?," and "What will it cost?"

The first question is easily resolved: simply ask your customers! You'll get an earful! Answering the remaining questions requires design, creativity, and continuous improvement. My hope is that on the pages to follow, you'll find some ideas that will spur your own teams into satisfying and rewarding action.

The Eight Critical Success Factors in Electronic Commerce and E-business

THERE ARE DOZENS, if not hundreds, of factors that affect businesses' relationships with their customers, but after listening to success stories from companies that have implemented successful e-business initiatives, I've identified eight critical success factors. Here they are:

1. Target the right customers.
2. Own the customer's total experience.
3. Streamline business processes that impact the customer.
4. Provide a 360-degree view of the customer relationship.

5. Let customers help themselves.
6. Help customers do their jobs.
7. Deliver personalized service.
8. Foster community.

You'll learn about each of these principles in the chapters that follow—what they mean, why they're important, and how you can implement them yourself.

I strongly recommend starting with the first success factor, targeting the right customers. If you don't start there, the rest of the factors may be well executed, but you'll be wasting time on the wrong customer population.

After that, however, there are no hard-and-fast rules to decide which success factor to work on next. Indeed, most of these factors are interrelated, and you'll find, as you begin to focus on one, that you've gone a long way towards finding solutions to others.

The companies used as examples in this book have all demonstrated innovation and successes in one or more of the critical success areas. However, none has successfully conquered them all . . . yet. I believe that eventually organizations with insight, dedication, and imagination will address all the factors I have laid out, even without having this list available. I offer these guidelines to shorten the discovery process for these innovators and to provide businesses not yet embarked on customer-facing initiatives with a "road map" of what I believe to be the most important, and rewarding, avenues to pursue.

A Handbook for Successful Implementation

FOR THOSE OF you who want to embark on your own "Customers.com journey," I offer a free handbook you can order from our Web site (www.customers.com). In it, I summarize both the business and organizational best practices I've witnessed, as well as the information technology architectures and approaches that seem to make the most sense. I highly recommend that you read the stories that form the meat of this book as well. What I've found is that concepts and how-tos really only take root when they're embodied in a story. As human beings, we tend to learn best by example. And it's easier to remember and extrapolate from the stories we're told and can retell to others.

In the *Customers.com Handbook*, I also offer you a description for a design and planning workshop I've evolved over the years that could help you jump-start the process. Sure, I'd be happy to facilitate such a workshop for you. But I want to describe it to you so that you can do this yourself, if you choose to do so. It requires high-level commitment, having the right players in the room (including representative customers and other key stakeholders), and lots of goodwill.

Continuing the Discovery Process

OF COURSE, THIS book represents only a snapshot in time and a cross section of examples. If you'd like to follow the progress of the case studies presented here, or if you want to learn about many other organizations that have embarked on similar initiatives or join in dialogue with others who are attempting this journey, I invite you to visit our Web site: www.customers.com.

PART ONE

Five Steps
to Success in
Electronic
Commerce

How to Create a Profitable Electronic Business Strategy

'm shopping for a new bank. My current bank is one of the world's leading financial institutions. But it just doesn't serve my needs anymore. When I move my personal accounts, if I'm satisfied, I may move my company's accounts, too. The banking services I want aren't hard to find in today's electronic marketplace, although the bank that offers them may not be based in Boston, where I live. But that won't matter to me as long as I can get the features I need and the kind of relationship I'm seeking. Global competition is a reality today.

I want a bank that will let me interact with it seamlessly by telephone, by ATM, from my handheld PalmPilot, and over the Internet. I want to be able to get cash anywhere in the world at any time of day. I want to see all my account information consolidated in a single electronic up-to-the-minute statement. I want to be able to look at my bills electronically, question a line item if necessary, and authorize and schedule their payments. Then I want the resulting expenses organized according to categories I specify, totaled by month, and compared against my original budget. I'd like to be able to see the current value of all my investments. And I want to be able to easily transfer money among my accounts, my investments, and any other banks or investment firms with which I may have dealings.

Of course, I need to be able to perform these transactions any time of the day or night from anywhere in the world, securely, via the Internet, by using a Touch-Tone phone or from a wireless handheld device. I'd like my bank to offer me other financial services—car insurance, homeowner's insurance, mortgage, investments, loans, and lines of credit—at competitive rates so that I can have the convenience of one-stop shopping for most of my financial needs. I expect personal service from the people I interact with. I want them to know who I am, what accounts I have, and what problems I've had in the past. When I'm dealing with the bank electronically, I expect fast, secure, accurate, and highly personal service—no hassles, just an enjoyable relationship. When I find this bank, I'll be a very loyal customer because I will have invested a lot of my time in setting up automated bill payments, deposits, and transfers, and entering my investment portfolio. The bank, in turn, will have learned a great deal about me as a customer. As long as they don't violate that trust or make it hard for me to do business with them, I'm likely to be theirs for life.

Does this picture sound seductive? Of course it does. Perhaps you already have a bank that does all this (please let me know which one it is!). Or you may have cobbled together a reasonable facsimile, using a financial management software package such as Intuit's Quicken, along with an online connection to your bank, and one or more investment sites to track your portfolio. If you don't have a bank that offers this kind of electronically enabled one-stop shopping, then, like me, you're probably looking. As business and consumer customers, we're all interested in improving our quality of life. We gravitate toward the companies that make it easy for us to do business with them twenty-four hours a day, anywhere in the world.

What if one or more of your competitors figures out how to beat the pants off you by doing business electronically with *your* customers? What would happen to your business? Would you survive? Would you be able to catch up? Could you learn how to develop a counterattack fast enough to win those customers back? Could you implement such a strategy quickly enough to keep other customers from defecting? Frankly, I doubt it. As you'll see from the next few chapters, creating and implementing a profitable electronic commerce strategy takes focus, time, and resources.

Maybe you're not worried about losing your customers. After all, your customers don't shop on the Internet. They buy your products or services in stores, through catalogs, or over the phone. They interact with your salespeople face-to-face. Or they purchase through your distribution channels. What do you have to fear from competitors' electronic business initiatives? Perhaps you think they aren't relevant to your market.

Think again.

You see, today's electronic commerce isn't limited to shopping over the Internet. It's also not confined to supply-chain transactions between large trading partners. Electronic commerce (also known as electronic business) is doing business electronically—*all* the aspects of doing business. It embodies the entire business process—from advertising and marketing, through to sales, ordering, manufacturing, distribution, customer service, after-sales support, and replenishment of inventory—managing the entire customer and product life cycles.

When we engage in electronic business, we're applying today's electronic technologies to streamline our business interactions. Those technologies include the Internet, but they also include advanced telephone systems, handheld digital appliances, interactive TVs, self-service kiosks, smart cards, and a whole host of emerging technologies. All of these customer-facing technologies are supported, behind the scenes, by integrated customer databases, call centers, streamlined workflows, and secure transactional systems. They require systems to talk to one another seamlessly, reliably, and securely across company boundaries, geographic boundaries, and time zones.

Sounds complicated, doesn't it? How do you get it right? The real secret of success in electronic commerce today revolves around customers. A successful strategy involves building and sustaining business relationships with customers electronically.

Reaping the Benefits from Electronic Commerce

To whet your appetite, here are a few concrete examples you'll be reading about shortly:

- Dell's on-line customers buy $6 million worth of products each day. These products provide a 30 percent higher profit margin than those purchased by its non-self-service customers.
- *The Wall Street Journal* has targeted a new market segment and has retained 85 percent of those new customers while growing its original customer base.
- Cisco Systems has saved over $550 million per year in customer service for the last three years and now does 62 percent of its $5-billion-per-year business over the Internet.
- National Semiconductor provides extremely targeted current information to one third of its potential global market without spending a dime on direct mail or advertising, since over 500,000 design engineers come back to its Web site every month.
- American Airlines reaches 1.7 million interested prospects each week through electronic mail, again without spending any advertising or telemarketing dollars.
- Wells Fargo has halved its cost per transaction, enjoys higher average balances per customer, and has reduced customer defections by 50 percent for on-line customers.

- The National Science Foundation automatically disburses $2 billion per year in grant monies electronically, reducing mountains of paperwork.
- Tripod built a vibrant, on-line community of more than 1 million members that was so valuable to advertisers that the company was purchased in early 1998 for $58 million—$1 million per employee!

Sounds good? It should. How can your company begin to reap some of these benefits? Here's the winning strategy I've gleaned from more than forty companies that have already implemented successful electronic commerce strategies. It's a five-step process. And, in the next five chapters, I'll explain each of the steps in more detail. They are:

1. Make it easy for customers to do business with you.
2. Focus on the end customer for your products and services.
3. Redesign your customer-facing business processes from the end customer's point of view.
4. Wire your company for profit*: design a comprehensive, evolving electronic business architecture.
5. Foster customer loyalty—the key to profitability in electronic commerce.

---

* "Wired for Profit" is the name of a service offered by Ernst & Young.

FIGURE 1

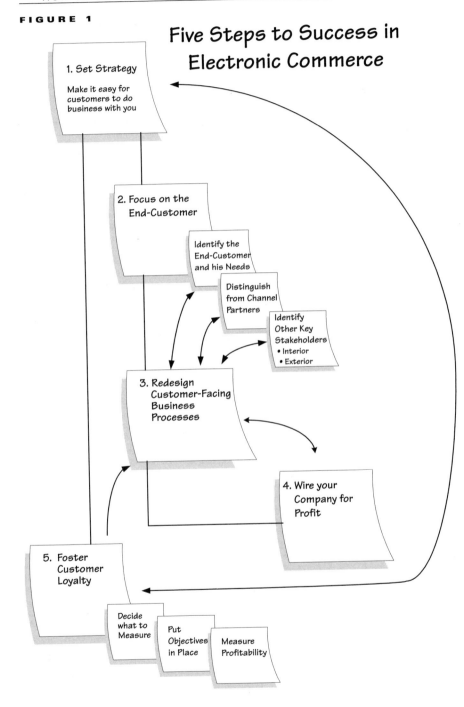

Five Steps to Success in Electronic Commerce

1. Set Strategy

Make it easy for customers to do business with you

2. Focus on the End-Customer

Identify the End-Customer and his Needs

Distinguish from Channel Partners

Identify Other Key Stakeholders
• Interior
• Exterior

3. Redesign Customer-Facing Business Processes

4. Wire your Company for Profit

5. Foster Customer Loyalty

Decide what to Measure

Put Objectives in Place

Measure Profitability

Make It Easy for Customers to Do Business with You

canceled my subscription to *The New York Times* this year. It's not that I don't enjoy reading the paper; I do! And my husband is addicted to the crossword puzzle in the Sunday magazine section! But I got tired of hassling with the company over my subscription. The *Times* tried to make it easier for customers to do business with it, but it didn't succeed. For example, it only used to take calls between 9 A.M. and 5 P.M. Eastern Standard Time, which was a real drag. I don't deal with things like newspaper subscriptions during my working day! Finally, last year, it launched a new twenty-four-hour automated system for handling subscription starts and stops. I was delighted! I had become accustomed to the convenience of using a telephone-based system to suspend my *Boston Globe* delivery every time I went out of town. I was expecting, since *The New York Times* had acquired *The Boston Globe*, that I could use the same convenient system. Well, it acted the same. I could call the toll-free number, enter my phone number or my account number (whoever has the account number handy?), and punch in the date I wanted to suspend delivery and the date I wanted it to resume. So far so good. Just like the *Globe*.

What went wrong? Everything! Obviously the systems behind the automated phone service weren't well integrated. I happened to return to my home in Boston unexpectedly about two weeks after I had suspended delivery. What did I find? Two weeks' worth of *New York Times*es piled up outside my door! Not only were they a soggy mess, but their presence provided an obvious message to would-be burglars! I called to complain. This time I talked to a person (after calling within the required nine-to-five time window). She looked up my account, said that they had no record of the delivery suspension, but that she would take care of it. I decided I wouldn't entrust my transactions to the *Times*' automated phone system again!

But that wasn't the end. Soon I began receiving bills for summer delivery of *The New York Times* to my home in Boston. First, I called a neighbor to check to be sure the papers weren't still being delivered. Then, after receiving reassurance on that score, I called the *Times* to complain again. This time I was told that their system clearly showed my delivery as suspended and that I should just ignore the bill. But the bills kept coming! And soon the collection notices began to arrive. I kept calling the *Times* and receiving the same answer: "Your delivery is suspended; we don't show you owing us any money; just ignore the bills." Well, this is pretty hard to do when the bill collector's notices keep arriving in the mail and making you feel like a deadbeat. So what did I do? I don't have the time or energy for this kind of annoyance. I paid the bill for the amount they claimed I owed (the two weeks of unwanted delivery of soggy newspapers that never got adjusted correctly out of their system), plus another period of delivery that mysteriously started on July 7 and ended on August 1 (which I had never asked for and which didn't actually occur!). Then I canceled my subscription. From now on, when I want the *Times,* I go to the store and buy one.

We've all had experiences like this one, where computer systems get in the way of our ability to do a simple business transaction and ruin our relationship with a company we used to enjoy doing business with. As technology becomes more and more ubiquitous, we need to ensure that it doesn't act as a barrier between our companies and the customers we're trying to serve and build relationships with.

Harness Technology to Streamline Customer Interactions

Now THAT THE Internet is upon us and the World Wide Web has captivated the hearts and minds of marketeers around the world, it's high time to reflect on what this fundamental shift in the business landscape means for *your* organization. Global networks are not new, but they're now pervasive. Electronic commerce is not new, but it's now become mandatory for organizations of every size and type to conduct business electronically. Integrated voice response systems and call centers aren't new, but they're now playing a much more fundamental role in the electronic delivery of service to customers twenty-four hours a day. Handheld electronic gadgets aren't new, but they're becoming more and more powerful and pervasive. You can continue to let your business use these technologies in a piecemeal fashion. Or you can think more strategically and reap the benefits that all the players profiled in these pages now enjoy.

So why not take a comprehensive look at how you can focus all of your information technology investments behind a single, winning strategy: *make it easy for your customers to do business with you!* This simple phrase packs an incredible amount of power. With this mantra, you can cut through organizational inertia, bureaucratic bungling, departmental fiefdoms, and line-of-business barriers. With this focus, you can rationalize your information technology investments and avoid duplication of effort. With this objective, you can marshal your employees, your suppliers, and your distribution partners into a seamless virtual organization with a shared vision and purpose: making it easy for your customers!

Most companies have been investing heavily in the use of information technology since the 1950s. Both the pace and the size of those investments continue to increase and show no sign of abating. However, in the past companies have been able to invest in a scattershot way: they've used technology to improve manufacturing, streamline accounting, coordinate and communicate with employees and partners, and improve product development and marketing. Today, you no longer have a choice in how you spend your Information Technology (IT) dollar. Instead of investing in new human resources, manufacturing, or financial systems, you need to be investing at least 50 percent of your IT dollars in making it easy for customers to do business with you.

I had lunch with a friend the other day. He's the CIO of one of the largest states in America. After we talked about all the initiatives he had under way—data center consolidation, Year 2000 conversion, major new applications under development—I asked, "If you could focus on anything you wanted to, how would you be spending your time?" He answered right away. "I'd spend fifty percent of my time doing what it takes to make it easier for companies to do business with this state." He absolutely understands the urgency of his situation. If businesses find it difficult to do business in his state, they'll set up shop elsewhere.

How will you know where to start? First, try doing business with your own company. I have. It's embarrassing. As a customer, you experience all the frustrations that your customers experience. And you'll notice that these frustrations aren't confined to customer service. A lot of them have to do with simple things. How do I find the right phone number to call? How do I find out what products and services you have? How do I get the right prices for my situation? How do I negotiate the terms and conditions? How do I place an order? What happens when I do? How do I know you can give me what I want when I want it? How much do your people know about me and my dealings with your organization? How do I question a bill? How do I know if payment has been received? How do I tell you what new products and features I'd like you to offer? How do I tell you how you could make my life easier? What happens when I do? The list goes on and on. And the back-end systems and business processes that are affected reach across your entire company. We're talking about streamlining product information, ordering, transactions, fulfillment, delivery, inventory management, accounting, taxation, and so on. And we're talking about doing this across departments, product lines, and distribution channels, all with a single focus: making it easy for the end customer to do business with you.

Start with the Basics

AS YOU EMBARK on your electronic business voyage, don't ignore the customer fundamentals:

- Don't waste our time!
- Remember who we are!
- Make it easy for us to order and procure service!
- Make sure your service delights us!
- Customize your products and service for me!

Don't Waste Our Time!

What's the biggest time waster in your life today? If you're like me, it's probably dealing with organizations that don't value your time or your patronage.

I live in Massachusetts. I used to dread having to renew my car registration each year. I had to drive to the Registry of Motor Vehicles, find a metered parking place, wait in several lines, be subjected to near abuse by rude clerks, and, if lucky, leave with my renewed registration and the new stickers for my license plates before the time on my parking meter had run out.

Today, renewing my registration is a piece of cake. I receive the renewal notice in the mail, get onto the Internet, fill in a form, supply my credit card number, and get a $5 discount to boot! Within a day I receive an e-mail with a confirmation number. In about a week, the new registration form arrives with the stickers for my license plates.

Here's another example. I often enjoy going out to the movies on Saturday night. But many of the theaters that play the movies I want to see are quite small, and Saturday is a popular time. There's nothing I hate more than waiting in line for a movie and then discovering that it's sold out at the last minute, when it's too late to make other plans. So I call 333-FILM. I can select the movie, find the nearest theater, and book my tickets, all in a couple of minutes. That way when I arrive at the theater, my tickets are waiting for me. The surcharge is more than balanced by my time savings. The movie theaters that offer this feature are the ones that get my patronage.

What are some other examples of time-saving features I'd like to be able to use that today's technologies enable? When I know I'm going on a business trip, I'd like to just enter the dates and locations in my electronic calendar and have the calendar automatically send the request to my travel reservation system. I'd expect an electronic agent to look up my personal profile and the business rules that I've entered (for example, "*If* it's a cross-country flight, and I have the frequent-flyer miles available, *then* upgrade the class of service"), and within minutes, I should get back an e-mail with some proposed itinerary choices and seating assignments. I could check off the flights I want, ask or answer questions, and e-mail back my selection. If it's a complicated trip, I'd want to press a button and get my agent on the phone. He or she would be looking at the same itinerary and choices I have in front of me, we'd discuss the other options, I'd decide, and I'd be off the phone. My flights would be booked and the reservation details and confirmations entered into my company's electronic calendar, which I could then synchronize with my handheld PalmPilot.

If my plans change, I'd like to be able to reschedule the flights, hotels, cars, and so on, by simply moving the trip on my electronic calendar and having all the reservations rebooked. If I need to cancel it, I should be able to do so by deleting the entry from my calendar and confirming that that is what I want to do. Of course, I expect all the travel expenses to flow automatically into my company's expense-reporting form, so that I can add incidentals and submit the expenses for reimbursement. What I've just described exists today, or is very close.

Remember Who We Are

Like you, I get lots of solicitations, both in the mail and by phone. Of course, the phone calls are the most annoying. But the ones that really make me mad are the ones from the companies I'm already doing business with. *Fortune* magazine called me the other day asking if I wanted to subscribe. When I said I'd been a subscriber for more than thirteen years, the operator said, "Thank you, we're sorry to bother you." American Express routinely sends me offers to join its exalted ranks. I've been a loyal American Express "member" for more than twenty years. I fail to understand why companies that have otherwise excellent customer databases do not manage to merge these databases with the outside lists they purchase when they're soliciting new business.

My local phone company has no idea who I am. Yet I have four phone lines coming into my home in Boston and four lines coming into my home in Boothbay, Maine, as well as a cellular account. I called once to ask if the phone company could consolidate my phone bills for me. The customer service rep said no. It frustrates me that my phone company doesn't have a complete picture of all the dealings I have with it. I'm sure I'm missing opportunities to save money, to avail myself of other services, and just to be treated as the special customer that I am, not to mention the annoyance of receiving nine separate phone bills each month.

It's not just affluent customers who deserve to be remembered and recognized, either. In a number of states and countries, social services recipients now have their benefits disbursed to them electronically. They use a standard bank ATM card to access these funds. But there are many other services they may be eligible for. They should be able to use the same bank card or smart card to securely access information about all the programs for which they may be eligible, to apply for those programs (job training, child care, medical benefits, housing assistance, transportation services, employment opportunities, and so on), to check on the status of those applications and programs, and to update their own family profile information. The fact that these services are being offered by different agencies and service providers shouldn't require the person to run around to all those different offices or to have to make a myriad of phone calls, each time repeating much of the same information about his or her current situation. Everything he or she needs should be right at his or her fingertips, consolidated.

My father is in his eighties. He's concerned about the fact that his medical records are kept in a file folder at home and that each different specialist or doctor he visits has only a partial picture of the whole. He'd like to have his entire medical history stored on a smart card that could be accessed by any physician he consults. Any recommendations, prescriptions, or procedures a physician authorizes would be entered as updates to my father's personal electronic medical records. This electronically stored medical information could then be accessed by his insurance providers so they'd be able not only to pay the bills but also to assess the efficacy of the treatments.

What about privacy issues? Who has access to this rich individual or family profile information? It's very clear to me (and to my father) that the customer always "owns" his or her profile. He or she controls it, keeps it up to date, and decides who can access that information. Most of us will trade convenience, accuracy, and personalized service for anonymity as long as we know that none of our personal profile information will be accessible to anyone we haven't authorized to see it. Will there be occasional mishaps and privacy scares? You bet! That's part of the shakedown period for learning to live with these new technologies. But I for one am willing to take the risk. I believe that the security technologies available today are strong enough to protect my personal information.

Make It Easy for Us to Order and Procure Service

In 1997, I signed up for AT&T's 500 number "follow me" service so that my customers, friends, and family wouldn't have to keep track of my whereabouts and my various phone numbers (home, office, vacation, cell phone, and so on).

The first problem occurred when I signed up using AT&T's friendly Web site. I supplied all the information it requested. I even got to select my own 500 phone number. And I was told my order had been placed. But nothing happened.

After waiting two months for the promised welcome packet to arrive in the mail, I finally looked up the customer service number and called to find out what had happened. They had no record of the Web transaction. So I had to repeat the entire transaction over the phone.

When they finally sent me my "welcome kit," my "personal" 500 number was in my husband's name, not mine! I was really annoyed that I had to call back and set the record straight. (I knew why they were having the problem. The bill for my home phone service is in my husband's name.) It took about fifteen minutes of consultation before the customer service representative was able to ascertain that it would indeed be possible to issue me a personal 500 number in my own name, linked to that account.

The rest of the relationship has been just as rocky. The voice mail feature didn't work. I didn't understand how to set up PIN numbers. Each of these transactions required several frustrated phone calls on my part. Am I using this service today? No.

By contrast, I recently ordered three laptop computers from Dell. I knew which model I wanted. I had the specs I needed. I was able to select the configurations and options I wanted for each one. And within a few minutes I had filled in the order form on the Web. The only stumbling block was when I came to the payment field. I wasn't going to pay by credit card. My company was going to send a check. There was no explanation of how to handle that situation. So I called the number on the screen, and my sales rep explained what I needed to enter in the field: "Prepaid." He said he could complete the order for me, but I'd get a discount if I continued the process over the Web. So I turned back to the screen, entered "Prepaid," and hit the "Order" button.

Within half an hour, I received an e-mail confirming my order. Then, an hour later, the same phone rep called with the address I needed to send the check to and the confirmation order number. He told me that it would take ten days from the time I sent the check until I received my laptops: five days for the check to arrive and be processed, five days for Dell to manufacture and ship my computers. Five days later, the computers arrived at my office—five days sooner than I had expected them. I was delighted!

As a customer, I expect to be able to get *all* the information I need to place an order from your Web site. I want to be able to answer my own questions, get accurate pricing information, know whether the product I want is in stock and exactly how long it will take to get delivered. I want to be able to find out whether it will work with other products I already have. If I or my company already has an account with you, I expect you to have all my payment information on file and to ask me simply to verify it. If I am dealing with you for the first time, I want to be able to complete the entire transaction from start to finish without picking up a phone, if I choose to do so. If I do want to talk with someone, I expect them to have all my information in front of them, including everything I've just filled in at the Web site and what products I was looking at.

Yet many organizations seem to have a hard time understanding and acting on this fairly simple set of customer requirements. They're taken by surprise when customers who used to require a lot of hand-holding now want to make their own purchases and transactions. Charles Schwab was the first investment firm to recognize and capitalize on this trend. It took two years for Merrill Lynch, PaineWebber, and Prudential Securities to begin to offer on-line trading services to their customers. These full-service firms hadn't wanted to compete with the discount brokers. Yet their customers demanded the ability to access their own information and to do their own trades. Today's customers want to be in control; they'll ask for help when they need it.

Make Sure Your Service Delights Us

All of us have war stories about terrible experiences with merchants, car dealerships, government bureaucracies, or travel providers. I won't bore you with mine.

By contrast, my experiences with the Hertz #1 Club Gold have amazed and delighted me. The van takes me right to my car. I see my name in gold lights (and who doesn't enjoy seeing one's own name in lights?) above the car. The trunk is open, the keys are in the car. The map is already there. All I have to do is drive out the gate and let the guard check my driver's license. Even when I arrived eighteen hours late to pick up my car (because of flight snafus), my car was there waiting for me!

Ordering from Amazon.com is also a pleasant, reassuring experience. I can browse by topic or author, read reviews, pick the books I want, and order them using the credit card number Amazon already has on file for me. I can double-check my past orders to make sure I didn't already send that book to Uncle Harry. And, when I place my order, the entire process is extremely reassuring. Within a few minutes I receive an e-mail further acknowledging my order. And over the next few days, I receive e-mails each time the different books I ordered are shipped out.

When I unpacked a box of books from Amazon.com last summer, I found a handwritten Post-it note on one of them. It said, "We know you ordered the softcover version of this book, but it's out of stock, so we sent you the hardcover copy for the same price." That little handwritten note cemented my love affair with Amazon.com.

Good service is proactive service. It's not sitting passively by assuming everything is fine. United Parcel Service discovered this when Federal Express began tracking all the packages it shipped by air and using that status information as a selling point with customers. At the time, UPS's management was not impressed. After all, the company had a 99 percent delivery success rate. They worried only about exceptions—the packages they weren't able to deliver. Customers knew the service was reliable. But once FedEx threw down the gauntlet of tracking every air shipment and making that information available to customers, the entire industry changed. Now it became a requirement for shippers and recipients to know exactly where their packages were at any moment in time and to be able to act on that information (reroute packages, speed up delivery, and so forth). UPS has caught up and actually surpassed Federal Express in its use of package-tracking technology. In 1997, UPS shipped just over 3 billion packages. Every package was tracked at least four times in its journey. When the package was received and signed for, the digital signature was stored electronically along with the date and time. And, as with Federal Express, you can look up the status of your packages on UPS's Web site. Both companies now work aggressively with their customers to encourage them to provide shipping notification to their end customers ("Your order was shipped on 12/23/97; it will be received before 5 pm on 12/24/97"). Reliable service isn't good enough. Today's customers want to know the status of what you're doing for them.

Customize Your Products and Service for Me

Most of the products I buy for my family or my business aren't fully customizable. When I ordered my laptops from Dell Computer, for example, I wanted to order one machine without a CD-ROM drive, since I already had one I could use. So I sent off an e-mail to Dell asking if this model could be configured without a CD-ROM drive. "No, all of our laptop configurations include the CD-ROM drive. Dell Online." This was the terse reply I received. So much for custom-configured computers! (On the other hand, I understand the logic behind that decision. Most products are available only in certain preconfigured packages. This helps keep costs down.)

I even understood why the return e-mail they sent back was so impersonal in nature. Other Web businesspeople have complained to me about the escalating costs of customer service when customers get chummy with the customer service reps who have answered their e-mail inquiries. The customer often replied thanking the rep and asking questions about the local weather or the local sports team. This would spawn a volley of nonessential e-mails that the customer service rep would have a hard time cutting off.

Nevertheless, I would have preferred a more personal response from Dell rather than one that seemed to have been sent by some electronic agent, which responds to all requests with the identical impersonal message. And I would like to have been given the choice to receive the standard model in five days or a custom-configured model in thirty days, perhaps even at extra cost.

Today I have a personalized newspaper that's continuously updated twenty-four hours a day (from *The Wall Street Journal Interactive*) and I receive lots of alerts and notices in my e-mail letting me know about new products or news items that I've asked to be notified about. For example, Hewlett-Packard's SmartFriend sends me a note anytime something in which I've expressed an interest is posted on HP's Web site. I get e-mail from Amazon.com every time a new book in my field is listed. And I get a mailing about discount airfares from American Airlines each week. Do I feel overwhelmed? No—these are all alerts I've asked for. I know what they are, and I can turn them off at any time. I like the personal service these companies are offering. It helps cement my relationship with them.

Can You Afford *Not* to Make It Easy for Your Customers?

So why am I telling you all these mundane details about my dealings with different organizations? I want you to think about your life. Think about the organizations and people you deal with in your different roles as a consumer, parent, taxpayer, businessperson, purchaser, or influencer of buying decisions. When do you enjoy these interactions? When do you find them a hassle?

If you're like me, you enjoy dealing with organizations that respect your time, treat you as a valued customer, cater to your individual needs, and re-assure you at the same time they're fulfilling their promises. When they can't fulfill, they make it up to you with panache. You continue to feel good about your relationship with them.

Now turn the tables around. How well does your organization do? How much do you know about the actual experiences of the end consumers of your products or services? You may be assuming that customers are satisfied and being well taken care of by your employees or the people who actually sell and distribute your products. You may feel that the customer satisfaction surveys you send out are giving you a good handle on customers' experiences. You may have so many customers that you feel it's impossible ever to get to know their individual needs and tastes. You're probably wrong on all counts. Today's e-business technologies make it cost-effective and easy for customers to interact with you directly, tell you more about themselves, and get better service. However, before you decide to invest in all the behind-the-scenes work you'll need to do to provide this seamless service to your customers, let's take a look at who your customers are.

Step 2:

Focus on the End Customer for Your Products and Services

Without customers, you have no business being in business. Everyone has customers. Businesses have customers: the business or consumer who *uses* the end product or service they produce. Government agencies have customers: the citizens and residents they serve. Nonprofits have customers: the people whose needs they serve.

Yet if you ask most organizations who their customers are, you'll receive a convoluted answer. A car manufacturer may reply that his dealers are his customers. An insurance provider may describe his independent agents as his customers. A nonprofit may describe its donors as its customers. A government organization may consider taxpayers to be its customers. A consumer products company may describe retailers as its customers. Many companies consider their wholesalers or their distributors to be their customers because these are the people with whom they interact on a daily basis. Certainly, keeping wholesalers, distributors, and retailers happy and attending to their needs is critical. Surely, keeping taxpayers and donors informed and on board is vital. *However, the real customer for any business is the end consumer of the product or service it produces*—the person or company who *uses* that product, not the ones who *distribute* the product to the user or even, necessarily, the ones who pay for it.

For a business, the end customer is the one who consumes the product or service it provides and usually, though not always, the one who pays for it. Often the person who pays is doing so on behalf of the end user of the product. For example, a librarian who buys the research materials for a corporate library is not the end user of the information.

Sometimes it's an even more indirect relationship. National Semiconductor figured this out. It targeted design engineers as its end customers. These are the people who spec National Semi's chips into the products they design. They are the "users" of National Semi's products. Yet the actual purchase of the product is made by a purchasing agent on behalf of a manufacturing operation, once the product containing the chip has been designed.

The purchasing agent may pay the bill, but he doesn't necessarily know about the quality or content of the product or service. Yet, if the end users don't value the research you produce, the car you manufacture, the cereal you package, the films you bring to market, or the machine tools you produce, you won't remain in business very long. Setting up a direct feedback loop between you, the producer of a product, and the end consumer of that product is vitally important to ensuring your continued success in the market(s) you serve. For the first time in history, it's now becoming cost-effective, possible, and even imperative to create and sustain electronic feedback loops with your end customers.

If your actual end customers don't value your product or service, sooner or later you'll be out of business. The length of time it takes for customer dissatisfaction to put you out of business depends on the degree to which you're insulated from direct customer feedback. A business that sells directly usually knows it's in trouble before a business that sells through channels does, for example. A nonprofit that doesn't fulfill its mission to serve the clientele it's chartered to serve will not be able to raise the funds required to continue functioning. And a government organization that does not serve its residents, many of whom are taxpayers, will eventually be voted out of office (although the civil servants often remain!).

Electronic Commerce Lets You Interact Directly with End Customers

THERE'S A PROFOUND REVOLUTION afoot as a result of electronic business technologies. Every organization, no matter how big, now has the wherewithal to interact directly with its end customers. Every company, no matter how decentralized, now has the ability to consolidate customer information and to gain a much better picture of who its customers are, what products and services they buy, and how they like to be served. Every business, no matter how much it relies on indirect sales channels, now has the opportunity to begin electronically linking its channel partners with its end customers and participating in the dialogue between them.

Can you afford not to take advantage of this new capability if your competitors do? I doubt it.

Can You Find Out Who Your Customers Are?

MANY ORGANIZATIONS KNOW who their customers are. Others don't. Manufacturers that sell big-ticket items, such as automobiles, are more likely to know who their customers are than manufacturers who sell low-priced consumer goods, such as toothpaste and detergent. The latter may know only the names of customers who complain about the quality of the product—a small percentage of the actual customer base. Yet even that small percentage of vocal, disgruntled customers could become a valuable asset to the company if they could be wooed into being vocal, loyal customers.

What if it was possible to know who actually buys your product without breaking the bank? Even if there are millions of customers to track, the demographic patterns by themselves would be invaluable to your company for product planning and development. Procter & Gamble and Microsoft both have tens of millions of customers. Yet both are making a concerted effort to learn much more about each customer. Procter & Gamble sells laundry detergent, yet the company invests heavily in end-user research. Whether I am buying software, phone service, or laundry detergent, it's important for you to know who I am and to try to get and keep all of my business in your category.

How Microsoft Is Getting to Know Its Customers

FOR EXAMPLE, MICROSOFT probably has close to 100 million customers. Most bought their products through indirect channels. The software came bundled on a PC, was ordered through a catalog, or was picked up at a retail outlet. Yet the company is finally making a concerted effort to build a comprehensive customer database. Within a few years, Microsoft will know a lot more about its end customers than it does today. The evolution of Microsoft's customer information strategy is informative and may sound familiar to many of you.

For many years, the only end customers Microsoft knew about were the ninety enterprise accounts it had and the 25 million or so people who had sent in warranty registration cards. The latter were collected in a marketing database, which is maintained by an outside mail house, and combined with purchased lists. Customers and prospects are segmented and targeted with direct mail for special promotions or invitations to seminars. In 1993, the company developed a data warehouse. Called "MS Sales," Microsoft's data warehouse and decision support system tells the company how it's doing by region, product, channel, and type of customer. As a by-product, it gathers a lot of information about which companies are making purchases. But until December 1996, Microsoft didn't really have a database that was designed primarily to profile its customers' interests or to communicate directly with them. That was triggered by the World Wide Web.

As customers came to Microsoft's Web site and began interacting with the company, they started leaving information about themselves behind (their e-mail addresses, their mailing addresses, what products and services they were interested in). But each of the different areas of the Web site was developed and maintained by the different product-marketing groups responsible for their own product lines or targeted customer sets. So all that information was being scattered, and much of it was duplicative. In fact, when Pieter Knook, general manager of Microsoft.com, took on the task of developing a single Interactive Marketing Database for the company, there were already seventy-two different smaller databases that were collecting customers' e-mail addresses! Now, there's a single database in which customer profile information is gathered from the Microsoft Web site. As you interact with the site, any information you specify is captured in your profile. You can then check your profile and update it at any time. The obvious next step is for Microsoft to link the Web-based customer profiles with the customer account information it has already gathered in its other systems.

What If Your Distribution Channel Owns Your Customers?

MANY COMPANIES HAVE delegated customer intimacy to their distribution channel as part of their overall strategy. Often the distribution channel "owns" the customer in exchange for services rendered. There is nothing wrong with delegating customer service to the channel that is best equipped to satisfy the customer. What is a problem, strategically, is letting that channel withhold information about your customers as part of that trade-off.

Consumer products companies have a difficult time keeping track of actual customers. There are so many of them, and they purchase commodity products. Yet these same companies pay millions of dollars each year to purchase information that purports to tell them the demographics of the consumers who have purchased their products and those of their competitors. In addition, they're constantly running promotions and giving away coupons. And it's absolutely vital that they track the efficacy of each promotional program. Nevertheless, there appears to be a perverse blind spot that keeps many companies from trying to gather end-consumer information.

Several years ago, when working with one consumer packaged goods company, I discovered an interesting institutional reluctance to gather actual consumer information. This company reaches the majority of its retailers through brokers. The brokers are the ones who are expected to nurture the company's relationship with the retailers. The retailers, in turn, are the ones who understand the specific demographics of their end customers and the concomitant needs of that clientele. Yet that valuable information—what the end customers actually needed and wanted—was not making it back to the company's headquarters. The brokers hoarded that information because it increased their value both to the company and to the retailers they served. Brokers would communicate the needs of their retailers when new in-store display strategies were being formulated or when the marketing department explicitly did a survey. But the company hadn't made it a condition of doing business for the brokers to supply detailed information about the retailers or the retailers' customers, the actual consumers.

Interestingly, this "hands-off" policy persisted even with the company's direct accounts. When the company developed tight working relationships with some of its largest retailers, such as Wal-Mart, it added direct account management. Yet the sales force was still operating under the old modus operandi.

The company gave the retailer what it asked for—in Wal-Mart's case, just-in-time inventory management. They were great at serving Wal-Mart, but they weren't in the habit of asking questions about what end consumers wanted or needed.

So when Wal-Mart approached its account rep and offered to give him the detailed daily purchase records for the products sold in each store, he politely declined the offer. When the marketing department got wind of this, they went ballistic! Why should it be paying third-party services, such as Nielsen, for *estimated* demographic information about who was consuming the company's products when it could pinpoint the exact daily sales in a single store in a single town? The sales department felt it was doing its job satisfying its "customer," Wal-Mart. The fact that the marketing department could use this information to target consumer buying patterns better was not of concern to them.

New Advances in Identifying Consumer Customers

IN THE PAST few years, technology has been put to work in exactly this type of consumer identification. Using a combination of product bar code identification and customer ID cards, many large retailers have moved from the practice of providing newspaper coupons to a system of customer ID cards. Customers used to apply for check-cashing cards at the local market; now these cards also entitle the customer to discounts on "special" items. We still get our weekly circular from the supermarket, but instead of cutting out paper coupons, the advertisement tells us which products are discounted with use of the card.

In the check out line, we present our ID card to the cashier, who scans it into the system. Then our groceries are scanned. We get discounts, and the supermarket knows exactly what we bought and can provide this information to its suppliers. This is a win-win situation for everyone. The customer has a choice about whether or not to use this ID card. He can opt not to have such a card and forgo the discounts. Or he can receive "payment" for giving the retailer the ability to link his purchase records with his identity through the use of discounts.

A number of retailers have begun making very good use of this customer information. For example, Radio Shack, which sells consumer electronics items in the United States, has saved millions of dollars each year by targeting its direct-mail promotions based on the information gleaned from these customer records. In Sweden, one grocery store chain not only issues discount member cards and tracks purchases, it also entices customers to "bank" with it by letting them keep their grocery money on deposit and paying a higher interest rate than the local bank!

What If Your Customers Are Truly Anonymous?

MOST PHARMACEUTICAL FIRMS have no idea who their customers are. They may know, if they're lucky, who the doctors are who prescribe their drugs, since they have salespeople calling on doctors. But even that correlation is problematic. In fact, it's been such an arm's-length relationship that an entire multimillion-dollar business was spawned simply to plug that information gap.

In the late 1960s, an enterprising IBM salesman who was calling on the pharmaceutical industry spotted this information gap and proposed to IBM that this would be an excellent business opportunity. IBM passed. And the company that later became IMS was formed. (IMS was acquired by Dun & Bradstreet in the 1990s for a hefty price. The IBM salesman, my brother-in-law, retired early!)

The business model was simple: gather information from the point of sale and sell it back to the manufacturers. Pharmaceutical companies distributed their products through wholesalers to distributors to the retail drugstores where the products were actually sold to end customers. But the drug companies also sustained large direct-sales organizations. The salespeople were known as "detail men"; their job was to call on doctors in their territory and provide them with the details on their firm's products. It was a "soft sell." And of course, they were calling on the prescribing doctor, not on the ultimate consumer of the product—the doctor's patient.

Salespeople felt they knew if they were successful. If the doctors asked them questions about the product and its side effects, and if they asked for more free samples, they were probably prescribing the drug. But this wasn't something the detail man could prove to management, since the doctors weren't going to give him a list of the patients to whom they had prescribed the drug.

IMS went to drugstores and offered to pay them for the detailed reports of every drug sold to every customer, promising to maintain the confidentiality of the information, which it did. It then went to every pharmaceutical company and offered to sell it the detailed demographic information that would tell it how many of each product it was selling in each drugstore. The company's sales management could then do a rough geographic correlation of drugstores to physicians to sales territory. So even in a situation in which it is virtually impossible to garner direct customer information, it *is* possible to garner information about your customers' demographics. And it's also possible to entice some percentage of the people who actually use your products to identify themselves in exchange for special incentives, as in the case of the supermarket card discounts.

How to Leverage Customer Information

I'M NOT GOING to propose that you sell your customer information to others. In fact, that's the last thing you should do. It will anger your customers, and it will weaken your franchise. Instead, I propose that you gather and use customer information to improve your relationships with all of your customers. Don't barrage them with direct mail or with unsolicited e-mail. Do ask them what products and services they'd like to know about and how they'd like to receive that information.

Over time, as you learn more about your customers, you'll be able to separate out the truly profitable customers from the ones who actually cost you money, but first, find out who they are and make it easy for them to do business with you. This will cement customer loyalty and should increase your profitability.

Patty's Rx for Apple Computer: Focus on Your End Customers

In the next few chapters, I'll be showing you the best practices a number of companies have used in their electronic commerce strategies. So I'm ending this chapter with a concrete example of how these best practices might be implemented. Let's take a look at how one company that most of us know and love, Apple Computer, could have focused on its end customers as a successful strategy for revitalizing the company when it went into a tailspin in 1996 and 1997.

I'm saddened by Apple's downfall. I'm no longer a Macintosh user, but I was, and I have six family members who still use Macs. Three summers ago, my husband made the switch to the PC. Ah, I remember that summer well: hot and getting hotter by the moment. Although my husband is a very sophisticated computer user, it still took him a full two months to get acclimated to Microsoft Windows, swearing the whole time! The cost—in irritation—of switching from the Mac to the Windows PC was very high. But my husband felt he had no choice. His work requirements demanded that he use a PC.

Then, of course, we both switched to Windows 95. Oh, I know Microsoft claimed this would be the most "Mac-like" of experiences, but that claim proved to be mostly hollow. For my husband, Windows 95 still fell far short of the experience he had grown to know and love on the Mac.

The moral of this story is that the Macintosh had, and still has, a lot going for it in intuitive interface and ease of use. However, the biggest thing it has going for it are loyal, die-hard customers such as my parents, my son, my daughter-in-law, and my brother-in-law. But has Apple ever communicated with any of these people? Nope. In fact, I'm pretty sure that Apple doesn't even know who any of them are, even though they have been loyal Macintosh users for years. All of them sent in their warranty cards and registration forms. Yet none of them has ever received any communication from Apple. The only indication that anyone even noticed they had purchased a Mac was the subscription come-ons for *MacWorld* magazine that began to arrive in the mail.

You'd think, given Apple's recent difficulties, that it would want to know who its loyal customers are. Apple could build a whole comeback strategy simply by targeting its existing customers.

How Apple Could Make a Comeback

I F I H A D a company that was under a lot of competitive pressure, such as Apple, I would do many of the things Gil Amelio tried to do in his brief tenure as CEO there. I would cut costs. I would focus on core products. I would introduce new best-in-class products. I would keep my prices low while not completely sacrificing profit margins. But first and foremost, I would find out who all my loyal customers are, what I need to do to keep them happy and loyal, and how I can forge strong relationships with them. Amelio never took this approach. Steve Jobs doesn't seem to have figured this out either.

Apple's problems were not ones that mass marketing and advertising would solve. The company had a business problem for which one-to-one relationship building would have been the ideal solution. Here are the steps Apple (or any company, for that matter) should be taking:

1. FIND OUT WHO THE END CUSTOMERS ARE. Of course, given the tens of millions of customers Apple probably still has, finding out who they are could be a daunting task. But it's certainly not an insurmountable one. I'd start with the information I already have. All those registration and warranty cards have to have gone somewhere. There's probably a lot better use that could be made of that database than simply selling the names to *MacWorld* magazine so that it can solicit subscriptions. Next, I'd take a page from Microsoft's book and offer rebates to all my dealers and resellers for every valid customer name and address they give me, along with whatever profile information they can easily capture at the point of sale without annoying the customer. Like Microsoft again, I'd begin to ID customers as they come to my Web site and build profiles as they give me information about themselves, including, in particular, their e-mail addresses, so that I could reach them cost-effectively.

2. MAKE LOYAL CUSTOMERS FEEL SPECIAL. I'd encourage loyal customers to register on my Web site as loyal Mac users. (But I wouldn't charge

them $19.95, as Apple did for customers joining its Apple Club! What an insult!) I'd ask these customers to provide profile information about who they are, what kinds of Macs they have, what software they run, and what they use their computers for. In exchange, I'd offer them benefits (discounts, advance software downloads, and so forth). As American Airlines has done on its Web site, I'd make the "Mac Members" part of the site special, seductive, useful, and rewarding so that these customers would want to come back over and over again.

In fact, I'd even consider launching a frequent-buyer program for loyal Mac customers. Like General Motors' Saturn division, I'd offer enticements to current loyal Mac users to stand up and be counted, such as discounts on the latest and greatest machines, T-shirts, and mugs, and points for buying Mac software or for using on-line services that can be redeemed as partial payment for my next Mac. My goal: to convert my loyal customer base from feeling sheepish and defensive about the choice they've made to being proud defenders of the "Apple Way."

3. **BUILD COMMUNITY.** Once I had these loyal Mac customers coming to my Web site, I'd get them interacting with one another. I'd encourage them to start discussion forums on topics of interest to them, to share Mac experiences, to troubleshoot one another's problems, and to make suggestions for product improvements. I'd offer them free e-mail accounts for life and a place to design and post their own home pages so they could strut their stuff in front of other members of the Mac community.

4. **BUILD A CUSTOMER DATABASE.** I'd combine all of the customer information we gathered into an exquisite customer information database—one designed to be extensible and to be updated and queried constantly and used interactively to generate custom e-mails and physical mailings. I'd combine customer transaction information with their profile information. Then I'd make this information available to them on the Web site and ask them to update anything that wasn't correct.

5. **LET CUSTOMERS PLACE THEIR OWN ORDERS.** I'd also take a page out of Dell's playbook and let customers configure and order their Macs online. Customers who prefer to buy direct from Apple could do so over the Web. They could compare models, get technical details, and try out different configuration and pricing options. For each configuration they put together, I'd make sure to show them the date this par-

ticular model could be shipped, so they could make informed trade-offs.

6. **LET CUSTOMERS CHECK ORDER HISTORY AND DELIVERY STATUS.** Then, of course, like Dell, I'd ship directly to the customer and maintain the order history, the configuration detail, and shipping and billing information on-line for the customer to come back to later.

7. **LINK CUSTOMERS AND DISTRIBUTION PARTNERS TO MY COMPANY ELECTRONICALLY.** For customers who already have a good relationship with a reseller, or for those who prefer to buy from a reseller, I'd create a three-way Web-based relationship management application. My end customers could interact directly with the dealer from whom they bought their Mac or the one from whom they were receiving service. But my company would be able to participate in that dialogue and learn from the interactions.

8. **GIVE CUSTOMERS THE INFORMATION THEY NEED TO TROUBLESHOOT THEIR OWN PROBLEMS.** To make sure that my customers remain completely delighted with their purchases, I'd offer them easy-to-use do-it-yourself service on the Web. I'd let them access the same knowledge base and troubleshooting scripts the technical support specialists in my call centers use. That way they could walk themselves through a problem and possibly find the solution on their own. And I'd give them a button to push to access a call center professional when they got stuck. When the phone connection was made, the technical support rep would know who the customer was, what configuration he or she had, and how far he or she had gotten in the knowledge base.

9. **PERSONALIZE THE CUSTOMER'S EXPERIENCE.** I would give each customer a "personal Web site" for his or her interactions with Apple. It would start with the customer's profile information and anything the reseller wanted to add to make him or her welcome. It would include all the information about each machine the customer had bought and what software he or she had. And it would alert the customer to any new software upgrades or hardware peripherals he or she might find appropriate. It would be the first place the customer would go to get support (filtered for the products he or she was using). And it would be one place the reseller could use to communicate special offers to the customer.

10. **SEGMENT CUSTOMERS BY PROFITABILITY.** Once I had collected all this customer information, it would be much easier to begin to segment the database based on the profitability of each account or at least of

market segments. This would tell me where to focus my energies in targeting special services and loyalty programs. I might be surprised to discover that many of my consumer customers—the ones I thought were only marginally profitable—actually bring lots of business my way by recommending Macs to family members and friends. I may also discover that there are market niches it costs me too much to support because they require a lot of hand-holding or the sales cycle is just too long.

Obviously, I've outlined quite an ambitious plan for Apple and one that would take a good deal of investment to execute. Yet there are certainly elements of this strategy that could be implemented quickly and relatively inexpensively.

Building the kind of customer information base I'm suggesting would take a lot of time and money. Yet getting started by giving loyal Mac customers a way to sign up on the Web and enter and maintain their own profile information would be a minor add-on to Apple's current Web site. Compiling an e-mail list and reaching out to loyal Mac customers wouldn't be expensive at all.

So there are many elements of this strategy that could be put into place for a small investment of time and effort. If I'm right, and if Apple's customers responded favorably to being courted, the profitability from their repeat business would help fund additional investments.

Can Apple Afford Not to Do at Least Some of This?

WITH THE TECHNOLOGIES available today to build exquisite customer databases, to let customers build and maintain their own profiles, to enable them to tailor their own Web experiences, to communicate with them based on their areas of interest, and to build and deliver products on demand, there's no excuse for Apple *not* to reach out to its customers. What other ammunition does Apple have?

What About You?

IN THE ELECTRONIC commerce world, knowing who your customers are and making sure you have the products and services they want becomes even more imperative than it is in the "real" world. Location plays much less of a role. When you are shopping on-line, it doesn't matter if the store you want is in the local mall or on the other side of the globe. The corner grocery needs only to approximate what customers really want because the convenience factor brings in the business. But when you eliminate this advantage—when customers can go anywhere to get what they want—you'd better know what they're looking for.

Your competitors are busy finding out exactly how customers want to interact with them electronically. And you need to do the same. But if you aren't asking the right people, your end customers, the most elegant online processes won't bring in the business.

FIGURE 2

An Rx for Apple:

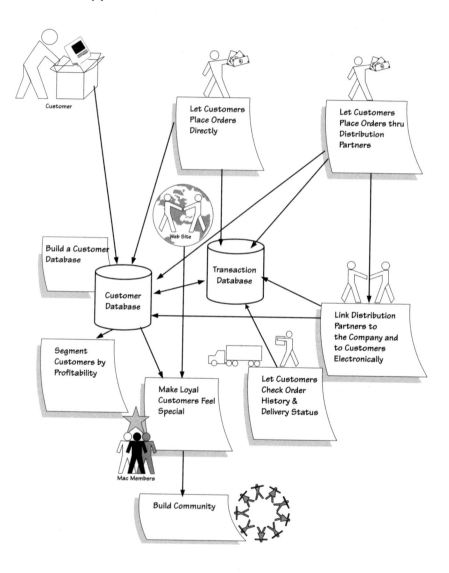

Step 3:

Redesign Your Customer-Facing Business Processes from the End Customer's Point of View

All of the electronic business technologies mentioned in this book—the Web, integrated voice response (IVR) systems, kiosks, e-mail, handheld digital appliances, cell phones, and "smart" call centers—are customer-facing technologies. They're new electronic channels through which customers can now interact with your firm. One of the wonderful advantages of thinking about your business freshly with these new technology assists in mind is that it requires you to do something you should have done long ago: redesign your company from the customer's point of view.

Redesign Processes from the Outside In

BACK IN THE heyday of reengineering, many companies focused on the wrong things. They streamlined business processes, all right. They reengineered their businesses to make them more cost-efficient. But they left out the most important piece of the equation. They didn't start from the outside—the end customer—and work in. Instead, they worked from the inside out, streamlining administrative processes, manufacturing operations, procurement processes, and so forth. These were all valuable initiatives. Many of them saved companies a great deal of money and made them leaner and more productive. But they haven't affected the revenue side of the equation. Most of the reengineering efforts that took place in the 1990s didn't involve the end customer, so they didn't focus on the key priority of making it easy for customers to do business with the firm. They haven't made a difference in keeping customers happy and loyal, coming back for more, and telling their friends about your great products and service.

Once you begin to experiment with a customer-facing Web site, you'll discover that customers will tell you exactly what they want and need with great precision. And you'll probably learn, to your dismay, that in order to really streamline tasks from the customer's point of view, you'll have to do major rework on your existing enterprise systems and business processes. What your Web site highlights, in an unflattering way, is all the black holes that exist in your company's operations. Today you have people who know where the problems in your processes are. They do workarounds. They fill the gaps. They do their best to provide your customers with seamless service. Yet behind the scenes there are usually a number of handoffs back and forth between departments: information is passed along verbally or informally. Someone will make adjustments to a standard process or product in order to accommodate a customer's needs. Someone else will ensure that the order is filled, the billing problem resolved, the delivery expedited. Yet once customers begin interacting with you via the Web, that safety net falls away. Your company is left standing naked in front of its customers and channel partners. Every wrinkle shows; every blemish spoils the customer's ability to help herself to information and transactions.

So these customer-facing technologies are a blessing in disguise. The competitive imperative of making it easy for customers to do business with you twenty-four hours a day across a variety of channels of interaction will cause you to streamline most of your behind-the-scenes operations.

How Customer-facing Technologies Spawn Business Process Changes

ONE OF THE new opportunities that electronic commerce technologies affords is that of getting directly into the hearts and minds of your end customers. Then you can work backward from what they want and need to design or redesign your business processes to meet their needs better. Take Hallmark for example. Hallmark Cards, Inc., a $3.6 billion company with a 44 percent market share in the United States, is a classic consumer products company selling millions of greeting cards to millions of anonymous customers through retail outlets.

Like most companies that sell through retail outlets, Hallmark kept close tabs on what cards sold in different demographic areas and continuously refined its product offerings to meet those needs as well as to keep up with the times. But when the company actually asked consumers what they wanted, it discovered that what its customers could really use was a reminder service—some way of reminding them to go buy a card and a gift for someone's birthday or anniversary. Hallmark took that requirement to heart. Today, on Hallmark's Web site (Hallmark.com), you'll find a handy reminder service. You enter the important dates you want to remember and specify when you want to be reminded—a week before, three days before, the day before—and you'll receive an e-mail reminding you of your friend's or relative's special occasion.

Hallmark now has, for the first time in its history, a database of customer profile information. It knows who some of its end customers are, when they need to send remembrances, and to whom they need to send them. So Hallmark and its business partners can develop new services and offerings. For example, a colleague of mine told me how delighted he was to receive a phone call from his local Hallmark store reminding him that his wife's birthday was coming up in a week and that last year he'd sent her a bouquet of balloons. How would he like to send her a teddy bear with a bouquet of roses this year? He was so happy to be reminded and to be offered an easy, enticing offer, he said yes on the spot and whipped out his credit card!

What I like about the Hallmark story is that it's a great example of a mass-market company that was able to begin to build a one-to-one relationship with its end customers in a cost-effective way using electronic commerce technologies.

Another example you'll be reading about in these pages is General Motors' OnStar service. Here's a case where a car manufacturer asked its end customers what they really valued and wanted. It turned out that what they cared about most was security and convenience. So GM went into an entirely new business, that of providing twenty-four-hour assistance to drivers using the cell phones in their cars and a global positioning system (GPS) to locate them and help them find their way to where they need to go. I'm betting that GM's OnStar service will become a big business, and one that won't be limited to GM cars. Once GM realized what capabilities these new technologies made possible, it was able to formulate an entire new set of business processes designed to keep customers for life.

Or take electronic ticketing. Now that the technology allows us to do away with paper tickets for airlines, trains, and buses, we can book our travel in advance, change our reservations at the last minute, and just turn up with a credit card or an ID to receive a boarding pass and seat assignment. From the end customer's point of view, this is wonderful because it means you no longer have to worry about losing tickets or exchanging them if you weren't able to use them. From the travel agent's perspective, it saves the expense of delivering and exchanging tickets. And from the airline's point of view, it eliminates a very large expense as well as the delays in revenue recognition that result from the time-consuming reconciliation process. One travel industry executive explained to me that more than 20 percent of the cost of getting a customer onto a plane is "exhaust": the aftercosts of reconciling tickets with fares, refunds, and exchanges. So by streamlining the reservation process from the end customer's point of view—eliminating the need for paper tickets—travel providers are also streamlining their own business processes, thus cutting out useless costs.

The Role of the Middleman in Streamlining Business Processes

WHEN WE THINK of electronic commerce, we tend to think in terms of disintermediation: taking the middleman out of the loop. After all, if I can buy computers from Compaq directly from their Web site, why do I need the PC dealer I used to buy from? What added value does that middleman provide? I've been fascinated to discover that while there is a fair amount of disintermediation going on with electronic commerce technologies, there's an equally vibrant industry of middlepeople who have sprung into being precisely to serve the needs of companies that want to make it easy for customers to do business with them.

Here's one example: getting your PC repaired. Anyone who has tried to order a spare part for a discontinued IBM laptop has probably had the same difficult experience I've had. You call IBM. They tell you they no longer stock these parts and give you the numbers of a variety of dealers, one of whom *may* have the part you're looking for. It's up to you, the customer, to call around to find a dealer who has the part in stock. Meanwhile, the dealer who has the part you're looking for has no way of knowing you need it. There's got to be a better way, and there is.

PC Service Source is a middleman. It stocks spare parts and handles warranty service for more than thirty manufacturers, including Hewlett-Packard, Compaq Computer, Toshiba, Motorola, Dell Computer, and AST Computer. As the end customer, you're not aware that you're dealing with PC Service Source. You start by calling the PC manufacturer or the dealer from whom you bought the machine. What happens?

When you call Compaq to request information on spare parts or warranties, your call is passed through to PC Service Source. The PC Service Source customer service rep will access your warranty records, see if the part you need is in stock, and ship it to you directly, requesting your credit card number if there is a charge. From the customer's standpoint, you get the service you need during a single, seamless phone call.

Or if you call the dealer from whom you bought your PC, the dealer can access PC Service Source's Web-based ServiceNet for dealers. While you're still on the phone, the dealer can enter your information, access your warranty records directly, and check to see if the necessary part is in stock. He can then order the part to be shipped to you or to his office and capture the billing details. The transaction is complete, and you, the customer, are satisfied. Why? Because a middleman provides a very valuable service to both the manufacturer and the dealer, which results in better service to the end customer.

Here's another example of a middleman whose purpose in life is to make it easier for companies to serve their end customers better. CheckFree Corporation defines its niche as that of enabling the existing trusted financial intermediaries—banks—to become more valuable to their end customers: the consumers and businesses they serve. CheckFree is the company that provides the infrastructure that enables more than 2 million customers to pay their bills automatically through their banks. And CheckFree is the leading supplier of bill presentment services for Web-based banking. If you want to go on-line and actually *see* your telephone bills, your electric bills, and all of your recurring bills before you pay them, chances are that CheckFree's software and bill presentment service will be what your bank uses to make it easy for you, the end customer, to do on-line banking.

To be sure, not all middlemen will survive in the era of electronic commerce. Brokers, agents, and middlemen who assume that customers will continue to work through them to gain access to product information, pricing, and basic service are doomed. However, those who recognize customers' increased desire to help themselves and who focus on making it as easy as possible for the customer to transact business will prosper. Their ongoing challenge will be to ensure that they continue to offer services that the customer really values and can't do on his own. Middlemen such as CheckFree and PC Service Source, which specialize in working behind the scenes to complete the supplier's base offerings in order to provide a total one-stop-shopping solution to end customers will thrive.

Key Ingredients of Successful Business Process Design

OVER THE YEARS, I've noticed something very interesting about business process design work. No matter how you map out your customer-facing business processes, you always wind up with the same picture. There are many different scenarios: customers placing orders, customers changing orders, customers accessing information, customers checking their status, customers checking account balances, customers requesting service, and so on. In each case, the process begins with a request the customer is making of your company—or an offer you're making to the customer—and continues through a series of steps, or business events, that enable that request or offer to be consummated. Right below the process flow you almost always find a symbol that looks like a bucket or a barrel with arrows pointing in and out of it. That bucket symbolizes a repository of information about the customer. This is where people or systems go to look up information about customers—address information, order history, preferences, negotiated terms and conditions, profile information, account information, and so on. In practice, this information may not be stored in a single physical database. The implementation details are unimportant. What is important to recognize is that in order to redesign your customer-facing business processes, you will need some way to store and access information about your customers.

The term "business event" may have a technical ring to it, but it's not a technical term. It's a business reality. Every day, hundreds of events take place in our dealings with our customers. Each necessary step in any business process—place an order, check credit, check inventory, ship product, bill customer, collect payment—is a business event. Each of these events triggers interaction(s) among people and applications within your company or with outside partners. And the result of each event changes the status of that step in the process. Business events are the second critical ingredient in business process design.

If you were to take a bird's-eye view of your business from a customer's standpoint, you'd see a series of interactions spawned by the end customer that trigger a series of business events that ripple through your company and through your distribution partners' and suppliers' companies. This web of customer-triggered interactions is the extended nervous system that supports electronic commerce. In the next chapter, I'll describe how you can design an infrastructure that will let you participate fully in e-business.

Wire Your Company for Profit*: Design a Comprehensive, Evolving Electronic Business Architecture

You can get started in e-business by creating a Web site and then evolving it to meet your customers' and business partners' needs. That's what most companies have done and will continue to do. There's nothing wrong with that approach. However, over time, you're going to encounter two major sets of issues. First, you'll begin to realize that, in order to do a good job with your Web site, you're going to need to integrate it tightly into many of your company's back-end systems. Ideally, you'll want to design a generalizable integration strategy for all those applications, not a piecemeal approach. Second, you'll begin to recognize that you could use many of the same features you design into your Web site to enable customers to help themselves using Touch-Tone telephones, kiosks, or handheld devices. You can even use much of the same information and streamlined processes in the call centers where your sales and service people are interacting with customers on the phone. And you can reuse a lot of the processes and information you develop for your end customers to serve your channel partners. So again, it's a good idea to generalize your thinking beyond building a Web site to designing an architecture that will support electronic commerce both today and in the future.

So how should you approach the task of evolving an infrastructure to support your e-business strategy? As a business planner, you cannot simply hand this question over to your technical team; you'll need to think through some key policy and organizational issues. As a technology guru,

---

* Apologies to Ernst & Young, whose service "Wired for Profit" debuted in October 1997. I was involved in the promotion and launch of the service.

you'll have your own ideas, but you'll need to build consensus across organizational boundaries. Let me give you some suggestions. First, we'll look at the key issues that typically confront business and technology executives. Then I'll suggest a conceptual framework that you can both use to help crystallize your thinking. Next, I'll point to a handful of hot technologies you should be aware of, and finally, I'll walk you through the five stages most companies go through in evolving their electronic commerce initiatives, and then you can decide where you are.

Business Challenges: Who "Owns" the Customer?

THE BIGGEST CHALLENGES your organization will probably face in designing an integrated customer-friendly e-business environment will involve the ownership of customer information. If your business is organized around product lines, your customer information may be fragmented across product lines. So if a customer has bought products from more than one line of your business, you may not currently have a consolidated set of customer profile and transaction information.

Another challenge will arise from the different functional departments that interact with customers at different points in their relationship with your firm. Marketing, sales, order entry, customer service, billing, manufacturing, fulfillment, delivery, and quality control are just a few of the functional groups the end customer or channel partner may need to deal with. Enabling the streamlined business processes we discussed in the last chapter requires smooth handoffs across each of these departments, with as little human intervention as possible (remember, we want to make it easy for customers to help themselves).

Ideally, you want to establish clear ownership both for the customer information and for the business processes that affect the customer. As you'll see from many of the examples in this book, that ownership often seems to gravitate to a global sales or marketing vice president. But there are many organizations that don't have an executive position with that kind of purview. If yours is one, you may need to form a customer steering committee or appoint a new "customer czar."

Technical Challenges: Integrating Information and Applications

THERE ARE TYPICALLY two major technical challenges involved in rewiring your company to support customer-facing business processes. The first involves pulling together all of the relevant information about each customer across product lines and departments. The second challenge has to do with enabling work to flow automatically from one application to another—from order entry to credit check to accounting to inventory, for example.

There is no one right way of consolidating customer information. Generally speaking, you want to link customer information that resides in different databases and applications. You may choose to do this by actually copying and transforming all the relevant customer data into a central data warehouse (as Bell Atlantic did). Or you may simply access scattered customer information and assemble it at the time it's needed (as Wells Fargo did). Whichever approach you take, you're probably going to need to add quite a bit more customer profile information to your customer databases than you've had in the past.

Similarly, there's no one "right" way to link applications together. But the best approach will be to use some form of middleware—software that's specifically designed to let applications interact with one another across a network. Generally speaking, you'll want to leave most of your existing applications alone, simply sending messages to them and receiving information back. There have, though, been cases—Bell Atlantic is the most notable—where companies have taken the opportunity to redesign a number of core applications so that they would be better able to support streamlined business processes across product lines.

Four Useful Concepts to Bridge Business and Technology

OVER THE PAST several years, there has emerged a set of conceptual building blocks that I've found really useful in helping companies design their electronic commerce architectures. What's nice about these constructs is that they're not technical mumbo jumbo. They're concepts that every businessperson can understand and appreciate. Yet to a technically trained application designer or systems architect, these constructs pack a lot of power. Once they've been identified and agreed upon by the business folks, the techies can use them to build very flexible, extensible systems.

And that's what you're looking for in the design of an e-business architecture. Here they are.

1. CUSTOMER PROFILES. If you're going to create customer-facing applications that take advantage of e-business technologies to deliver personalized service in a cost-effective manner, you'll probably want to use customer profiles. A customer profile is where the customer gives you his preferences and where you note important things you've learned about the customer. For example, GM's OnStar service already had basic information about each customer—name, phone number, address, the GM car the customer is driving—but after a year, OnStar discovered it needed to add much more information: what gas credit card the customer uses, who else in the family drives the car, what kind of restaurants the customer prefers. These aren't just "nice-to-know" features that a customer service representative would see when on the phone with a customer; they're actionable pieces of information that can be used to launch applications. In OnStar's case, when a customer asks for directions to the nearest gas station, the system will highlight the ones whose credit cards he carries. When his wife requests help finding a place to stop for lunch, the OnStar system will retrieve the restaurants from its database that will be most acceptable to her. As another example, American Airlines already had customer profiles containing customers' seating and meal preferences, but it wanted to extend and enhance that information: which airport does the customer typically fly out of? Where does the customer like to go on weekends? This allows American to send targeted e-mails out to customers promoting special bargain weekend fares—in my case, from Boston to San Francisco.

2. BUSINESS RULES. Every business is run using a set of implicit and explicit rules. "If a customer orders 100-plus parts, give him this discount." "If the customer's credit is good, approve the order." "If you order this product, these are the options currently available." These are all examples of explicit business rules. Others, such as "If she's a long-time customer and she needs an expedited shipment, waive the freight charges," may be implicit rules—things people do that haven't been codified in policy manuals or software. Business rules go hand in hand with customer profiles. By combining the two, you can begin to target the right information, products, and offers to your customers. For example, I stipulated a business rule in my Hertz car rental profile: "If a rental car with the Never Lost option is available, offer that car

first." Now I don't need to ask for this special service; Hertz's computer systems will automatically offer me that option.

3. BUSINESS EVENTS. In the last chapter, I mentioned business events. Why bring them up again? Because once you identify all the key business events—e.g., check bank balance, transfer funds from savings to checking, pay phone bill—in a given business process, you've identified all the places in which systems have to interact with one another. If the business people can agree on what all the key events are that affect the customer, the technical people can ensure that information and tasks flow smoothly from one system to another for each event.

4. BUSINESS OBJECTS. Business and technical people need a common language to describe their business. Business rules and business events are part of that language, and business objects are its fundamental building blocks. A business object is an entity in your business that has an agreed-upon definition. For example, "customer," "account," "order," and "product" are all examples of business objects. Business people need to describe these explicitly enough so that all the important nuances are captured. What's the difference between a retail customer and a wholesale customer? A checking account and an investment account? An order for a product that we have in inventory and an order for a product that needs to be manufactured? And so on. Each type of customer, account, or product will have different behaviors and attributes. In order to design a streamlined set of business processes for the customer, the business folks will need to describe these business objects to the technical folks. They can then use that understanding to build the applications that will allow the customer to interact with these objects electronically.

How will these concepts help you deal with the organizational and technical challenges I described at the outset? From an organizational standpoint, you can collect customer profile information, business rules, and business events from each group within your company that owns a piece of the customers. Then, by pulling this information together into a common business model, each group will be able to see where its information fits. This is essentially what Hertz did when it set out to build a single global customer profile for its #1 Club Gold program.

From a technical standpoint, you'll be able to use the business events that each group has identified to create interfaces among the applications that need to interact with one another. You'll use the business rules and customer profiles to develop front-end applications that will respond appropriately to each customer. And you'll use the business object definitions to design the components of your new applications.

In the Handbook I offer as an adjunct to this book, you'll find a technical road map that describes how a technical team can use these concepts to design its e-business architecture, as well as a description of a workshop you can run to quickly capture all the key customer profile information, business rules, business events, and business objects that will enable you to jump-start your electronic commerce projects.

"Hot" Technologies That Businesspeople Engaging in E-commerce Should Understand

MANY TECHNOLOGIES ARE involved in implementing an electronic commerce infrastructure. I'm not going to bore you by covering them all. However, there are two caveats I'd like you to bear in mind. First, use the Internet both inside and outside your company as your common networking infrastructure. You can make it secure. You can make it private. But you should take advantage of all the technical standards that are rapidly evolving on the Internet. Second, think about using the World Wide Web itself as the development environment for most of your customer-facing applications. Even if your customers aren't helping themselves directly via the Web, you can probably design a call center application, an integrated voice response application, or even an application that will run on a customer's handheld terminal, using the Web as your platform. The best approach is to link all of the back-end systems that impact customer-facing business processes into the Web. Keep all of the common customer profile, product, accounting, and order status information in a Web-accessible format. Then develop different user interfaces and functions for each of the different channels through which customers interact with your organization.

There are four emerging technologies in particular that business folks should know enough about to be able to have a golf course conversation about them. They're all strategically important to electronic commerce.

1. SMART CARDS. Think of a smart card as a bank ATM card with the ability to store information and perform transactions. For example, a smart card could hold your customer profile information. It could store your frequent-flyer numbers and your current frequent-flyer account balances and let you purchase an airline ticket by debiting those miles. Or it could store your medical records (my father's dream). It can even

hold cash for you and act as an electronic wallet, allowing you to pay for the subway, bus, taxis, or newspapers in any currency (since currency conversion is automatic at the point of sale). At the Hong Kong Jockey Club, one of the world's most prestigious horse-racing enterprises, customers have been known to load up to $50,000 into their smart cards so they can conveniently place bets during an afternoon of racing!

Why is it important to understand smart cards? Because within the next few years, they're going to become ubiquitous. You'll use them to access your computer, your bank, and your grocery store, and to perform most other services. The smart card, along with a password, a fingerprint, or an eye scan, will identify you uniquely to all the computer-based services you use. The smart card may not be in the form of a plastic card; it might be a ring, a watch, or anything you carry on your person that can communicate with computers and telephones. It identifies you and stores vital information.

Since your customers will begin to have smart cards, you'll want to be sure that your applications work with the smart card the customer already has so he doesn't have to complicate his life by having as many different smart cards as most of us have plastic credit cards and membership cards today. Who will issue smart cards? Transit authorities, banks, universities, airlines, and government agencies, to name a few. In different parts of the world, different players are taking the lead. In many European and Asian countries, the local government issues smart cards that are used for social services. In the United States, banks are likely to issue them to consumers because they are less expensive for them to support than credit cards are.

2. DIGITAL CERTIFICATES. A digital certificate enables two entities to establish each other's identity for electronic commerce transactions. Think about it. If a person isn't standing in front of you, able to show you some form of identification, how do you know she's the person she claims to be? She identifies herself with a digital certificate. Businesses need to have them too, so that when they collect money from people or submit filings to a regulatory agency over the Net, the party on the other end knows he is dealing with the business he thinks he's dealing with and not some imposter. Digital certificates can be stored on smart cards and in computer systems. They certify the authenticity of the person performing the transaction.

3. XML. XML stands for Extensible Mark-up Language. But you don't need to remember that. What you do need to know is that it's time to

start using XML to identify all the information about each of your products—the type of product, its attributes, its price—everything that a person or another program might need to know about it. XML is rapidly becoming the lingua franca of electronic commerce. Within two years, all electronically distributed information, and all product descriptions, pricing, shipping and ordering information, will be coded in XML.

4. **JAVA.** In the movie *The Graduate*, the young protagonist, played by Dustin Hoffman, is given career advice by one of his father's friends. "Plastics," the man tells him. "Get into plastics and you won't go wrong." For the past two years, I've been doing the same thing to every young person I come across. "Java," I tell them. "If you learn to program in Java, you'll never be without a job!" Why should you care what the hottest programming language is? Three reasons: There will be more Java programmers available than any other talent pool. Programs written in Java take less time to produce because it's much less error-prone. And Java will run on any platform, from a TV set-top box, to a cell phone, to a Web site, without any modifications.

Now you know all you need to know about electronic commerce technologies to impress your friends and neighbors at the next backyard barbecue!

Now let's walk through the five stages most companies go through with their e-business initiatives. You've probably already mastered a couple of these stages with your company's Web site or with an automated voice response system. The first four stages are relevant no matter what kind of customer-facing technologies you use. The fifth stage—fostering community—is germane for Web-based initiatives.

The Five Stages of Electronic Business

COMPANIES TYPICALLY GO through five distinct stages in their e-business initiatives:

1. Supplying company and product information (brochureware)
2. Providing customer support and enabling interactions
3. Supporting electronic transactions
4. Personalizing interactions with customers
5. Fostering community

1. Supplying Company and Product Information (Brochureware)

"Brochureware" is the term commonly given to a "first-generation" Web site, one that simply provides marketing information and company background information. There's a consensus in the business community that this isn't a very profitable stage. Yet it's generally considered a prerequisite. I've heard lots of people say to me, "Our company has a Web site, but it's only brochureware." They're embarrassed that their company's Web site is little more than an electronic brochure. However, before building a house, you need a foundation. Brochureware is a useful first step because it allows people outside the company to get an overview of the business and its products, history, and financial status, or even just find a mailing address.

A number of companies have also done a great job of providing useful company and product information that is accessible via Touch-Tone phone: hours of operation, current product availability and pricing, driving directions, mailing address. This is the phone-accessible equivalent of a first-generation Web site. The major difference is that when designing a phone-based information system, you focus only on the "must have" information and leave out all the "nice to have," or ancillary, information.

You can use a Web-based information system for informational kiosks as well. However, by the time you're ready to invest in a kiosk, you'll also be ready for stages 2 and 3.

2. Providing Customer Support and Enabling Interactions

Customer support is the next stage. And here's where the real payoff begins. If you have a group of consumer or business customers who are currently, or likely soon to be, Internet-enabled, this is where you want to put your emphasis. As Michael Dell, CEO and founder of Dell Computer, says, customer support is the most beneficial—and least applauded—application on the Web. Customers want to help themselves to information, both before they make a purchase and afterward. They want to research their choices and make informed decisions. Once they've placed an order, they want to check on the status of that order. They want to get help understanding how to make the product work without waiting for someone to answer the phone and answer their questions. By and large, Internet-savvy people are delighted to help themselves. And woe to the company that doesn't provide enough information via the Web! As Phil Gibson, interactive marketing director for National Semiconductor, commented, "Every time we don't post product information on our Web site, our customers give us grief. They want to know everything *we* know about our products."

You can also develop interactive automated phone systems that give customers the ability to help themselves to information, check on the status of their shipment, see if payment has been received, check on the balance due, and perform basic interactions (starting or stopping delivery of a newspaper, for example). How do you know which support functions customers need? It's easy. You simply log the volume of phone calls and e-mails your company receives by type of inquiry, and you will quickly see what categories the highest numbers of inquiries fall into. These are the functions you want to make available via Touch-Tone phone.

Customers' handheld devices, like cell phones, pagers, and personal digital assistants (PDAs), can be used in much the same way that an automated phone system would work. You provide a way for the customer to submit very focused, but frequently requested, queries from their handhelds. For example, actual flight departure time and gate information is something travelers need before they leave for the airport. You can provide this information in response to a customer inquiry, or you can supply that information each time the customer travels on your airline, based on the customer's profile.

Kiosks are another great way of letting customers interact with your organization. Customers should be able to identify themselves by account number and password, make inquiries, and help themselves to the information they need. Today, the most cost-effective way of designing a kiosk is by using the Web as your development and deployment platform.

3. Supporting Electronic Transactions

Once you have a Web site that explains your products and services and lets customers help themselves, the logical next step is to enable customers actually to purchase goods and services from the Web—the transactions stage. There is nothing more annoying to prospective customers than to be ready to place an order on the Web and be told that they have to "call 1-800 . . ." To be fair, some customers may choose not to place an order over the Internet for a variety of reasons. They may like talking to someone to close the sale. They may need additional information in order to feel comfortable making the purchase. Or they may not feel comfortable sending their credit card information over the Internet, despite assurances that the site is secure. However, you'll probably be surprised at the number of customers who will be willing to order from you electronically, particularly customers who are repeat buyers. You may also be surprised at the amount of transactions people are currently doing over the Web. One customer did $100 million worth of business with Cisco Systems over the Internet last year without ever talking to a person!

By the same token, customers should be able to perform routine transactions over the phone without talking to a customer service representative. If you're ordering something you've ordered in the past, paying a bill, transferring funds, or buying stock, you can easily handle these types of transactions using your Touch-Tone phone.

4. Personalizing Interactions with Customers

So now you've got a highly informational and interactive Web site. The customer can help herself to all the information she needs to make a purchasing decision. And she can go to the Web site to answer any questions she has about the product or find out about the status of her transactions with your company. What do you do next to ensure that she'll keep doing business with your firm? You ask her to tell you more about herself. You build and maintain a profile about her particular interests and preferences. How does she prefer to have you communicate with her? By phone, e-mail, or fax? Which of your products or services does she care about? Perhaps she's interested in only one of the six product lines you offer. Then you personalize the Web site for her, so that every time she comes back, you greet her by name, show her first the things she cares about, and offer her things that fit her profile. Every time I return to Amazon.com, for example, the home page welcomes me by name and suggests several new books that are similar to books that I've bought in the past. This gives me a warm and fuzzy feeling each time I go back to this virtual bookstore.

The more of himself a customer leaves with your company, the greater the hold you have on him. Financial services' Web sites are the best example of this "stickiness" phenomenon. Once a customer enters all the companies whose bills he wants to pay automatically and the number of shares of stock and mutual funds he owns (so the value of his portfolio can be updated automatically), he's going to be really reluctant to have to enter all the information again at some other company's Web site. Once a customer has made an investment in a business by giving it the information he wants it to have in order to streamline the process of doing business with it, unless it betrays the customer's trust, he's likely to stick around.

5. Fostering Community

Once you've established a level of trust and a one-on-one relationship with a customer using electronic tools, you can move to the next step: fostering a feeling of community among your customers. You'll be surprised at the extent to which customers like to help one another out with technical problems, give one another tips, and swap experiences. Cisco Systems was able to capitalize on customers' willingness to help one another early in its history. By encouraging customers to answer one another's technical questions, the company was able to increase the level of customer support it offered without adding hundreds more support engineers.

People like to feel they're part of the in crowd. That's why so many Web sites offer "members only" areas. American Airlines recognized this when it set up a separate area in its Web site for their AAdvantage frequent flyers. Microsoft understood this when it set up separate areas for CIOs and developers.

People also like to contribute their own ideas and thoughts. *The Wall Street Journal Interactive Edition* capitalizes on the fact that many of its customers like to voice their opinions about hot topics in the business news. By creating forums where customers can enter into dialogue with one another about issues they're passionate about, the *Journal* makes those customers feel much more connected to the *Journal*. The customer who voices an opinion on-line is going to return day after day to see how others have reacted.

Tying It All Together

So what's involved in designing an infrastructure for electronic business? You start with your end customers. You redesign the key business processes that impact those customers from the outside in. You do this by capturing all of the key business events, specifying business rules, and defining each of your core business objects. Then your technology team can take that evolving blueprint and use the Internet and the Web as their design platform for customer-facing applications. They'll pull customer information together across product lines and functions and add extensible customer profiles. They'll use the business rules you've defined to trigger automated workflows across departments and applications. They'll design information databases and knowledge bases and code the information in them in such a way that your partners', suppliers', and customers' electronic commerce applications will be able to locate the information they need and act on it. And they'll design a series of customer-facing applications—for the Web, for kiosks, for integrated voice response systems, for call center personnel involved in telesales, telemarketing, and customer support, and for the variety of electronic systems and devices that your customers will be using to interact with your company. These customer-facing e-business applications will be tightly integrated into the rest of your operational systems, and they'll extend back out across the network to your suppliers, distributors, bankers, and all your other business partners.

As you read through the case studies in this book, you'll find that no one company has built its infrastructure in exactly this way, but many have come close. And if you were to ask most of these folks how they'd design their electronic commerce infrastructures if they were starting today instead of two to three years ago, I suspect they'd tell you that they'd follow a process very similar to the one I just outlined. But before we move on to tell the stories of the pioneers who have been homesteading on the electronic commerce frontier, let's look at the last strategic step you'll want to take before you embark on your journey: figuring out how you're going to measure your success.

Foster Customer Loyalty, the Key to Profitability in Electronic Commerce

On average, U.S. companies lose 50 percent of their customers in five years. How many leads must you pursue to get an order from a new customer? How long will it be before the profits from additional orders pay back the cost of acquiring that new customer? In some industries, recouping the cost of acquiring a new customer takes years. It's no surprise that firms that keep valuable customers are more profitable than those with little repeat business.

Electronic commerce lets you build cost-effective, loyalty-enhancing relationships with your most profitable customers. When you make it easier for them to do business with you, you "lock them in" to a level of convenience and a set of habits that's hard for competitors to beat. Customers who do business with you electronically are also more likely to upsell themselves into higher-profit-margin products and services, as both Dell Computer and Wells Fargo can attest.

The best way to measure the results of your electronic commerce initiatives will be to base your return on investment on increased customer loyalty at a lower cost to serve. That's what American Airlines, Bell Atlantic, Cisco Systems, PhotoDisc, and iPrint have done. It works! Even if the business model for your electronic commerce initiative is based on advertising revenues, loyal customers who keep coming back for more will lead to increased advertising rates, as both *The Wall Street Journal* and Tripod found.

First let's take a look at the economics of customer loyalty. Then we'll examine a few of the issues involved in measuring and achieving customer loyalty.

How a Loyal Customer Feeds Your Bottom Line

QUANTITATIVE DATA SHOW that improving customer retention has a profound impact on a company's bottom line. Firms that are able to attract and keep the right customers are significantly more profitable than those whose customers defect after a few transactions. There are several revenue and cost elements to measure in order to understand your relationship with individual customers and the effect that increased customer retention has on profits. Figure 3 depicts the various revenue components of customer loyalty.

A number of elements can be measured that relate to achieving higher revenues via customer retention, including:

- BASE REVENUE. *BASE REVENUE* is the revenue you receive from a given transaction, regardless of customer relationship or loyalty or product discounts. The longer you keep a paying customer, the more of this base revenue you receive.
- GROWTH. When the initial transaction creates value for a customer, he buys additional products from you. Your revenue from that customer grows as your share of that customer's buying dollar grows.
- REFERRAL. *REFERRAL REVENUE* occurs when your satisfied customer refers her associates to your firm. The longer your relationship with a customer lasts, the more new customers are referred to you.
- PRICE PREMIUM. Contrary to popular belief, loyal customers will pay more for your products than will a new customer who isn't necessarily convinced of the value of your offerings. If the customer is satisfied with the value you deliver, why would he incur the trouble and risk of trying another product? Loyal customers are not tempted to defect by competitors' discounts, and they do not require discounts to continue to buy from you. The more satisfied the customer is with the relationship, the greater the premium the customer will pay.

You'll also need to look at elements that impact how much you need to spend to keep the customer pool viable. Significant considerations in this area include:

- NO-COST ACQUISITION. The most successful loyalty-based businesses spend nothing on acquiring new customers. Customers never—or rarely—defect. Revenues increase as these customers buy more each

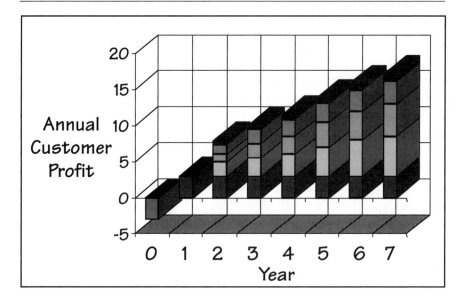

Once acquired, a loyal customer boosts the firm's profits by making more purchases, paying higher prices, and being less expensive to work with. He also refers his associates to your firm, eliminating the cost of acquiring those customers.

year. Your new customers are referred to you by your satisfied and loyal customers. And the new customers fit the profile of your best customers.

- **EXPERIENCED CUSTOMER.** The loyal customer costs less to work with. He has learned your product line and processes. He doesn't call the wrong department, asking for products your firm doesn't provide. While you may have provided him with special tools to support the relationship, such as worksheets, electronic access, or on-line product configurators, you save a great deal of money because he can help himself in a number of transactions, and when you work together, he is prepared for an efficient exchange.

The customer pool cannot remain stagnant, however, if your company wishes to grow. By retaining the majority of your customers while soliciting new ones, you benefit on both sides:

- BY INCREASING CUSTOMER INVENTORY. You will certainly lose customers each year. That's business. And you must replace these customers as they leave. Take as an example a firm that finds 10 percent new customers each year and loses 10 percent of existing customers. There is no change in the size of the customer inventory. If this firm retains 5 percent more customers, without having to spend additional money to acquire new customers, its customer inventory will grow by 5 percent per year. In fourteen years, it will have twice as many customers as today. The firm will have grown substantially just by keeping customers longer.
- BY INCREASING CUSTOMER TENURE. The positive effect on profit of *more* customers is overshadowed by the even more positive effect of *more valuable* customers. Customers probably buy more from you each year, generating more revenue and more profit. In Figure 3, you can see that a seventh-year customer contributes substantially more profit than a first-year customer does. The longer a customer stays with you, the more valuable she becomes.

Measuring the Retention Effect

WE'RE ACCUSTOMED TO thinking of customers in market segments: urban male teens, high-income singles, active senior citizens. It's important to understand that we need to look at *individual* customers in doing retention analysis. On average, if your company is making money, your customer base is profitable. However, in every market segment you identify, some customers contribute profit while others make you take a loss.

For example, in the banking industry, customer profitability analysis has been honed to a fine art. One bank that performs such analyses has discovered that the 20 percent most profitable customers account for more than

100 percent of its profits! The remaining 80 percent of customers erode that profit down to the figure that appears on the bank's income statement.

Another pioneer in customer profitability analysis is an electronics manufacturer. This firm, convinced that it was servicing too many customers, began producing profit-and-loss statements by customer. This immediately identified the set of customers responsible for losses and those contributing the greatest profit. Using this information, the firm now concentrates on its best customers, with prices that no longer subsidize unprofitable relationships.

We need to be able to measure this profit and loss by customer, just as we do by product. So our measurement system has to focus on measuring customers as individuals, not as members of a market segment. And measuring profit by individual will require new cost data and new analysis.

Business decisions that increase customer retention require information that may not have been collected or assessed before. The list of useful data includes:

- Customer revenues and costs over time
- Referrals from the customer
- Reason for defection
- Cause of loyalty, or what the customer values in your product

New information enables new analyses, supporting a new set of decisions, such as:

- Determining profits per customer
- Identifying the most and least profitable customers
- Understanding the characteristics of your best customers
- Tailoring marketing campaigns to acquire the right customers
- Analyzing how to improve your value to customers
- Assessing how to reduce defections

Measuring Customer Revenue

MANY COMPANIES ROUTINELY measure revenue per customer in order to calculate sales commissions. Generally, order and billing systems store customer revenue information and generate customer revenue reports by territory and by product. Reporting revenue per customer presents no real challenge to today's financial applications.

But for a few industries, it isn't obvious what a customer is. Is it a household? Or individuals in a household? AT&T regards each phone line in a household as belonging to a separate customer entity. Bell Atlantic, on the other hand, has consolidated all members of each household into a single customer.

Once a decision on what constitutes a customer has been reached, achieving a common customer identity across product lines may be the next challenge. In a product-focused company, each line of business has a different customer identification number, and no line of business is looking at any one customer's overall relationship with the firm. In this environment, arriving at a common definition of the customer presents a serious obstacle to assessing customer revenue and profitability.

Measuring Customer Costs

THE CHIEF DIFFICULTY in analyzing profit is measuring cost. Accounting systems are helpless with regard to measuring actual costs. They can measure historic costs, and they can suggest an average direct and indirect cost for a product. They can allocate a portion of corporate overhead and sales and marketing costs to a customer or product. But measuring the actual cost to take an order, make one unit of the product, and deliver it to a customer is just not possible.

The standard financial accounting model hides the value of loyalty. It is designed for external reporting, not management use. Its focus is capital assets and depreciation, cost of goods sold, and work in process.

Accounting systems typically allocate sales, general, and administrative (SGA) expense across product lines. But this category can account for as much as 25 to 30 percent of total costs, and it includes substantial customer care expense. SGA costs need to be tracked per customer to understand the service cost. Simply allocating a blanket percentage to all customers doesn't give a true picture.

In the past decade, accounting systems have been under fire to improve product cost and profitability data. Today's information is still not accurate. Activity-based costing (ABC) offers important additional data and analysis that can improve cost estimates. ABC models the enterprise based on business events (for example, costs to place an order, deliver a product, service a customer) and associates the events with activities and processes. The resulting costs are assigned to cost objects, which can be customers, products, or processes. Once you've begun to model your business with business events and business objects, you'll be better equipped to adopt an ABC model.

Implementing an ABC system to analyze customer profitability is no simple matter. First, an ABC model is developed to analyze customer-driven costs. To avoid falling into the trap of an endless implementation cycle for your ABC efforts, start by focusing only on the business events that impact your customers. Next, multidimensional analysis is used to establish the cost to serve the customer. Finally, profit-and-loss statements are structured to highlight the relationships between product-driven and customer-driven activity costs.

Measuring Customer Profitability

At the beginning of our customer analysis, we may not be certain what the costs per customer are. We aren't sure what period to inspect for profitability or whether a customer is a person or a household. It isn't clear when we should look at standard costs or actual costs or when we should include allocated costs. Yet we want to get started building a picture of customer profitability in order to have a baseline for our electronic commerce initiatives.

Given our inexperience and the imprecision of our data, it's important to be able to experiment with different analyses. A good first step is to divide your customer base into quartiles by profitability. But don't use a static picture (the most recent financial reporting period, for example). Instead, take a few different time periods; view profits calculated from actual costs, with no allocations, over twenty-month, twelve-month, and three-month moving averages.

The top quartile will be your most profitable customers. The bottom fourth will be your least profitable customers. As a starting point, you can target your electronic commerce initiatives for your most profitable customers. Next, you may want to examine ways you can use electronic commerce technologies to reduce the cost of doing business with your least profitable customers while at the same time increasing the revenues derived from that group.

Evaluating Defection and Loyalty

Keeping customers is not a matter of lavishing attention upon them in the hope that they will remember your firm. Customers stay with your firm because of the value that is provided.

There are hundreds of entertaining defection stories describing how a company alienated a customer. But most often customers defect not in anger but because of their perceived value of a product offering. New products appear on the market, or an established competitor comes up with a more innovative pricing scheme, feature set, or delivery option. The customer suddenly views this alternative as having more value. Also, customers' habits or needs may change, changing their perceived value of the attributes of your product line.

For example, Wang Laboratories had a near monopoly in word processing systems and provided outstanding customer service. But by the early 1990s, Wang's word processors didn't measure up in price and function to the new PCs arriving on the market. Despite the high quality of Wang's service, customers defected. For a number of years, Wang failed to notice these defections because the company was still booking lots of orders from new customers.

Customers generally don't say good-bye. Like old soldiers, they just fade away. If you don't have a system in place to identify defectors, you might not even notice that they have disappeared.

Of course, your order data might reveal declining purchases by a particular customer, but this information comes to attention only if you are looking for it. You might track buying patterns of a sample set of users, or you might periodically survey a portion of your customer list to ask what they buy and from whom, but again, you must go and look for that information. To stem the defection tide, you need to maintain and actively monitor some key information:

- How many defections have there been?
- What do the defectors have in common?
- Why did they defect?

For example, Dudley Nigg at Wells Fargo discovered that he could decrease defections by 50 percent by offering on-line banking services. Customers who would normally have changed banks when they moved out of Wells's banking territory no longer did so if they were on-line customers.

Finding and Keeping the Right Customers

So NOW WE know who the right customers are—they're the profitable ones identified in our profitability analysis. Next we need to identify and understand the characteristics of these customers. Some customers may be people who prefer long-term relationships; some might simply be profitable because they are rather passive, proving to be undemanding and predictable. But in general, the right customers are those whose needs match the value you deliver.

Having identified their characteristics, you can take marketing actions designed to attract the right customers. Similarly, knowing the characteristics of unprofitable customers helps you design programs to avoid attracting them.

But, you say, isn't this the same kind of target marketing you're already doing—male urban teens and so forth? Not at all. Segment marketing is based on generic demographics; marketing by customer characteristics is based on developing highly subjective (to your company) profiles of individuals whose demographics may vary widely.

Customer profitability analysis will inevitably discover a large number of profit-draining customers. What do you do with that information? The obvious answer is to turn these customers around, making them profitable by reducing the cost to serve them or by increasing the revenue attained from them.

Failing that, customers should be encouraged to defect to a provider that is a better match for their needs. Now, wait a minute. Am I actually advocating taking steps to intentionally discourage a customer? Difficult as that may seem, it is safer than asking your stockholders or your top-tier customers to subsidize the bottom tier.

A high customer retention rate is proof that the firm is delivering better value than customers can find elsewhere. When you understand what that value is, you can offer more of it to your customers, thereby increasing your share of their purchases.

What is the value that you offer to your customers? Beyond the basic product quality and features, customers value organizations that are easy to do business with!

Challenge: Moving from a Product-centric to a Customer-centric Model

TOO MANY COMPANIES are product-centered. Companies with multiple product lines often treat each one as an island of business. For each product, there are dedicated salespeople, support people, product development, billing, and so forth. There is little communication across product boundaries.

In this model, the customer is the anonymous target of marketing campaigns, and the financial systems are designed to evaluate product market share, product costs, and product contribution to profits. But when you think about it, that's taking things backward. Revenue and profits come from customers, not products.

Adding to the problem, sales efforts seem to focus on identifying *new* customers—qualified leads—rather than on delighting the existing customer base so that each customer will spend more and more on the organization's products and services. The cost of finding new customers often outweighs the initial purchase each customer makes.

Customers—even corporate customers—are people, and people appreciate and value being treated with courtesy, respect, and appreciation. When a customer calls or accesses your Web site, he wants to be recognized. At a minimum, he wants you to know his name, the products and services he buys, how long he has been a customer, how valuable a customer he is, his special requirements, his latest request for assistance, his latest order, and who handled his last call. (Notice that this minimum is quite a lot!)

If the employee he interacts with does not have this information, the customer will be frustrated and feel undervalued. A customer should never have to ask, "Don't you know who I am?" (See Figure 4.)

Organizations that are aligned by product and function can't satisfy a customer's need to be recognized and remembered. They can't deliver a consolidated view of a customer. Their applications and data are segmented by product line. There is no single concept of "customer." If your company is product-focused as opposed to customer-focused, you're going to have a more difficult time using electronic commerce technologies to build and maintain customer loyalty. You'll need to pull customer information together and streamline business processes across product lines in order to be successful.

Customer Focus Will Become the Norm

TODAY, COMPANIES THAT are measuring customer profitability and have organized themselves to retain customers have a strategic advantage. In the very near future, customers will expect you to know who they are and deliver what they need. Within two years, companies that identify and leverage customers will be the norm. Firms still selling product families to anonymous customers will be struggling to remain profitable.

The customer-focused organization may seem to be a far cry from where you are today. But taking a step in that direction can have a substantial impact on your firm's bottom line.

So take that first step today. Identify some of your most profitable customers, and then design electronic commerce solutions to help cement your relationships with them. See what happens. Your firm will learn a great deal from the exercise, and a little bit of success will make the next steps seem easier. Make sure to start out by knowing the retention rate for the set of customers you've targeted and the costs of serving those customers. Then you'll be armed with the metrics you'll need to measure the results of your electronic commerce initiatives.

FIGURE 4

PRODUCT-FOCUSED ORGANIZATION

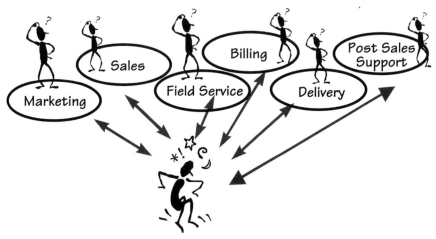

Don't you know who I am?!!

Our customer is struggling to explain his situation, once again, to yet another compartmentalized, product-focused department. The willing and helpful employees he talks to just don't have the information they need to help him. The customer talks first to one, then to another, getting no closer to solving his problem.

PART TWO

Eight Critical
Success Factors
and Case Studies

How to Assimilate the Critical Success Factors and Case Studies

In the next eight chapters we're going to examine each of these eight critical success factors (CSFs) in detail:

- Target the right customers
- Own the customer's total experience
- Streamline business processes that impact the customer
- Provide a 360-degree view of the customer relationship
- Let customers help themselves
- Help customers do their jobs
- Deliver personalized service
- Foster community

They sound so simple, so prosaic. Yet as I "unpack" each one, you'll see that there are many subtleties involved in getting them right! There are scores of organizations whose e-business initiatives serve as testimony to each. So I've peppered the descriptions of the CSFs with lots of examples from all kinds of companies, including nonprofits and government agencies, from all over the world.

After each CSF discussion, I'll tell you the stories of two different companies that have done a good job of implementing that particular CSF (as well as some others). At the beginning of each of these case studies, you'll find a chart like the one shown here:

Critical Success Factors in the "X" Story	
⋆ Target the right customers	✓ Let customers help themselves
Own the customer's total experience	✓ Help customers do their jobs
✓ Streamline business processes that impact the customer	✓ Deliver personalized service
Provide a 360-degree view of the customer relationship	Foster community
⋆ = Featured in this discussion	✓ = Touched on in this discussion

The purpose of the chart is to help you navigate through the story. Since all the case studies are best practices, each one illustrates several of the CSFs. The stars indicate which CSFs are the focal point of the story. The check marks show you which other CSFs you can expect to find discussed in the case.

Selecting the Case Studies

How DID I select these particular companies to feature? It was truly difficult. I had over forty companies from which to choose. Basically, I selected the ones I felt best illustrated the CSF success factor I was trying to highlight. The companies chosen have all done a great job of making it easy for customers to do business with them. And they're not finished yet. But that's not to say that they've done the best job or that there aren't other companies or organizations that are equally impressive. The other characteristic that the sixteen companies I've chosen to spotlight have in common is that they were all willing to share their experiences in enough detail to be useful to someone who wants to learn from watching others.

Of course, my research hasn't stopped here. I've written up many more case studies than you'll find in these pages, and I'll continue to do so. Be sure to visit our Web site, www.customers.com, to get an up-to-date listing. And if you'd like me to chronicle your company's initiative, drop me a line at pseybold@customers.com. I'll be happy to take a look at what you've done.

The Technical Stuff

BECAUSE I'VE WRITTEN this book for an audience of both business executives and technologists, I've tried to tell each story from the business and organizational perspective without getting mired in the technical details. Yet I know that many of you will want to know a bit about what kind of systems and technologies were used, so I've included a boxed section in each case like the one shown here:

Evolving the Technical Infrastructure

This is where I give an overview of the technology approaches used, and some of the thinking behind the architectural choices made. This section is for techies only!

My Prescription for Action

TOWARDS THE END of each case study, you'll see a section titled "Patty's Rx." This is where I offer my own observations about what I think the company should do next to improve its e-business initiative. There's always room for improvement! And, of course, as a consultant, I can't resist the urge to offer my two cents' worth. What you may find interesting about this section is what has transpired since these prescriptions were written (about six months before the actual publication of the book). Six months is a long time in Web time! So the chances are pretty good that a number of improvements will have been made by the time you read these prescriptions. You'll get a chance to see whether the things I thought were important made it to the top of the priority list. (Of course, all these companies prioritize their efforts based on what their customers want—not on what some consultant suggests!)

Take-Aways and Lessons Learned

AT THE END of each case study, you'll find a list of "take-aways." These are the key points I hope you'll assimilate from each story. They're the points I thought you'd find useful for your own initiatives. Of course, if you're like me, as you're reading about another company's situation, all kinds of ideas will start firing in your head about your own organization. So your take-aways may be quite different from the ones I've left for you.

After each pair of case studies, I've provided a summary of the lessons I learned in researching both initiatives that I thought you'd find useful. What I'm hoping you'll take away from this book is not just the stories of what American Airlines or Cisco Systems has done but the patterns that emerge when you look at a group of companies that have pioneered in using electronic commerce technologies to make it easy for their customers to do business with them.

Synthesizing the Best Practices

AT THE END of this book, I've provided a summary chapter highlighting more of the patterns that cut across all of the different industries, organizations, and critical success factors. There's no end to the learning in this field. The more you know, the more you still need to experiment and explore. So this synthesis is not meant as a definitive set of best practices. Rather, you should view it as one way of stimulating your own thinking. What other patterns did you notice? What approaches did others take that you'll want to emulate (or avoid)?

Finally, if you're ready to embark on your own Customers.com initiative or refine one that's already under way, you'll want to order the *Customers.com Handbook* from the Customers.com Web site (www.customers.com). In it you'll find two "road maps": one for the business people on your team, another for your technology folks, as well as a workshop you can run that will jump-start your Customers.com project.

Target the Right Customers

American Airlines and National Semiconductor are great examples of companies that have carefully targeted their World Wide Web initiatives to the right customer: the one that makes a difference to the bottom line. American targets its Web site at its most loyal customers: its 32 million–plus AAdvantage frequent flyers. These customers can plan travel, reserve and electronically ticket their flights, apply for upgrades, and locate partner hotels and restaurants offering AAdvantage miles.

National Semiconductor targets the people who have the greatest influence on the decision to purchase their products: design engineers. More than 500,000 of them use National Semiconductor's site each month to search for appropriate chips, download data sheets and software simulations, and order sample lots.

We'll take an in-depth look at what each of these companies has done in a few pages. But first, let's lay the groundwork. What are the steps you'll need to take in order to emulate their success?

- Know who your customers and prospects are.
- Find out which customers are profitable.
- Decide which customers you want to attract (or keep from losing).
- Know which customers influence key purchases.
- Find out which customers generate referrals.
- Don't confuse customers, partners, and stakeholders.

Know Who Your Customers and Prospects Are

THE FIRST STEP is to know who your end customers—and your prospective customers—are and then to learn as much about them as possible. You may feel that there's no reasonable way to accurately find out who your customers are, particularly if you sell through indirect channels. But that's no longer true, as we've seen from Hallmark (which offers customers a reminder service), Quaker Oats (which lures customers to its Rice-A-Roni site for recipes), and many, many others. With today's cost-effective customer outreach technologies—ranging from Web sites to e-mail to member cards—you can identify at least a reasonable subset of your customer base.

So do everything you can to identify and woo your end customers. Offer them incentives to identify themselves to you—special benefits they'll get by declaring themselves as loyal customers. You may be surprised by how much information customers will willingly volunteer if they think you actually care! The important thing is never to betray their trust. Never send customers offers or reminders they haven't asked for. One woman ditched her supermarket card when she received a letter from the store reminding her that it was time to buy tampons! CVS, the U.S. drugstore chain, got into trouble with its customers when it sent out reminders about prescriptions that were due to be renewed. Even though the mailings were done as a service to customers and offered suggestions about less expensive generic drugs they might want to consider, consumers got up in arms at these unsolicited reminders. They considered them an invasion of their privacy. So be circumspect about how you use customer information. Make sure that customers are clear about what they're going to get in return for identifying themselves to you. And don't do anything that might violate their trust.

Find Out Which Customers Are Profitable

OF COURSE, SOME of your customers will be more profitable than others. It is therefore imperative that you identify your most profitable customers. American Airlines' frequent flyers account for the majority of ticket sales and the resulting profit. They're profitable, not only because they fly often but because they're educated travelers who typically require fewer explanations and less hand-holding than the occasional traveler.

When Wells Fargo began to revamp its call center operations, the company focused on its high-net-worth customers—the ones who brought the bank the most profits, due to the many fee-based services they used. Making it easy for those customers to transfer funds, redeem bonds, and invest in certificates of deposit and money market funds with a single phone call was critical to keeping their business.

When AT&T began to streamline customer service, it targeted its small-business customers. The products and services offered to these 9 million customers are standard across the country, which makes them cost-effective to provide. By making it easier for these customers to upgrade their service, add a new service, get repair work done, or adjust a bill, AT&T lowered its costs while improving customer satisfaction and loyalty.

So as you're analyzing profitability, look not only at the revenues each customer segment represents but also at the costs to service that customer segment. And be sure to look at the lifetime value of these customers. How much profit will a certain customer segment generate over its lifetime, measured in increased sales, lower costs of doing business, referrals, and higher-profit-margin business?

Decide Which Customers You Want to Attract (or Keep from Losing)

WHEN DOW JONES initiated its Web-based version of *The Wall Street Journal*, the company set its sights on a very clear target market. With newspaper readership dwindling because younger people don't have the daily newspaper habit, *The Wall Street Journal* wanted to find and attract people who don't read a daily business newspaper but who care about business events. They thought they'd find them on the Web, and they did. More than 65 percent of the paying subscribers to *The Wall Street Journal Interactive Edition* are not subscribers to the print newspaper.

Reader's Digest has a similar problem. Most younger people wouldn't think of picking up the magazine; they associate it with their grandparents. It's not the kind of publication they'd think of reading. Yet the company's largest source of revenues and profits is the sale, by direct mail, of the kind of household "how to" books that most young families would find valuable. So *Reader's Digest* uses the Web to target the consumer segment it's losing: parents of young families. It does this by offering "how to" advice on topics of interest to this target audience—such as "how to raise drug-free kids"—and by building community around those topics.

Bell Atlantic wanted to keep from losing its residential customers as cable companies, cellular companies, and long-distance companies began to move into its territory in the mid-Atlantic region of the United States. So the company put a full-court press on its efforts to streamline customer service—to make it easy for customers to receive all their telecommunications services from Bell Atlantic. Then customers wouldn't have an inclination to stray.

So think about which new customers you want to target and which ones you want to keep from defecting. How can you take advantage of technology to cost-effectively attract them and keep them happy?

Know Which Customers Influence Key Purchases

A CUSTOMER ISN'T always the person who calls in the order or writes the check. Often, the real customer is the person who influences key purchases, passing the paper pushing onto a clerical staff member or a purchasing department.

A number of companies have struck proverbial gold by targeting the influencers, rather than the purchasers, of their products. National Semiconductor realized that it was design engineers who spec'd National Semi's chips into the product they were designing. Although it could be months before a new product was in production and an order came through from the purchasing department, getting technical specifications and product samples into the hands of product designers was the crucial first step. The company's Web site has provided the most cost-effective means to that end.

Similarly, Community Playthings, manufacturers of day care equipment and specialized furniture for special-needs children, identified physical therapists as key influencers. Physical therapists who work with children in school settings rarely approve or initiate purchases. They do, however, recommend what equipment should be bought. An added incentive to identifying these influential therapists is that many of them are itinerant, traveling to a number of schools during the week. Thus, even though it's the school or the day care center that actually orders the products and pays the bills, finding and educating a single physical therapist can result in multiple sales. Community Playthings has modified its customer database not only to include the employees at the schools and day care centers to which it sells equipment but also to maintain the names of the physical therapists and to link them to the different schools over which they have influence.

Another company doing an excellent job of identifying customers, prospects, and influencers is Pioneer Hibred. Pioneer Hibred is the leading producer of seed for growing corn, wheat, barley, and other crops, with a market share of 75 percent in the United States alone. The company maintains an exquisite customer database that includes every farm operator in the United States whether or not he is a customer. The company has tracked weather conditions, seed and fertilizers used, and crop yields per acre for both customers and prospects for over ten years. But it also recognizes the important role of influencers and has added this category to its customer database. Influencers include such people as agricultural consultants, as well as nutritionists from companies such as Frito-Lay, who are concerned about what type of corn seed is planted.

Who influences the purchase of your products? How can you establish a direct relationship with them? How do you track them, communicate with them, and ensure that they have accurate, timely information about your products and services?

Find Out Which Customers Generate Referrals

SATISFIED CUSTOMERS ARE your best source of referrals. Community Playthings, for example, discovered that 60 percent of its customers were repeat customers, indicating satisfaction. Although this $25 million manufacturer spent $600,000 a year on direct marketing, that effort generated only 12 percent of new business. Yet an equal 12 percent of sales came from referrals—which didn't cost the company a penny! Community Playthings has now eliminated most direct marketing from its strategy, concentrating on identifying and delighting existing customers, who then generate repeat sales and refer new business.

My company, the Patricia Seybold Group, clearly sees the benefits of key influencers and referrals. As a consulting firm offering strategic business guidance about the use of information technology for e-business, we spend a lot of time meeting with technology vendors to evaluate new products. Most of these vendors are represented by public relations firms. These PR representatives often recommend our products and services to their new clients. Recognizing this referral trend, we have focused more and more on our relationships with the PR firms, ensuring that they understand our offerings and we understand how they operate.

It's in your best interest to make it attractive for current customers to recommend new customers. Magazines do it all the time! "Sign up a new subscriber and we'll extend your subscription for a year!" Indeed, one of my company's most successful marketing campaigns in terms of cost relative to return, was focused on generating referrals from our longest-standing customers. We offered a lobster dinner for two to be flown to a customer's home for every new paid customer that customer referred. Not only was this "Lobster Buddy" program very successful, it was popular with the customers who liked the personal nature of the premium.

What are you doing to generate referrals from your customer base? How could you use information technology to better track and stimulate the referral process?

Don't Confuse Customers, Partners, and Stakeholders

THERE ARE MANY people who are vital to your business, but not all of them are customers. It's important to differentiate between end customers—consumers of your products—and partners or stakeholders. Partners may be the people who deal directly with the customer on your behalf, such as agents, brokers, or distributors. Stakeholders are the other people involved, from internal employees to outside regulators or bankers, who care a lot about your business and contribute greatly to it but aren't the people who *use* your products. This isn't to say that you should ignore partners and stakeholders, but they should come second in your thinking about how to make life easier for the end customer. If you get into the heads of your end customers, you'll be better able to help your partners and stakeholders streamline the business processes that impact your customers.

The National Science Foundation, a U.S. government agency that distributes grant money for scientific research, wanted to streamline business processes for its end customers—the researchers who apply for grants—as well as for key stakeholders, such as university development offices, department heads, and administrative and financial staff. So far, the foundation has had a somewhat easier time streamlining the administrative and financial processes than it has making the process of submitting grant proposals easier for the actual researchers.

Yet if you make it easy for the end customer, you usually make it easier for other stakeholders, such as channel partners. Fruit of the Loom wanted to make it easy for people to be able to buy logoed T-shirts at sporting events and rock concerts. So it streamlined the entire process of getting relatively small quantities of T-shirts delivered quickly through its distribution channel to the silk-screen operators in the venues where these events took place.

Are you clear about who your end customers are? Can you find ways to serve them better while improving your relationship with your channel partners and other key stakeholders at the same time? If you focus on the end customer without ignoring the needs of all the rest of the key stakeholders required in the relationship, chances are you'll make the right decisions for the long term.

Examples: American Airlines and National Semiconductor

As YOU READ these two case studies, think about your own organization. What have these companies done that you may be able to emulate? What I like about each of these examples is the fact that each of these companies was absolutely clear about which customer segment it was targeting. And both have continuously refined their offerings to meet the challenging expectations of those sets of customers.

TARGET THE RIGHT CUSTOMERS:

American Airlines
www.aa.com

Executive Summary

American Airlines was the first major airline to develop a Web site that let passengers plan their trips and book reservations, as well as access real-time flight information. What was different about the approach American took is that American's Web site was designed specifically for the company's 32 million most profitable customers—its AAdvantage frequent flyers. Along the way, American learned some important lessons. It learned that customers value proactive e-mail notifications. It discovered that customer profiles are important in order to be able to tailor offerings for each customer. And it discovered the value of the Web as an interactive marketing channel.

Critical Success Factors in the American Airlines Story	
✶ Target the right customers	✓ Let customers help themselves
Own the customer's total experience	✓ Help customers do their jobs
✓ Streamline business processes that impact the customer	✶ Deliver personalized service
Provide a 360-degree view of the customer relationship	Foster community
✶ = Featured in this discussion	✓ = Touched on in this discussion

American Airlines Targets Its Most Loyal Customers

WHEN JOHN SAMUEL saw his company's corporate Web site (www.amr.com) in late 1994, he immediately realized that the company was missing an important opportunity. Instead of putting AMR's annual report on-line, it should be answering all the questions that customers have, from "What time is Flight 1474 arriving?" to "How do I travel with my dog?" In fact, he suggested that customers be able to make reservations over the Web, reducing distribution expenses for American while providing convenience and control to customers.

At that time, John Samuel was the director of American Airlines' distribution planning division—the group responsible for overseeing the airline's computer reservations systems. He also closely coordinated with American's reservations offices and understood that more than 50 percent of the calls coming into the reservations centers didn't result in actual bookings. Samuel figured that if he could lure a fraction of the people who call American's toll-free number for flight information, fare quotes, and travel planning tips onto the Web, he could save the company money. And, if he could make even a tiny dent in the $2 billion per year that American was spending on travel distribution costs by letting customers book their own travel over the Web, that would more than justify the investment in this new channel.

Cater to the Frequent Flyer

BUT SAMUEL'S VISION for this new Web channel didn't stop there. He realized that, at the same time he was saving the airline money, he could be cementing relationships with American's most loyal customers, its frequent flyers.

American's frequent-flyer program, AAdvantage, has more than 32 million members. In surveying these customers in 1995, American had ascertained that a whopping 87 percent of them had computers at work or at the office and more than 70 percent owned a computer at home. And, a fall 1997 survey of American's most frequent fliers indicated that a full 100 percent have access to a PC. So, it comes as no surprise that many of American's flights are filled with passengers using laptop computers. One of these—the flight from Austin, Texas, to San Jose, California—has so many computer users on it, it's now affectionately called "the Nerd Bird." Additional surveys revealed that 70 percent of AAdvantage members would like to do business with American electronically. What these busy, wired customers valued most was control over their own travel planning and rescheduling. "Our best customers are relatively busy folks. They'd like to be able to do their travel planning on their own time and at the time that's best for them, which may be in the middle of the night," Samuel explained.

So Samuel proposed that a separate group be formed within the airline to assume responsibility for this new channel, American Airline's Web site, with the tending of the corporate AMR site left to the corporate communications folks. In early 1995, he put a small team together—about six people in all—to manage American's electronic interactions with its customers, whether over the Web or using PC software. This distribution-planning group was chartered to develop and maintain new electronic distribution channels for American Airlines. The group has its own profit-and-loss statement. Its success was to be measured by how much money it saved the airline in distribution and customer communication costs.

Launching the Original Web Site: Access to Information

JULIE SHOHET IS the product manager for the Web team. She is a businessperson, not a technologist. She knew what kinds of questions American's customers typically asked. They're questions such as: "Is the flight from Chicago on time?" "Do they serve lunch on board?", "How far is the airport from downtown?" "How do I pack skis?" "What movie are you showing on your westbound flights this month?" The first thing Julie's team did was to take the information that was used by the call center operators and rework it for Web access.

When American Airlines' Web site opened for business on May 17, 1995 (as a subsection of AMR.com), it was chock full of detailed information. You could find out about baggage requirements and limitations, movies and meals, airport layouts, and other logistical information.

During the summer, the Web team added access to airline schedules. You entered the cities you wanted to fly from and to, and the dates of arrival and departure, and you'd receive a listing of all the flights that matched your criteria. Although American's flights appeared at the top of the list, other airlines were listed as well. Why? Because customers who called American's hot lines were often comparison shopping. They couldn't make a decision until they knew what other flights were available.

The next critical piece of information that customers needed that would save wear and tear on call center personnel was flight arrival and departure information: gates and times. By October 1995, American was the only airline that published real-time flight information on the Web. Departures, arrivals, schedule changes, and gate assignments were updated every thirty seconds.

Toward the late fall, Shohet's team readied the first sensitive information for the Web site: they were adding the ability for customers to get fare information on-line.

Why was this sensitive? In the airline industry, fare quotes are considered a form of advertising and are carefully scrutinized. So the team had to reassure American's legal department that all the fares quoted on the Web site had gone through the same business process used for all published fares.

By the end of 1995, American's customers and prospects could get much of the same information on the Web that they could get by calling on the phone.

One of the hurdles Shohet's group had to overcome was getting each department within American Airlines—airports, reservations, movies, meals, baggage handling, AAdvantage program—to take responsibility for maintaining "its" information on the Web site. AMR's chairman, Bob Crandall, and other company executives helped a lot. They were firmly and vocally behind the Web site. Yet, Shohet explained, "In some departments, it was like pulling teeth. Gradually, over the first ten months, people became more educated and interested regarding the Internet. I sent out a memo and said, 'Your department has an opportunity to promote AA's products/services to our Internet customers. However, you must be responsible for providing accurate information and maintaining it.' " Eventually, each group began to take pride of ownership in its part of the Web site. By the end of 1997, at least forty different people across the company were maintaining content for their parts of the site.

Once Shohet's team got the basics handled, it was time to make good on Samuel's vision of making it easy for AAdvantage customers to do business with American conveniently and cost-effectively. So by February 1996, AAdvantage customers could log onto the Web and access their own account information. They could see how many miles they had accumulated to date and which flights, hotel stays, and restaurant meals had been credited. Customers responded enthusiastically, logging on and registering in droves. Samuel's group encouraged members to come back by holding auctions for transatlantic flights and vacation packages.

The Biggest Surprise: The Popularity of Proactive E-Mail Notification

WHAT WAS THE most surprising thing that happened along the way? A simple idea mushroomed out of control. In early 1996, Samuel's team decided that it would be relatively straightforward to send an electronic mail message listing the "specials" for the week (discounted tickets available for travel over the upcoming weekend) to any customer who wanted to subscribe to this service. They had no idea how popular this offering would be. Within thirty days, they had 20,000 subscribers; in a couple of months, the mailing list had climbed to 100,000. And, within a year, more than 775,000 people had subscribed to the NetSAAver fares e-mail lists. By early 1998, American was sending 1.7 million e-mails out each week! Although other airlines have since copied the idea of promoting discount airfares by e-mail, American was the first to do so and remains in the lead with the largest e-mail list.

The unexpected popularity of these proactive e-mails led American to restructure its electronic mail delivery systems twice within the course of a year. It also led to new functionality on the Web site. American added a NetSAAver fares booking module that lets customers quickly find the bargain flights and book seats on-line. Customers don't have to be AAdvantage members to receive the e-mails about NetSAAver fares, but they do have to be AAdvantage members to book a NetSAAver seat on the Web.

This has, to no surprise, contributed to increases in AAdvantage membership enrollment.

Adding On-line Transactions

LATER IN THE summer of 1996, American Airlines unveiled a new set of interactive offerings it dubbed AAccess: American Airlines' Interactive Travel Network and a new Web site address, www.americanair.com. At this point American added the ability for AAdvantage customers to make and change reservations on-line and have tickets mailed to them. By the fall, AAdvantage members could book using electronic ticketing, so they could change flights up to the last minute and not worry about having to exchange tickets. American also offered incentives and promotions. Every time you booked a flight via the Web, you received bonus frequent-flyer miles. Every on-line promotion resulted in a spike in bookings which was sustained after the promotion ended. In fact, bookings from the Web site initially grew 22 percent per month every month, exceeding Samuel's most optimistic expectations. On-line booked revenue came in at 98 percent above plan for 1997 and continued to grow at a substantial pace from month to month in 1998. John Samuel's vision was becoming a reality. "We're making our Web site the best place for AAdvantage members to do business."

Over the next twelve months, Samuel's team continued to enhance the Web site and, in particular, its functionality for AAdvantage members. Members could find restaurants and hotels offering AAdvantage miles close to their destination, select a restaurant based on type of cuisine and relative expense, and view or print out a map showing how to get there.

By the spring of 1997, AAdvantage members could request upgrade coupons and reserve upgraded seats in first or business class via the Web. By the fall of 1997, American had done away with a significant annoyance its frequent flyers complained about: the need to use and keep up with upgrade coupons or stickers at all. American Airlines had gone paperless.

One of the discoveries American made along the way was that customers wanted much more reassurance about reservations they had made electronically than they needed when they were given paper tickets. Sure, customers could view the status of their reservations at any time. And yes, they could print out a copy of the reservation and take it along with them. But they needed more. So American began sending confirmation e-mails to each customer every time he or she booked or changed a reservation. This was the reassurance customers were seeking.

Evolving the Technical Infrastructure

For the first two years, the actual programming for the Web site was done by American's sister company, **SABRE**. The SABRE Decision Technologies (**SDT**) division developed the infrastructure American needed, leveraging, at least in part, the work it was doing for its own Web site, Travelocity. American Airlines already had a very-large-scale booking and reservations system, the existing mainframe-based **SABRE** system. Thus the design challenge became how to surround the existing **SABRE** reservations system with the components needed to enable the development and evolution of customizable and consumer-friendly booking capabilities on the Web.

Surrounding the Reservation Service with Mix-and-Match Components

The **SDT** development team tasked with delivering **SABRE** functionality to the Web took a modular approach. First, they thought of the existing **SABRE** reservations system as the "reservation service." Second, they realized that delivering information over the Internet had unique needs that hadn't been contemplated in the design of the various input and output capabilities that already existed for **SABRE**. Therefore, they divided the problem space into functions—Input/Output, Authentication, Session Management, and so on—and implemented each function as a separate, customizable component. This service- and component-based architecture met the needs for a first-generation system. As new functions, like electronic ticketing, have been added, it's been a fairly straightforward process to add and swap components.

The Next Steps: Consolidating Profiles and Adding Personalization

As 1997 drew to a close, American Airlines had embarked on a major redesign of the massive databases underlying its Web site. One problem it needed to solve was the "multiple-profile" problem. Up until then, customer profiles had been kept in a few different places. One set of profile information resided in the **SABRE** reservations system. Another set, for AAdvantage members, was kept in the AAdvantage DB2 database. Finally, as the NetSAAver fares subscriber base grew, American created an Oracle database to track information about these subscribers. Now the company is in the process of consolidating and linking all of this different profile information.

Another related engineering project American Airlines embarked on at the close of 1997 was the redesign of its content databases. In order to be able to personalize the site for each visitor, the company needed to tag most of its content so that different types of offers could be served up to different groups of customers. Samuel realized that this would probably be the most time-consuming job of all, since American Airlines had well over 3,000 pages of information that needed to be broken up into smaller, tagged information objects and moved into an object database. When the project was almost complete, Samuel said that it had taken even longer than he had projected. In fact, he cautions groups embarking on a similar exercise to estimate how long they think it will take to codify all their information for different customer sets and quadruple that estimate!

American opted to use BroadVision's One-To-One software platform to add personalization to its Web site. It selected two different system integrators and design firms to assist the SABRE group in implementing the personalized marketing and booking capabilities.

The electronic booking tool that front-ends the SABRE system also had to be redesigned so that it could interact with the AAdvantage customer profiles and be responsive to the business rules that each customer might choose to specify. This required developing a separate fares database—one that would give American much more flexibility than that maintained within SABRE. Now that it is using a business rules–driven approach, American needs to be able to associate metadata tags with its fares—to flag certain destinations as "golf," "beach," "skiing," and so on. Samuel expects to be using XML to tag this information in the near future.

Moving to Personalization

IN JUNE 1998, American Airlines launched a new release of its Web site. In addition to streamlining navigation and offering improved functionality, the major advance has been personalization for AAdvantage members. American starts with the profile you already have on file in the AAdvantage database. This contains your name and address, how many miles you've flown on American, how many frequent-flyer miles you've earned and redeemed, and whether you are a gold or platinum-level AAdvantage member, for example. As you use the newly revamped travel planning and booking tool on the Web site to make reservations, you're given the opportunity to add choices to your profile. For example, if you specify an aisle seat or a special meal, there's a box you can check to add that preference to your profile. As you make reservations for other people—say, other family members—you can create profiles for them as well. Each AAdvantage customer can have up to ten linked profiles. Each profile can also have multiple credit cards associated with it, and these cards can be named, for example, Personal, Business, and so on. So you no longer have to specify American Express, Visa, or Mastercard.

What does American do with all of this profiling information? In the first release, the company will use your AAdvantage membership tier (gold, platinum), your home airport, and flight and fare information to trigger business rules. So you'll be able to request alerts any time the fare between Boston and San Francisco falls below $400, for example. Then you'll be able to click on those fares to see which dates they're applicable to. Or you'll be notified about special rates or new flights available from your home airport, or be told if there's airport construction there that could cause delays. You'll be offered benefits that are specific to platinum members, for example. In the next release of American's personalization program, due by the end of 1998, you'll have the ability to set your own rules, such as "Tell me about fares under $500 to beach destinations leaving from my home airport." Once again, American has pulled out ahead of the pack by providing a level of personalization to its most loyal frequent flyers that outstrips its competitors' levels of service.

Results

ONE WAY AMERICAN knows it is serving customers with useful information is the steady increase in traffic on its Web site. As of March 1998, American was serving up 4 million page views per week, and over 530,000 customers have logged onto the on-line service since its inception. The June 1998 Media Metrix PCMeter ratings report confirmed it is still the most popular airline site on the Internet.

Thousands of AAdvantage customers are making regular use of the American Web site each week, for both travel planning and booking, accessing AAdvantage account and program information as well as researching airline product and service details.

Samuel's expectations were that customers might research and plan their travel using the Web, but would probably actually book flights by phone. He's been pleasantly surprised. Samuel planned to double 1997 revenues from the site in 1998, but by the end of the first quarter of 1998, revenues had already doubled! To put this into perspective, Web bookings still account for about 1 percent of American Airline's total revenues, or about $140 million. On-line bookings are by far the least expensive and the most profitable tickets American sells, however. And Samuel expects the percentage of revenues from the Web to grow steadily over the next several years.

What John Samuel and Julie Shohet and their team are most excited about, however, are the incredible opportunities they are discovering for interactive marketing using the Web. Take the ability to sell "distressed inventory," for example. Before he took over the distribution planning function, Samuel worked in American's yield management group. He knew how complex the formulae are that American and other airlines use to maximize the profitable yield on passenger seats. For each flight, a certain percentage of seats is reserved for frequent business travelers, who tend to book at the last minute. But within forty-eight hours of a flight, the airline wants to sell off as much of that inventory as it can. Where else but on the Web would it be cost-effective and possible to have "sales" on particular seats within forty-eight hours of departure? How else can you notify travelers that you have special prices available on certain flights at such a low cost? And now that the technical work has been completed to support profiling and personalization, the company will be able promote specific flights to the particular customers who typically fly those routes.

Patty's Rx for American Airlines

American Airlines got a head start on its competition, but by the fall of 1997, many airlines, including American's archrival, United Airlines, had caught up and actually surpassed some of the functionality American offers. For example, United offered customers graphical seat selection before

American did, although American beat United to the punch with personalization. Here are some of the other issues American needs to address.

1. **INTEGRATE TRAVEL RESERVATIONS ACROSS CHANNELS.** Today, when you book a flight using a travel agent or by calling American Airlines directly, you can't see any record of that reservation when you log onto the Web site. Similarly, if you book on the Web site but call your travel agent to make a last-minute change in your itinerary, the agent will not be able to access the reservation you made on the Web (unless you supply the reservation number). This is annoying to customers. We want seamless interactions with American's reservations system. Obviously, once a travel agent gets involved with the reservation, that agent will need to receive a commission from American. But what the customer wants is a seamless experience. Whether customers book travel themselves or call American on the phone or use a travel agent for any part of the itinerary, all the information should be easily available to any party who may need to access and change it. This is one of the areas of functionality American is tackling now.

2. **DO A BETTER JOB WITH INCOMING E-MAILS.** American Airlines receives a lot of e-mails from customers who use its Web site. As of the end of 1997, the company had implemented some basic automated e-mail handling filters to help categorize the mail and in some cases to auto-respond to customers. However, workflow changes that span multiple departments and sophisticated tracking software are warranted to more effectively and efficiently respond to customer e-mail. Not surprisingly, the company addressed this problem first on the AAdvantage section of its Web site, by giving AAdvantage customers the ability to send e-mail to the AAdvantage customer support representatives who answer the phones. These e-mails are logged into the same support database used to answer phone inquiries. That's a good first step. But the company really needs to have a more comprehensive and automated solution to handling the thousands of e-mails per week that it will continue to receive from customers.

3. **GIVE CUSTOMERS BUSINESS RULES FOR FREQUENT-FLYER MILE REDEMPTION.** American is very conscious of the importance that frequent flyer miles play in their customers' psyches. Having invented this game, the company is now at the mercy of it. Many AAdvantage customers expend a great deal of time and effort maximizing the number of miles they'll receive and optimizing their redemption. Today, AAdvantage members can opt to upgrade their flights at the time they book their

travel, and if a first class seat is available within the time period allowed, the upgrade will take effect and the passenger will be notified that the upgrade has taken effect. But why not make it even easier? Why not give customers a place on the Web site where we can enter, maintain, and change the rules we'd like to use when redeeming our miles? For example, "If I have more than 50,000 miles in my account and I'm flying a transcontinental flight, upgrade me automatically to first class." Then, any time this rule went into effect, the company could automatically send out an e-mail notifying me that I've been upgraded.

4. LET CUSTOMERS BOOK HOTELS, CARS, AND RESTAURANTS. Today, there are many travel sites on the Web where you can book not just your airline reservation, but also your rental car and your hotel. American needs to make its site a "one-stop-shopping" site for its frequent flyers. Once I've booked my reservation and found a hotel and a restaurant that offer me additional AAdvantage miles, let me book them directly from the American site, along with my rental car. It won't matter to me if American implements this by taking me directly to the hotel's Web site to reserve my room, as long as it passes all the relevant profile information and credit card information along so I don't have to reenter everything. All of American's AAdvantage partners would benefit greatly from this pass-through capability. And customers would love the one-stop shopping.

5. OFFER AADVANTAGE CUSTOMERS SMART CARDS. Most frequent travelers I talk with don't like having to carry lots of different plastic cards around, one for each airline, hotel, and car rental company. They are also weary of maintaining separate log-in IDs and passwords for each of these companies. A better solution would be a consolidated travelers' smart card. It might be based on the credit card I already use. It could contain my digital certificate(s), which would guarantee my identity to each company. And it could contain the most recent balances in my various frequent-traveler accounts, as well as my current itinerary. To board a plane or access a reserved hotel room, I would simply stick the card into a convenient card reader and type in my password or let the reader scan my eyes or my fingers for validation. I would use the same smart card in any device I used to access the Net in order to make new reservations or to change existing ones. American has already deployed smart-card readers at all of its airports. The company is still trying to figure out, however, what would make the most sense for customers. It's hard to imagine American Airlines approaching United

Airlines, for example, and suggesting that they partner in the creation of a single travelers' smart card. But it's not hard to imagine American convincing all of its AAdvantage partner airlines, hotels, car rental companies, banks, and so on, to combine forces.

"Take-Aways" from the American Airlines Story

1. Focus your electronic commerce efforts on your most profitable customers. Find out what they need and value. Cater to them and make it easier and easier for them to do business with you.

2. In deciding what information to put onto your Web site first, start with the most commonly requested information your call centers give out. If you can migrate a small fraction of those callers onto the Web to answer their own questions, you'll save money.

3. Think about marketing offers you can make electronically that it's not practical to do any other way. American discovered this with its phenomenally successful NetSAAvers Fares program—notifying customers each Wednesday about excess inventory for the upcoming weekend so that customers could grab these discounted seats.

4. Note that your Web marketing team doesn't have to develop all the content for your Web site. American's Julie Shohet has done a great job of convincing lots of different people throughout the company—about forty in all—that they "own" their portion of the Web site. It then becomes part of that person's job to ensure that the information in his or her section of the site is up to date and accurate. Employees vie with one another to have the best and most useful content.

5. You don't have to redesign your back-end systems in order to make it easy for customers to access them. You do need to treat those systems as "services" and design your Web front end as a set of applications that request information and functions from those back-end services.

TARGET THE RIGHT CUSTOMERS:

National Semiconductor
www.national.com

Executive Summary

Within two years of operation, National Semiconductor's Web site became a magnet for at least one third of the company's total potential worldwide market. More than 500,000 design engineers flock to the site each month to get the latest information about the particular chips they're interested in. National Semiconductor targeted its Web site for the customers at the very front end of the buying chain: the engineers who do the technical evaluations on the components they're selecting to build into the cell phones and other products they're designing. National Semi has also done an outstanding job of connecting its Web site to the rest of its business. Leads from the Web site flow directly into the opportunity management system. Customers' e-mails are answered by any of 8,000 employees. And every day National Semi's employees receive electronically distributed charts giving them data from the Web site: which products customers are interested in and which samples they ordered. This information is combined with distributors' forecasts by customer and actual sales to give everyone in the company an up-to-the-minute gauge of how they're doing on a product-by-product basis.

Critical Success Factors in the National Semiconductor Story	
☆ Target the right customers	✓ Let customers help themselves
✓ Own the customer's total experience	☆ Help customers do their jobs
✓ Streamline business processes that impact the customer	✓ Deliver personalized service
Provide a 360-degree view of the customer relationship	Foster community
☆ = Featured in this discussion	✓ = Touched on in this discussion

National Semiconductor Targets Design Engineers

IN 1994, PHIL Gibson, director of interactive marketing, and Ann Wagner, vice president of marketing and communications, of National Semiconductor approached their boss, Pat Brockett, head of worldwide sales and marketing, with the idea of building a Web site for the company. Pat approved the initiative with one caveat: "Target design engineers."

When engineers are designing new or improved products, they have to locate all the available parts they'll need. To do so, they consult parts catalogs and data sheets supplied by the manufacturers whose products they favor, talk to the manufacturers' representatives, and order samples they can try out. Once a part has been spec'd into a product design, it's the purchasing department, on behalf of the manufacturing organization, that handles the actual procurement.

Brockett knew that the person with the most influence over the actual purchasing decision was the design engineer who designed National Semi's chips into a product, not the procurement officer who actually placed the order for the components to be used in building that product.

Gibson and Wagner asked Rick Brennan to get the Web site up. Brennan put a small team together, and with the help of R. R. Donnelly, the printer that produced all of National Semi's product data sheets, they launched a Web site from which design engineers could download data sheets on demand.

Asking Customers What They Want

AS INPUT INTO the initial design, Brennan's team hired a marketing organization to run focus groups with design engineers, asking them what they wanted and needed from a Web site. Customer feedback came back loud and clear: "Don't bore us with corporate or marketing information; just give us the product information."

Then, every three months after the site went live, market researchers convened a group of engineers and asked them to compare and rate the National Semiconductor site against those of its competitors: Texas Instruments, Motorola, and Xylinx, in particular. Brennan's team combined this feedback with the feedback they received directly from users of the Web site.

What they found was that customers didn't want any of the attractive graphics they had used in the first iteration of the site. These took too long to display. Engineers also didn't want to wait to download the large data sheet files. Instead, they wanted to search for the products whose parameters met their criteria, scan abstracts of the data sheets, download the ones they were interested in, and order samples, all as quickly and easily as possible. "We want it functional; we want it quick; we want minimal graphics" was what customers told the market researchers.

Make It Easy to Search

In response to this customer feedback, the team totally revamped the Web site. They designed four different ways in which engineers could search for the information they needed.

The most valuable search tool was a parametric search engine. The engineer fills in a table with the parameters he or she cares about. He may be seeking a chip with a certain gain width, pin count, temperature tolerance, and/or price. He could ask to see all the 100-milliamp low-voltage regulators under $25, for example. This parametric search goes against National Semi's database of 22,000 possible devices and returns all of those that meet the search criteria within a second or two.

The second search engine was a text search capability. This lets the customer type in keywords or phrases, like "analog to digital converters," and returns a listing of all the documents on the site—data sheets, pricing information, or software simulations—that pertain.

Third, the customer can use a visual search capability to search by diagram.

Or the customer may choose to search National Semi's on-line catalog. This lets her search by category of chip, drilling down within the category of interest to see all the possible offerings.

Give Fast Access to Information and Transactions

Once the design engineer has found what he's looking for, the next thing he wants is to get all the relevant information. Tim Stuart, who had joined the Web team in late 1995, came up with the notion of product folders. Each product has its own folder. In it the customer finds all the information related to that product. This includes data sheets, pricing information, software simulations, detailed technical specifications, availability (when the device will be available and in what quantities), and a way to order samples.

Many marketing executives would be pleased if customers spent a fair amount of time browsing their company's Web site. Not Phil Gibson. He heard what his customers were saying. They wanted to come to the site, find what they needed, and get off again quickly. They had a job to do. This wasn't a leisurely shopping trip.

By monitoring customers' activity on the site very closely, the National Semiconductor team has been able to streamline customers' experiences continuously. When the site first went live in the spring of 1995, customers typically "hit" seven to eight pages on the Web site before they left. Twenty-two months later, customers were able to get onto and off the site with an average of 2.5 pages. They arrive at the home page, do a search, perform a transaction (for example, order samples, download a datasheet, or send e-mail to the product manager), and get off.

Extending the Reach to Procurement

ONCE NATIONAL SEMICONDUCTOR had succeeded in building tight relationships with the people who decide whether or not to use its electronic devices, Gibson and his team turned their attention to the rest of the company's value chain. Again, National took a very focused approach. They targeted purchasing agents, buyers, and component engineers. Each of these constituencies has different needs. But all are served by the new purpose-built "Purchasing Resources" Web site that National introduced in May 1998. This site includes interactive links to DigiKey, Farnell,

Newark, and Pioneer—several of National's catalog suppliers and distributors—for live ordering and real time shipments.

Purchasing agents and buyers have a critical problem that their Web site is designed to address. When a company is designing a new product, the engineers need fast access to small quantities of the parts they'll use to build and test the product before it's approved for production. Through this purchasing resources site, purchasing agents first locate the parts in question. Then they check on availability by accessing accurate inventory information from any of fifty distributors who stock the parts. Finally, they can order the small quantities they need directly from the suppliers who have already linked their order entry systems into National's Web site, or they can contact the others by phone. (Naturally, Gibson expects that many of the rest of National's distributors will soon integrate their back-end ordering systems into National's purchasing agents' site.)

The purchasing resources site also gives customers the ability to cross-reference product information, sign up for notification of product changes, create a personalized portfolio of information on specific National products, and enter orders on-line.

Component engineers are the people who are charged with finding new substitute or replacement parts for products that are already in production. They can use this same purchasing resources site to locate alternate parts, find out who has inventory, and procure the parts they need. National estimates that streamlining these aspects of customers' procurement processes has the potential to save the company and its customers about $100 million in procurement productivity and time over the next year.

Changing the Metabolism of National Semiconductor

IT'S ONE THING to have a great Web site for your customers; it's quite another to get a company the size of National Semiconductor (with 19,000 employees worldwide) to respond quickly to customers and to take full advantage of their feedback and input. Phil Gibson was painfully aware of the cultural challenges he faced. So he has worked hard to ensure that customer input penetrates to the core of the company.

Customer Inquiries Go Directly to the Responsible Parties

One important step the Web designers took to support Gibson's goal was to design e-mail forms on the Web site that would be automatically routed to the product managers and technical support people responsible for each product. When the customer sends off e-mail, it's routed into a database, tracked, and automatically sent on to the appropriate party within the company, based on the subject matter of the message. The customer receives an immediate acknowledgment that his message has been received and is guaranteed an answer within forty-eight hours.

The second thing Gibson insisted on was that there be no "dead ends." Once an e-mail form is routed into the company, it is automatically logged and tracked to completion. If the person who received it can't deal with the issue or answer the customer's question satisfactorily, the e-mail is automatically routed on to someone who can respond effectively.

So instead of having a small group of customer support people responsible for answering customers' inquiries, Gibson has more than 8,000 people who may receive and answer customers' questions. The automated workflow ensures that no one person receives more than his or her fair share of questions. And since all the questions and answers are tracked and logged in a database that's accessible to everyone in the company, National can ensure that questions are being answered consistently.

Sales Leads Go Directly to the Account Managers

Before he tackled the Web site, Gibson had overseen the selection, design, and implementation of the company's sales automation and opportunity management system. Once design engineers began visiting the Web, registering as users, and supplying profile information in response to on-line surveys, Gibson made sure that this information was automatically entered into the opportunity management system. So when a design engineer visits the site and looks up information on a particular device, that information appears in the opportunity management pipeline for the salesperson or distributor who handles his company's account.

Getting Product Feedback to Decision Makers Right Away

Gibson also understood how important it was for decision makers to be bathed in a constant stream of customer feedback. In order to make this information easy for executives to assimilate, Gibson's team customized software to provide graphical reports. These reports tally the number of inquiries received for each product, the number of data sheets downloaded, and the number of samples requested, for example. This information can then be easily correlated to actual product sales, giving National Semiconductor an "early-warning system" about which products are popular and which aren't.

Gibson's team also ensures that the anecdotal feedback from customers' e-mails and survey responses gets delivered promptly to the appropriate product managers and marketing managers. Often, customers will offer insights about competitors' products that can be immediately distributed to the field sales organization.

Streamlining Distributors' Interactions with National Semiconductor

LIKE MANY LARGE manufacturers, National Semiconductor sells directly to a very small market segment—about one hundred accounts. The rest of its business is handled through distributors who resell National Semiconductors' chips along with those from many other companies. Typically, a customer's purchasing department provides its distributors with a list of all the parts it needs to manufacture a given product. The distributors shop for the best prices and availability and provide quotes back to the buyers, who in turn negotiate with the distributors for the best final bids.

National Semiconductor has private Web sites that are used to support its independent distributors in Asia, Europe, and Latin America. At first, this Web site held mostly marketing materials such as slide presentations, brochures, product selection guides, "electronic pitch" packs—everything a distributor would need to close a sale.

In September 1997, National Semi added a new capability to its Extranet connection with its distributors: the ability for channel partners to register customer deals. Called TEAM, this channel sales-force automation system includes a registration form that lets the reseller enter the details of the customer's account, what device that customer is interested in, and what run rates he's projecting. In exchange for providing this information to National Semiconductor, essentially "registering" the pending deal, the reseller is guaranteed a commission and given a profit-margin incentive. The distributor benefits because he now knows what product orders are in the pipeline. And National Semiconductor benefits because it now knows more accurately what to manufacture. Within the first few months, more than 1,000 deals were registered. Within the first year, more than 6,000 deals were registered, solidifying $1 billion worth of forecasted leads. Gibson reports that the distribution sales managers love this new ability to "see" into the value chain. They can now easily get summaries of sales activity by distributor, branch, region, and country.

By the spring of 1998, distributors and their resellers had access to a fully automated configuration and quoting application on the Web, called BizQuote. This is an easy-to-use graphical front end that is linked directly to National Semiconductor's back-end systems. BizQuote provides lead time, quotes, and commitments. Until now, the only person able to generate a price quote to a customer or reseller was a branch manager. Now everyone in the channel has the ability to configure orders, quote them, and place them via the Web. Gibson estimates that BizQuote will save National's channel partners and its customers at least $20 million per year by reducing the cost of checking availability and placing orders.

Evolving the Technical Infrastructure

At first, National Semiconductor's Web site included links to all the data sheets that were hosted off-site at R. R. Donnelly's premises. This became problematic as traffic to the site increased. So, National Semi brought all the information together onto one very large Sun server running Netscape Commerce Server software, with a shadow server providing backup, and hosted it at a nearby Internet service provider's site with high-speed access.

Parametric Search Engine Written in Java

When it became apparent that a parametric search engine was needed for the Web site, Tim Stuart went looking for an off-the-shelf package National Semi could use. He found a small company, Cadis, that had the makings of what he needed, but the application it had developed was not Web-enabled. Stuart applied for and received one of National Semiconductor's "innovation grants" and used that money to fund Cadis's development of a Java-based parametric search engine. By March 1996, the search engine was up and running with a database of several thousand products. National Semiconductor had launched the world's first commercial Java application.

Combining Native Internet and Lotus Notes

The sales force automation system that Phil Gibson had championed is a Lotus Notes–based application from MFJ International called OverQuota. It contains National Semi's entire customer database and tracks all of the contacts anyone in the company has with each account. Notes (now Domino) also forms the basis of the automated workflows National Semi uses to route e-mails from the Web site through the rest of the company. And all product launches are managed using Notes workflows and databases. The sales force and manufacturing reps can monitor the proposed positioning and availability of new products before they're launched and offer valuable feedback from the field.

Using Pointcast to Broadcast Information Throughout the Company

Gibson's team also uses Lotus Notes as the vehicle through which it currently assembles product-related information from the Web site, combines that material with information pumped in from the manufacturing applications, and produces graphs and charts that are broadcast via Pointcast. All employees in the company have Pointcast on their PCs and can tailor their screen display to show only the products or categories of products in which they're interested.

Staging Information for Web Publication and Personalization

After two and a half years of running a production Web site, Gibson's team determined that it needed a much better way to control the staging of the information that was being authored, designed, edited, and posted by many different product groups around the company. To help with this organizational and document management problem, Gibson selected Vignette's Story-Server. This document management platform has allowed the company to set up document review cycles, to better control the distributed creation of information, and to enable the delivery of personalized pages for National Semi's large accounts. National's internally developed SiteCreator tool allows the sales forces to create, edit, and maintain Web pages through a simple browser interface. This can be done remotely from anywhere in the world. The user-friendliness of this tool requires no knowledge of HTML scripting, file structures, or link management.

Giving Distributors Access to National's Mainframe-based Systems

National's distributors are now linked directly to its mainframe transaction engine over the Web for queries, quotes, orders, and expediting using a tool from Enterprise Link called SmartTran.

Wooing Large Customers with Personalized Sites

IN MAY 1998, Gibson's team launched a facility that enables the salespeople who handle the company's major accounts to design personalized sites for each of their accounts. The account reps select the information they want to highlight for the account and link the personalized site to the real-time order-status information for that account. This customized Web site then becomes the place where most of the dialogue and discussion between the account rep and the key people at his customer account take place. By July 1998, the sales force had created approximately 200 such custom Web sites. Customers use these sites to review public and proprietary communications such as corporate contracts, prices, and lead times. They can also access valuable information such as newly released and preliminary product specifications, browse white papers and application notes related to their business, and share product development status for custom projects. And they can sign up for product notifications and receive special factory applications assistance.

Results

IN ITS FIRST two years of operation, the traffic at National Semiconductor's Web site went from zero visitors to 500,000 people per month. Forty percent of these customers have "bookmarked" the site, which means that they find it so useful they keep the address a single click away.

National Semi's site has been rated number one by design engineers in their search for semiconductor product technology and information across five separate studies the company has conducted over the last two and a half years. Why? Because Gibson and his team continually refine the site in response to customers' feedback and behavior.

The kind of kudos Gibson and his team receive from customers are "You guys are great, you sent me the samples right away," "I've never talked to National before; now I can," "I love using this Web Site. It's so fast and easy!"

There are approximately 1.5 million design engineers who make use of semiconductors worldwide. So National Semiconductor is in communication with over one third of the available market for its products each month. "That's fifty times more people than I can touch or establish a relationship directly with through any other sales channel that I have. It would be absolutely impossible for my call centers to handle this volume, or for my direct sales force to contact this many people!" Gibson exclaims.

As of December 1997, customers were pulling 11,000 data sheets per day off National Semiconductor's Web site. As Gibson points out, "That's 330,000 data sheets being handed out to customers every month on exactly the products they're interested in." Gibson points out that there's no way his 400-person direct sales force, his 400 manufacturing representatives, or his 8,000 distributors could match the reach of his Web site. Together, they touch only 8.5 percent of National Semiconductor's customers, accounting for 60 percent of the company's revenues. The other 40 percent of revenues come through catalog suppliers who stock National Semiconductor's chips and make them available to small quantity purchasers. The Web site plays an important role in giving all customers (large and small) all the information they need to make a product design decision.

Large Customers Bring National's Site In-house

What better way to measure the success of your customer-focused Web site than to have customers bring your site into their organizations' intranets. Quite a few of National Semi's largest customers have welcomed its site in behind their firewalls. In this way, their design engineers can access all the latest product information without going out over the Internet.

In fact, in 1996, Tektronix, one of National Semiconductor's largest customers, invited all of its suppliers to its headquarters, gave them a demonstration of the National Semi site, and suggested that they all use it as a benchmark for their own Web efforts!

An International Reach

When the company first launched its Web site in 1995, 95 percent of the visitors who came to the site were from the United States or Canada. Within two years, only 50 percent of the visitors were from North America; the rest came from other countries. In fact, National Semiconductor began receiving requests and orders from countries it had never sold to before.

Customer Feedback Has Shortened Product Cycle Time

In the past, when National Semiconductor launched a new product, it would take the company about a year to assess whether or not the product was going to be successful. Now the product manager can monitor customers' reactions on a daily basis. She can tell how many inquiries have been received, how many of those prospects accessed technical information, and how many ordered samples. She will receive customers' questions, reactions, and competitive feedback overnight. The result is that National Semi can now tell within three months of a product launch whether it has a winner or a dud on its hands.

Patty's Rx for National Semiconductor

It's hard to think of much that National Semiconductor hasn't done right with its Web site to date, but there are always areas for improvement with any initiative. As of mid-1998, here were some of the things I thought National Semi should be working on next.

1. ADD MORE SIMULATIONS. Although it's possible to download software simulations from the National Semiconductor site, most of these were written to run in proprietary systems. And not all customers have access to these systems. A logical next step, and one Gibson's team has its eye on, is to begin to offer Java-based software models and simulations for many of National Semiconductor's products so that engineers can plug in their own parameters and visualize the results. By writing these simulations in Java (which will run on any computer), they could easily be run from the Web site, or downloaded onto any of the customer's own systems.

2. BUILD COMMUNITY. While it's true that National Semiconductor's customers like to get onto the site, find what they're looking for, and get off again, it's also true that they have a lot in common with one another. It's likely that many have faced the same design challenges and come up with solutions that might be of value to others. I recommend that National Semi foster more dialogue among users at its site by posting stimulating and useful topics, encouraging debate, and moderating technical discussions.

3. COMPLETE THE DESIGN-PROCUREMENT-MANUFACTURING LOOP. Today, National Semi has the design cycle nailed. But there's a gap between the time an engineer selects a product to test and the time the order is

placed. And there's a handoff that occurs, both in the customer's organization—from engineering to manufacturing to procurement—and in National Semiconductor's distribution channels. The majority of National Semiconductor's devices are actually purchased through distributors. Although the company has made some impressive steps in collecting information from its distribution channel, it's now time for the company to turn its attention to bringing these distributors and their end customers much more closely into the information loop. Ideally, National Semi will want to track end customers' entire business process, from selecting a device through procurement and on to manufacturing.

"Take-Aways" from the National Semiconductor Story

1. Sometimes the most important customers to target don't actually buy anything from your firm. Yet they're the people who strongly influence the purchasing decision.

2. National Semi has done a great job of tracking what customers do on its site in order to continuously streamline its Web experience. By reading the logs of what paths customers took and what they eventually went away with, the developers can figure out how to make it easier for customers to come in, find what they want, get it, and get off with as few clicks as possible.

3. Note that customers may need several different ways to search for products and information. National Semiconductor offers customers four different ways to find the products they're seeking.

4. Handling customers' incoming e-mails is an important issue for everyone. National Semiconductor took this seriously. Each incoming e-mail is captured in a database, logged, and then routed to the right person to be handled. However, instead of simply routing all e-mail to the company's dedicated technical support group, Gibson chose to route them to thousands of product managers, marketing managers, and engineering groups. That way, more internal people would have direct customer contact.

5. Gibson wanted to be sure that everyone in the company could take advantage of the real-time customer information that was pouring in through the company's Web site. So his team organizes the data from the Web site by product category, combines it with actual inventory

and order data, and broadcasts the combined "dashboard" to everyone in the company on a daily basis. That way, everyone in the company knows what products are hot and which ones are running into problems.

6. Customers maintain their own profiles on the Web site. These profiles and Web visits are used to update the company's opportunity management system and customer database.

7. Distributors have their own extranet connection to National Semiconductor, including the ability to log sales that are in the pipeline, to "lock in" production capacity, and to place orders directly into National's mainframe-based production systems. This close electronic linkage with its distributors lets National do a much better job of production planning, and gives the company visibility into its end-customers' accounts.

8. National took a particular business process—the rapid procurement of a small quantity of chips—and streamlined it from the end customer's point of view. To do so, National built a seamless (from the customer's point of view) set of linkages to its suppliers. End customers' purchasing agents can access National's distributors' inventories directly in order to check prices and availability and to place small-quantity, quick-turnaround orders.

9. National provided its direct sales reps—the one who manage its largest accounts—with the tools they needed to be able to quickly design and deliver a personalized Web site to each major account.

Target the Right Customers: Lessons Learned

Who are the right customers? For American Airlines and National Semiconductor, they're the ones that make the biggest difference to the bottom line. In American's case, they're the actual purchasers and consumers of the service. In National Semi's case, they're the key influencers of the purchasing decision. They are the ones who actually use the product in their designs. While both companies' Web sites serve lots of audiences—investors, prospective employees, casual visitors, and occasional customers—the companies have focused whole sections of their Web sites on these most valuable customers. Most of the time and effort spent on maintaining each site is devoted to making it easy for these target customers to do business.

Find Out What Customers Need and Continuously Improve Your Ability to Provide It

NOTE THAT BOTH American Airlines and National Semiconductor began by doing fundamental market research. They found out what their customers valued and how they wanted to interact. National Semiconductor, in particular, has done an exquisite job of continuous improvement based on customers' actual behavior on its Web site, as well as in responding to specific requests. The fact that every three months the company monitors customers' reactions to its Web site compared to that of the competition demonstrates National Semi's vigilance to the possibility that a competitor could easily catch up and surpass its Web site.

Neither of these Web sites has been inexpensive to build or maintain. Yet both American Airlines and National Semiconductor are delivering better, more effective customer service at a lower cost to the company than they were able to do with call centers and direct-mail marketing. They are reaching and satisfying hundreds of thousands more customers with much more efficiently delivered and targeted information. And both companies have the measurable results to prove this. American Airlines is generating on-line reservations at a fraction of the cost of reservations made through travel agents or even call centers, and AAdvantage customers are helping themselves to information they used to have to call for or go without. National Semiconductor is reaching a much larger customer base with direct, tailored information than it could ever afford to reach any other way. The company's international sales are increasing as a direct result of its Web-site activities.

Provide Easy Access to Transactions

BOTH COMPANIES LEARNED quickly that while customers will use your Web site for research, they don't want to stop there. They want to follow a natural path from research to transactions to status reporting. It took American Airlines more than a year to get to the point where customers could actually book travel on-line. But in the meantime, the company provided value for its frequent flyers by giving them the ability to check the status of their accounts.

National Semiconductor supports a variety of transactions: customers can download data sheets and software. They can order product samples. These are the transactions that drive traffic to the Web site and keep customers coming back for more. The next step, linking in the on-line ordering of bulk quantities through distributors, will serve a different audience—purchasing agents—and complete the cycle.

Use E-Mail Effectively

AMERICAN AIRLINES IS doing a great job of using e-mail to reach out and touch customers on a regular basis. The sheer volume of its weekly NetSAAver e-mail traffic and its continued popularity are testimony to the fact that customers like to be offered special deals. This keeps American Airlines in their consciousness far more effectively than much more expensive advertising could do.

National Semiconductor does an even better job with incoming e-mail. By automatically filtering and routing incoming mail to the correct person, capturing these e-mails in a database, and tracking them to completion, National Semi is ensuring that it gets the most value from these customer interactions.

Change Your Corporate Culture to Be More Customer-centric

IN BOTH CASES, these customer-focused Web sites have had a dramatic impact on the "way we do things around here." For American Airlines, the Web site has become a catalyst for cross-departmental information sharing and pride. Instead of hoarding information, each department now vies with the others to see how quickly it can post all the new information about its products and services. In National Semi's case, the fact that product managers and designers receive direct feedback from hundreds of specific customers via e-mail from the Web site has actually influenced product development priorities.

National Semiconductor has done the best job of leveraging the information it garners from its Web site to impact decision making in the company. Because National Semi took the extra step of consolidating customer feedback into easy-to-grasp charts and disseminating these to each executive and product-line manager, these key decision makers are now able to monitor the pulse of their products. By seeing how many customers are accessing information, downloading samples, and placing orders, National Semi now has an exquisite "early-warning" system that enables it to change course quickly.

Own the Customer's Total Experience

did a lot of my Christmas shopping on the Web this year. And, I wasn't the only one. According to the Yankee Group, consumers spent $800 million shopping on-line between Thanksgiving Day and New Year's in 1997, compared to $300 million spent on-line in the same time period a year before. I expect on-line consumer sales of at least $2 billion in the 1998 holiday season.

What made it easy and fun to shop on-line? The fact that I knew exactly what to expect at each site and no one let me down. Whether I shopped at L. L. Bean, Wal-Mart, Amazon.com, Virtual Vineyards, or West Marine, I had the same satisfying, reassuring, and predictable experience. Often I knew what I was looking for: a book about urban planning for my architect brother-in-law, an extra-large floppy-brimmed sailing hat for my son-in-law, an interesting assortment of unusual California wines for my brother and his wife, a coveted "Tickle Me Elmo" doll for a good friend's two-year-old. In several cases, when I went to the on-line store, I was greeted like a friend: "Hi, Patricia Seybold, welcome back! Here are some things we think you'll like."

In all cases, I began my on-line interaction with a targeted search (although occasionally I'd detour to check out the "specials" the company was promoting). With each targeted search, I found an interesting assortment of relevant options from which to choose. What I enjoyed most was the ability to get lots of information about each item—pictures, detailed write-ups, ratings, recommendations, and sometimes other customers' reviews. The actual buying process was also easy and reassuring. In each case it was very clear what to do next: put the item into your shopping cart, fill in or double-check the credit card number and the shipping address, select gift-wrapping paper or a greeting card, select the type of shipping. It didn't matter if I stopped in the middle and came back the next day. My shopping cart was still "sitting" in the electronic aisle with the items I had selected, and I could pick up where I had left off. A couple of times, I decided I wanted to talk to someone. So I called the toll-free number and asked my questions ("Which of these two hats is really both sunproof and waterproof?"). Again I was greeted by name, my questions were answered efficiently, and I just placed the order over the phone.

But the on-line shopping experience didn't stop when I placed the orders. Then the e-mails began arriving: "We just shipped out these two books. We upgraded your shipment to priority mail. The other four books in the same order will be shipped shortly." "Linda Seybold signed for the wine you sent yesterday at 5:40 P.M." When the products arrived, they were carefully packaged and nicely wrapped (if that's what I had requested).

What worked for me was the fact that, in each case, I felt that I was dealing with a company with a "personality." The human touch came through. In fact, it came through better than it probably would have had I been battling crowds in a physical store. I could get information when I needed it, without having to look around for someone to ask or waiting in line at the checkout counter. In fact, there was no waiting, no annoyance; just satisfaction and peace of mind. These companies have all done a great job of giving me the total experience I really want and expect.

Of course, customers' needs change over time. Companies that recognize this begin to track customers' life cycles. They understand that a single person's financial needs change when she gets married and begins to think about having a family. They realize that children grow up and will need different products and services as they do. They understand the difference between a customer who is selecting and installing a product for the first time and one who is now rolling that product out to thousands of end users. For example, American Skiing Company—which owns and operates more than a dozen ski resorts—tracks each family member's skiing or snowboarding expertise and notes which lodge you stayed at the last time and whether or not you rented skis. If you just want to sign Timmy up for the next level of ski instruction, rent the same size boots for Sarah, and stay in the same room you had before, that's no problem. And you can make these arrangements by phone or over the Web.

Customers have different needs when they're dealing with you as businesspeople than they do when they're acting as consumers. If you rent a car from Hertz, whether for business or pleasure, many of your needs will be the same—automatic transmission, four doors, nonsmoking car—but others will be different. For business, a cellular car phone may be required, while on personal vacation travel, you may want a car seat for your toddler and a ski rack.

Above all, customers like to have a well-orchestrated, well-designed, predictable experience of doing business with you. Yet they also want to feel in control. They need to have the ability to call the shots, to tailor their own experience to fit their individual circumstances.

There are a number of things a company must do in order to build the kind of customer loyalty that accrues to companies that take responsibility for owning the customer's total experience.

They are:

* Deliver a consistent, "branded" experience.
* Focus on saving customers time and irritation.
* Offer peace of mind.
* Work with partners to deliver consistent service and quality.
* Respect the customer's individuality.
* Give customers control over their experience.

Deliver a Consistent, "Branded" Experience

A BRAND NAME doesn't just evoke a product; it also invokes a set of feelings in the customer. The more experiential the product or service, the more visceral the customer's reaction is likely to be. Today, there are a number of companies that have successfully "branded" the entire customer experience by setting customers' expectations about what it feels like to do business with them.

A personal favorite is L. L. Bean, which emphasizes the personal touch, a casual, friendly environment, the outdoor experience, and exquisite customer service. When I lived in Yarmouth, Maine, in the late 1960s, my husband and I would often visit L. L. Bean in the middle of the night. After all, there wasn't much after-hours activity in Maine, and L. L. Bean was open twenty-four hours a day to serve hunters and others who were driving long distances into the wilderness. Browsing and shopping at 2 A.M. and being surrounded by friendly salespeople, no crowds, and a warm, cozy atmosphere made it a special treat. But late-night entertainment isn't the only memorable part of the L. L. Bean experience. Their return policy is truly amazing. I once had a pair of well-loved L. L. Bean winter boots. After two years, the heels had worn down. Wanting to get the heels replaced, I took them back to L. L. Bean and waited in a surprisingly fast-moving customer service line, only to be told that Bean doesn't do repairs on this type of boot and, to my dismay, that this particular model was no longer being offered. But before depression set in, the customer service representative told me that I could help myself to a brand-new pair of any other kind of boot the store offered—for free! So I did. The notion that I could just keep swapping my used boots for a new pair each time they got worn out truly amazed me and has kept me a loyal and vocal L. L. Bean shopper.

When you go visit the L. L. Bean store on-line, you find the same consistent, branded experience I remember from shopping at 2 A.M. on a winter morning. Sure, you can shop and buy things on-line, just as you can browse and shop in the store or from Bean's paper catalog. But you also find what you'd expect to find at L. L. Bean: helpful, knowledgeable information about how to enjoy outdoor activities to their fullest—from advice on how to break in your hiking boots and which kind of socks will keep your feet driest to information about cross-country ski trails in a variety of state parks.

Focus on Saving Customers Time and Irritation

THE SINGLE MOST important thing you can do for your customers is to anticipate and eliminate snags and delays in their experience of dealing with you. Soon you'll be reading about all the ways that Hertz has found to eliminate delays for its customers. Another good example of a company that excels in doing this is American Skiing Company (ASC). Like Hertz, this company is intent on streamlining customers' experience in the physical world as well as in their electronic dealings with the company. Each interaction you have at the ski resort is streamlined, from renting skis and boots (they're waiting for you in your hotel room) to finding your way to the ski slope from the parking lot—an ambassador greets you, answers your questions, and shows you the way. Like Hertz, ASC offers a frequent skier's program, called Edge. Once you have an Edge card (which you can order ahead, or procure on-site) pinned to your jacket, you never have to wait in line for lift tickets again. The electronic card is scanned as you approach the ski lift, giving you access to the mountain. The same Edge card lets you buy anything the resort offers. Your account is automatically debited when you pick up lunch, take classes, rent skis, or use any of the resort's amenities. You can apply for your card over the Web site and check your account balance there too. Your family's profile information, including the hotel rooms you stayed in, the ages of your children, the sizes of their boots, and what classes each person took when you last visited any of ASC's eight properties, is also kept up to date.

Offer Peace of Mind

A GOOD CUSTOMER experience delivers service, product—and peace of mind. Let me give you an example. When the concept of Internet banking first emerged, what were customers most afraid of? Security. Security First Network Bank recognized that it could turn a fear into an asset, and it made peace of mind the core of its business strategy, beginning with its name.

Amazon.com and Virtual Vineyards both discovered the importance of peace of mind early in the lives of their businesses. Both companies reassure customers every step of the way as orders are placed. They notify customers that the order has been received, notify them again that the order has been shipped, and even, in Virtual Vineyard's case, monitor delivery.

One of the most popular applications at most commercial Web sites is the ability for customers to check the status of their orders. Dell Computer, Cisco Systems, Amazon.com, and many others offer this capability. It's a good example of one of the ways companies can contribute to customers' peace of mind. Customers like to be able to check on the status of orders placed, service requests submitted, payments sent, and billing adjustments made. Sometimes they want to check on the availability of items in inventory. In late 1996, Boeing began offering its airline customers electronic access to its database of spare parts. Before this, Boeing's customers could call a hot line to order a spare part or to check pricing or availability. And they could place orders using proprietary electronic data interchange (EDI) linkages. But once Boeing offered customers the ability both to access this information and to place orders using the Web, customers flocked to the site. Smaller airlines that had never bothered to create an EDI linkage with Boeing could now place orders quickly and easily via the Internet. But more important, customers could check on the availability of spare parts. Customers who might have called the hot line once a week began checking the Web site several times a day. They wanted to know which parts were available and where they were warehoused. If Qantas wanted to replace a part in Sydney, Australia, it wanted to know if the part in question was in the warehouse in Hawaii or the one in Seattle. Clearly, knowing that they could procure the part quickly if they needed to was important to Boeing's customers' peace of mind.

Another proven way to calm customers' apprehensions is by offering guarantees. Sunday River ski resort (an ASC property) guarantees that customers won't have to wait in line for the ski lift for more than eight minutes. If the wait is longer, you ride for free. They also guarantee that customers will learn how to ski or snowboard better in each lesson, or the next lesson is free.

Peace of mind is particularly important when customers are placed in stressful situations. Let's use my favorite example: delayed or canceled airline flights. The way airlines give unhappy customers peace of mind is by telling them *exactly* what's going on. What doesn't work is saying, "Sit tight, we'll let you know soon." What does work is saying, "We have a mechanical problem with the air-conditioning system. This type of problem usually takes thirty minutes to fix," or "We've had to cancel this flight, but you've all been rebooked on the next flight, which leaves in thirty minutes from gate 2A. Your seat assignments remain the same. Please have a cup of coffee on us, and let us know if you'd like us to call someone for you. We apologize for the inconvenience." Giving customers specific and accurate information about their situation goes a long way toward establishing and maintaining peace of mind.

Work with Partners to Deliver Consistent Service and Quality

Sometimes your company isn't the only one that interacts with your customer. What if the customer orders goods and services from you but they're delivered by a third party? Or what if you sell through distribution channels and partners that take orders, deliver products, and provide service and customization for the end customer? What if you have outsourced key functions, such as customer support or field service? The customer doesn't care how you get the job done. But the customer will absolutely hold you responsible for the quality of the outcome as well as the experience he had en route.

Most virtual companies—such as Amazon.com, Security First Network Bank, and Virtual Vineyards—rely heavily on partners to complete their offerings. Security First outsources virtually all of its operations. Yet from the customer's perspective, it feels as if you're dealing with a single, well-oiled organization. Everyone who deals with you has the whole picture about your accounts and the status of your dealings with the bank.

Outsourcing is likely to become the norm, not the exception, as more and more companies pare down to their core competencies and outsource key business functions. Luckily, there are a number of suppliers that have a deep understanding of the need to provide seamless service. Distributors such as Ingram Books, which handles most of the procurement for Amazon.com's business, become critical business partners in this scenario.

Third-party service providers, such as Altel, which handles customer service for Security First Network Bank, or CheckFree, which handles bill payment and bill presentment for Security First and many other financial institutions, understand the need to provide transparent service. The customer experiences the benefits but never "sees" the third party. If there's a problem, all the status information is immediately available both to the end customer and to the company he *thinks* he's dealing with. Delivery companies such as UPS and Federal Express encourage their customers to rely on them to fulfill the total experience promise. They understand companies' need not only to deliver products to their customers but also to provide those companies and their customers with the ability to track the status of their deliveries.

Respect the Customer's Individuality

It's not really possible to offer customers a "total" experience without treating and serving them as individuals. No matter how good and consistent the experience is, if you're made to feel like part of an assembly line, as you do at most fast-food restaurants, for example, you aren't as likely to become a loyal devotee. On the other hand, as soon as a business begins treating you like the important individual you are, your loyalty soars. L. L. Bean keeps a record of what you've purchased, building profiles on you as a customer. L. L. Bean knows I own a canoe, like Polartec clothing, and wear a size 10. Hertz knows I use my American Express card when I rent cars for business and Visa when I rent for personal use. They know I prefer four-door compact cars and that I am geographically challenged, so they'll offer me their NeverLost option when it's available. Sunday River ski resort knows that I have children, how old they are, how well they ski, and what kind of accommodations my family prefers.

Give Customers Control over Their Experience

No matter how well you orchestrate customers' total experience, you don't want to emasculate them in the process. As customers, we need to feel we're in control. So, for example, at Sunday River ski resort, when you sign up for ski instruction, you decide which level of class you should take by comparing yourself to skiers shown in a series of video clips and deciding which one skies most like you.

Security First Network Bank understood that customers didn't want just to access their bank accounts, pay bills, and be able to transfer money among accounts but also to be able to *manage* their money better. So SFNB provides customers with the ability to categorize their expenditures, generate reports, and manage their investments on-line. By letting the customer plan and control his finances, not just access them, SFNB meets the "total experience" challenge.

Examples: Hertz and Amazon.com

IN THE TWO case studies that follow, we'll look first at how Hertz "owns" the customer's total experience when dealing with customers in the physical world of renting and driving cars. Then we'll look behind the scenes at what Amazon.com does to own the customer's total experience when all of its dealings with them take place in cyberspace. First the physical world; then the virtual world.

OWN THE CUSTOMER'S TOTAL EXPERIENCE (IN THE PHYSICAL WORLD):

Hertz
www.hertz.com

Executive Summary

Back in the 1970s, Hertz executives learned the value of keeping customer profiles on file. Later, when the company decided to develop an enhanced customer loyalty program, it was able to extend that customer database and make it the focal point for all of the streamlined business processes that touched the customer. Hertz #1 Club Gold combines a series of technologies, ranging from electronic clipboards to in-car navigation systems to electronic sign boards, to make the customer's total car rental experience a pleasant one. The company's Web site was designed to support several different constituencies—leisure travelers, business travelers, professional travel agents, corporate travel departments—by leveraging the same basic information and application integration infrastructure.

Critical Success Factors in the Hertz Story	
Target the right customers	✓ Let customers help themselves
★ Own the customer's total experience	Help customers do their jobs
★ Streamline business processes that impact the customer	✓ Deliver personalized service
✓ Provide a 360-degree view of the customer relationship	Foster community
★ = Featured in this discussion	✓ = Touched on in this discussion

Hertz Focuses on a Hassle-free Experience

HERTZ HAS THE most popular frequent car rental program in the world. Why? Because Hertz understands that its customers want more than points. They want a better car rental experience. As a Hertz #1 Club Gold member, I am taken care of from the time I reserve my car on the Web to the moment I find my way to my final destination using Hertz's NeverLost in-car global positioning system (GPS). Hertz has made innovative use of electronics to eliminate unnecessary steps for its customers and has used customer profiling to ensure that each customer's preferences are honored from Atlanta to New Zealand.

Hertz was the first rental car company to recognize the strategic value of maintaining a customer profile database. The practice of keeping each customer's name, car class preference, credit card number, address, and company information on file was the brainchild of a customer service representative. In the early 1970s, this entrepreneurial rental clerk realized that she was seeing many of the same customers each week. She began to keep their profile information on index cards, so she could fill in their rental forms before they arrived. By 1973, the company had formalized this practice by developing an on-line customer profile database. They called this program Hertz #1 Club and marketed it as a way to save customers time.

In the late 1980s, Hertz marketing executives noticed a clear directive emerging from the customer satisfaction surveys they conducted regularly. "Why do I have to keep coming to the counter at the airport and wait in line to sign my rental forms?" their #1 Club customers kept asking. "Why, indeed?" these executives asked themselves. Brian Kennedy, executive vice president of Hertz marketing and sales, put together a task force to look at how Hertz could streamline all the processes that impacted its most loyal customers. He asked Janet Smyth, vice president of advertising and marketing programs, to lead the task force. Robert Bailey was the point person for operations. Kennedy dubbed this new initiative Hertz #1 Club Gold, and he articulated an ambitious goal: streamline *all* the processes that touch our customers. The timeline was ambitious too. He wanted the Hertz #1 Club Gold program up and running within two years, worldwide!

Why couldn't Hertz give its #1 Club Gold customers an annual rental agreement? Customers could agree to the conditions stated and update their profile information once a year. With the customer's credit card on file, customers wouldn't have to sign for the car each time. No more waiting at the rental counter! This was the first breakthrough the task force came up with.

Next, the task force looked at the process of getting from the air terminal to the car. Customers had made it clear that they wanted speed. They would value the convenience of being able to get off the airplane, get onto the shuttle bus, and be taken right to their car. But they didn't want this streamlined process to become an impersonal one. As the market researchers explained what customers really wanted, the architects, facilities managers, and operations staff listened carefully.

Then they discussed ways they could redesign the car lots to deliver convenience with a personal touch. What if there was an electronic signboard with customers' names in alphabetical order showing the stall number where their pre-assigned vehicle was parked and another sign above each car with the customer's name on it? The customer would get off the bus and see her name in lights! What if they placed canopies over the parking area to keep snow and rain off? That would allow them to leave the car trunks open, so that a customer could simply throw his bags into the trunk, close it, and drive off. What would the customer need to show to the security guard as proof of identity? How about his driver's license? That way, Hertz would check that the customer had a valid driver's license and ascertain his identity at the same time, while checking the preprinted rental record placed in the customer's vehicle to make sure the customer had the right pre-assigned vehicle.

Expediting the Car Rental Experience: Delivering the #1 Club Gold Program

KENNEDY WAS ADAMANT about the fact that the #1 Club Gold program had to be a single, global initiative. No matter where a customer traveled, his experience in dealing with Hertz needed to be the same. So the design team embarked on an international internal marketing campaign. They went from country to country, explaining the premise behind the program and laying out the requirements that would have to be met in each country. There were two sets of issues the team encountered. First, each Hertz operation outside the United States already had its own distinct customer database. Second, there were a number of important cultural differences in the way car rentals were handled in each country. For example, in France, cars were often rented with chauffeurs. The design team listened carefully to the objections and noted, in particular, all the different kinds of information that would be have to be kept in a customer's profile record to satisfy the different countries' needs. For example, many countries required the renter's passport number as well as the driver's license number to be listed on the rental agreement.

After the fact-finding mission, it became apparent that the only way to ensure a consistent customer experience worldwide would be to have a single global customer database with tight integration into the reservations and counter systems around the world. The plan was to migrate each country's customer database onto the newly expanded global database and to either replace or rework the other systems to meet the #1 Club Gold requirements. Janet Smyth and Brian Dickerson, Hertz's sales systems director, describe this international consensus building as a "pretty painful process." They were grateful, however, for the unstinting support of Brian Kennedy. Whenever they met too much resistance, they simply bumped the issues up to Kennedy, who had the clout to resolve them.

By November 1988, the Hertz #1 Club Gold program was piloted in four locations in the United States. Each of these pilots included the new electronic signs with the customer's "name in lights," as well as new systems for the operations people, who now needed to print out customer's rental records, place them in the car, and ensure that the car was ready to go when the customer arrived. Customers' reactions to these pilot sites were so positive that Hertz decided to continue with an aggressive rollout. Hertz launched its #1 Club Gold expedited car rental service in the United States in April 1989. The program rolled out in Canada in 1991, Europe in

1992, and Asia Pacific in 1993. Today, Hertz has #1 Club Gold service available at more than 600 locations worldwide. At thirty-eight major airports, Hertz offers canopy service with no lines. nothing to sign. Your name and car location are in lights, and your car is waiting in a weather-protected #1 Club Gold rental area, with the trunk open and backed into its preselected parking space. You just get in, show your driver's license and rental record at the exit gate, and drive off. At more than 600 other locations, customers go to a specially designated Hertz #1 Club Gold counter, present their license to the Hertz representative, get their car keys and rental record, and go directly to their car.

Helping Customers Find the Way to Their Destinations

HERTZ'S COMMITMENT TO improving customers' car rental experience has propelled the company into some pretty innovative uses of technology. For example, Hertz executives decided that providing a map wasn't sufficient in helping customers to their final destination, so in 1984, Hertz became the first car rental company to deploy terminals and kiosks with computerized driving directions (CDD) to their customers. This service provides customers with detailed directions to local destinations, including estimated time and distance, in six languages in the United States and Canada, and nine languages in Europe. The touch-screen terminals at airport counters allow customers to select a specific hotel, restaurant, or tourist attraction and print a set of detailed driving instructions from the Hertz location.

But this approach didn't work well for many of Hertz's business travelers' destinations. Typically, all they had was the street address of the business they needed to visit. So Hertz set about to streamline the process of giving exact directions to destinations without making customers stop at a counter and wait in line to talk to an agent. The solution Hertz chose was the use of a global positioning system (GPS) in selected cars.

GPS units had become more affordable, and Rockwell International had a unit in production that piqued Hertz executives' interest. Bob Bailey, senior vice president of quality assurance, became the sponsor for testing Rockwell's in-vehicle GPS systems. He did so by installing these units in the cars of the top Hertz executives. All the marketing executives and general managers who lived and worked around the Hertz Park Ridge, New Jersey, headquarters became guinea pigs for this new device. And they loved it! The company dubbed the system Hertz NeverLost and began planning to add it as an option for Hertz #1 Club Gold customers in the United States.

The next step was to try the GPS system out on real customers. Hertz's marketing team held focus groups with customers to determine their requirements and gauge their interest level. In 1995, the company piloted the use of these devices in nine markets in 600 vehicles on a test basis. The response was so positive that Hertz deployed an additional 7,500 units throughout its fleet a year later. In 1997, the Rockwell GPS division was acquired by the California-based GPS manufacturer Magellan Systems Corporation. Hertz's NeverLost system had the features that mattered most to customers: an easy-to-read display screen map; large, legible arrows showing when and where to turn; the ability to recalibrate the map quickly after the car emerged from a tunnel; and a system that could quickly propose a new route if the driver missed an exit or made a wrong turn.

Other capabilities on the customers' wish list included the ability to select from a list of attractions—amusement parks, hotels, hospitals, and so on—in the event that customers did not know the exact address of a "named" destination. Other features included listing fast-food outlets, the nearest ATM, local restaurants, and the nearest gas station.

Navigation Technologies of Sunnyvale, California, produced the mapping software for the Magellan units. The maps are stored on a PCMCIA card that is stored in a device in the trunk of the car and interfaces with the GPS. New map cards are released twice a year. In the United States, the maps of California are extremely detailed. Getting detailed geocoded (with exact latitude and longitude) street maps for every part of the world remains a challenge.

Currently, Hertz has approximately 8,000 Hertz NeverLost units in its U.S. rental fleet, more than ten times as many GPS systems as its closest competitor. Hertz reports that once customers have the experience of using cars equipped with the Hertz NeverLost option, they usually request the feature over and over again.

Magellan continues to refine and improve the system through the updating of maps, ancillary information, and real-time traffic routing.

During the 1996 Summer Olympics, in Atlanta, Georgia, Hertz created a custom database for the Olympic venues. And it used this opportunity to pilot the next improvement to the GPS system: a real-time feed of traffic information and suggested detours to avoid traffic congestion. The Olympics provided a unique opportunity for the test of these new features. In most cities, a driver finds out about traffic congestion and alternate route suggestions from a local radio traffic report. However, during the Olympics, Atlanta's traffic and public safety infrastructure implemented a traffic advisory service that could be received by taxis, buses, and any appropriately equipped car. This service broadcast not only voice but also geographically encoded data that could be integrated into in-vehicle systems. So by adding an additional receiver/transmitter in each car and adding some software to the devices, Hertz was able to give customers driving its NeverLost cars real-time traffic updates and automatic reprogramming of the system to offer new routes.

Streamlining the Car Return Process

HERTZ ALSO PIONEERED innovations in the car return process. In 1987, the company introduced Hertz Instant Return, in which a Hertz agent greets the returning customer at carside, enters the mileage and gas information, processes the return, and gives the customer a receipt in less that sixty seconds from a portable printer. Today, Instant Return is available in more than 110 locations in the United States and Canada, as well as in Australia and seven European countries. In 1997, Hertz decided to go one step further and introduced Hertz Return Centers, a covered area in the car return section of the parking lot that protects customers from the weather as they're getting out of the car, retrieving their luggage from the trunk, processing their returns, and boarding the bus. Hertz plans forty Return Centers by the end of 1999.

Adding Web Self-Service for Customers and Travel Agents

TODAY, HERTZ'S WORLDWIDE Reservations Center in Oklahoma City handles more than 30 million phone calls annually, and more than 50 percent of Hertz's 17 million reservations each year are booked through commissioned travel agents. Travel agents typically access Hertz's reservations system through the airlines' computerized reservations systems (CRSs), each of which charges a fee for each reservation. So, Hertz's Global Automation Marketing group began planning the company's Web initiative. It had two goals: first, to make it easy for customers to get information about rental rates and car availability and to make their own reservations from the Web; second, to give travel agents another way to interact with Hertz. What was unusual about Hertz's approach to the Web is that it targeted both end customers and travel agents with common Web initiatives.

Also, it offered travel agents the same commissions they'd normally get (by booking through any other computerized reservations system).

The first Hertz informational Web site was launched in November 1996. The following spring, the team had implemented the next phases: customer service and transactions. Prospects and customers could enter the dates when and location in which they wished to reserve a car, select the type of car they were interested in, and see if one was available. Hertz #1 Club and #1 Club Gold customers were quoted the type of rates that were on file in their profile (corporate discount, AAA discount, and so on).

As soon as Hertz opened its Web-based reservations system for business, the company was pleasantly surprised by the volume of traffic. Most of the customers who availed themselves of the site were existing Hertz customers.

Over time, Hertz continues to streamline and improve the Web-based front end for both its end customers and its travel agents. For example, not only can agents book reservations, they can also access the customer's corporate discount information and see pictures of the different kinds of vehicles offered—the latter is something they can't do from the standard CRS they use. And not only can customers get information and make reservations via the Web, they can also access reservations they've made through a travel agent. This is the kind of hassle-free interaction that Hertz's customers expect from the company.

Evolving the Technical Infrastructure

The biggest shift in Hertz's information technology infrastructure occurred in the late 1980s, when the company began to redesign its systems to deliver expedited service for its #1 Club Gold customers. But, because the company already had a customer profile database, this was not as traumatic as it would be for a company that had never had a central customer database. The evolution occurred as a natural progression. First, the #1 Club database had to be extended to incorporate additional information required for expedited service around the world. Second, separate customer databases being used in different locations around the world had to be consolidated so that Hertz had a single, global customer database. Third, new interfaces had to be interjected between the profile database, the reservations system, the rate system, the credit card authorization application, and the car inventory and availability databases (these are distributed around the world). The customer profiles now sit at the center of all the applications. Customers' preferences drive the interactions with the different application services. Finally, a Web front end was added.

Brian Dickerson led the information technology redesign effort for the Hertz #1 Club Gold program. He feels that Hertz was fortunate to already have its initial customer database with the original Hertz #1 Club as a starting point. This IDMS database already had the basic customer profile information for #1 Club members. In order to meet the requirements for the new #1 Club Gold members, they extended the original #1 Club database to handle all of Hertz's customers worldwide. However, #1 Club Gold members' profiles required additional information. This additional profile information was stored in linked DB2 databases. The combined global customer database is housed in Oklahoma City in mirrored data centers and accessed via global private wide area networks.

Next, Dickerson and his team set out to streamline the rest of the reservations process, deriving the information from the customer's profile.

Redesigning the Reservations Process

Dickerson explains the four steps that are required to deliver Gold service: "First, you have to find the vehicle class the customer wants. Second, you have to assign a rate to that vehicle, depending on the terms of the contract, applicable discounts, and current promotions. Third, you need to gain approval to debit the customer's credit card. Fourth, you need to print the rental record in advance and place it on a 'hangtag' in the actual preassigned vehicle."

The information systems team worked from that process description to determine what information would be required to complete each of those steps. For example, in order to know which vehicle the customer prefers, you need to start with the information contained in their profile. If the customer specifies a different type of car at the time a reservation is made, that new specification overrides the profile information (on a one-time basis). Once the customer's car preference is determined, the reservation system queries the vehicle availability database and provides the necessary information—vehicle type; date, time, and location for pick-up; date, time, and location for drop-off. After an available vehicle has been located, the reservation system queries the customer database for any contractual information that would affect the rate—for example, Is the customer eligible for a discount as a AAA member? Does the customer's company have a special contract with Hertz with negotiated rates? With that contractual information in hand, the reservations system queries the rate system and returns the rate for this transaction. When the customer has accepted the reservation, the reservation system requests authorization from the credit card authorization system to debit the customer's credit card.

Finally, on the day the customer is to pick up the car, the complete record is sent to the counter system at the pick-up location. There it is queued to be printed and placed as a hangtag in the car. And, if the customer's flight is delayed, or he misses the flight, there is a recovery procedure that is proactively initiated at the pick-up location.

Dickerson reports that Hertz was fortunate in that the four systems required to implement the streamlined reservations process—reservations, vehicle availability, rates, and credit card authorization—were already in place and working fine. These heavy-duty transactional systems implemented on IBM mainframes were already interconnected with high-speed hyperchannel links. The streamlining process involved integrating the customer profile information into the transaction flows.

To further enhance this process, in 1996 Hertz introduced its Gold Electronic Manifest (GEM) system, which gave courtesy bus drivers electronic manifests with each customer's record handy so they could greet each customer and ensure the customer's car was ready before proceeding to the #1 Club Gold car rental area.

Migrating onto the Web

In 1996, Hertz selected Microsoft's Internet Information Server running on Windows NT for Hertz's Web platform. A small technical team created CGI script interfaces to the customer profile database, reservation system, and rate engine. Thus the Web constitutes another front end into Hertz's existing back-end reservation systems. All of the business rules, customer profile information, and application-to-application workflows are identical to those experienced by Hertz's call center personnel or travel agents interacting via other computerized reservation systems (CRSs).

Customer Profile Issues

HERTZ IS ONE of very few companies that have been using customer profiles at the core of their information systems for over a decade. However, knowing when to update a customer's profile remains a thorny issue. For example, if a customer specifies a different kind of car or special equipment for a car at the time he reserves it, this new specification will override the specification in his profile on a one-time-only basis. So how does Hertz know when a customer wants the information in his profile permanently changed? At first, Hertz's reservation agents would ask the customer, "Do you want this changed in your profile, or is this a onetime change?" But what they discovered is that customers weren't predictable in answering that question correctly. Later, customers would book again and be distraught that the new specification had overridden their original one. This problem occurred particularly when customers alternated between renting cars for business and for leisure travel. Hertz's current resolution for this problem is to encourage the customer to explicitly change his own profile whenever he chooses to do so, but to assume that all other changes made at the point of reservation should be considered one-time changes only. Changes to the profile may be made by calling a customer service representative or by mailing or faxing in a paper form. Today, Hertz #1 Club Gold customers can update profiles on-line via the Web.

Results

HERTZ IS THE world's largest car rental company. And the company has been profitable every year since 1918. Since the Hertz #1 Club Gold program was launched in 1989, it has grown to more than 2 million members. Moreover, #1 Club Gold members account for more than 40 percent of Hertz's total car rental business in the United States and are by far the company's most loyal customers. Each time Hertz has added more convenience and service for its customers, they have responded by giving the company more business.

Patty's Rx for Hertz

Hertz is head and shoulders above its competitors in understanding how to deliver streamlined processes for its customers and in continuously extending those processes to encompass more and more of the customer's experience of renting and driving a car. Naturally, there are many more steps the company can take.

When traveling in Ireland in mid-1998, I discovered that Hertz's service at Shannon Airport was below par, and that #1 Club Gold service wasn't offered (although brochures describing the service were). So, when traveling internationally, check to be sure this particular service is offered.

The Web lends itself to the process of creating all the services of a corporate travel desk for both large and small businesses, and Hertz is working on leveraging this to provide better service. Hertz's large corporate accounts currently receive consolidated bills and reports each month. The corporate travel agent has access to all the functions that a regular travel agent has. Using the Web as a channel, Hertz now has the opportunity to extend that kind of functionality to much smaller businesses. For the first time in its history, the company has a cost-effective mechanism—the Web—it can use to provide tailored service to small businesses.

"Take-Aways" from the Hertz Story

1. Customer profiles are the first step. Start with a comprehensive set of customer profile information. Have customers maintain their own profiles.

2. Use a single global customer database. Accommodate local needs in the overall database structure. That way, customers will be assured of consistent service, with any local variations treated as "extras."

3. Start from the customer's experience in prioritizing business process redesign efforts. In Hertz's case, customers complained about having to wait in line at the airport counter. Hertz began its massive redesign effort by eliminating that step for customers.

4. Eliminate *every* step that wastes the customer's time. Hertz did this over and over again: creating electronic signage to direct the customer to her car, leaving the car trunk open, putting the map in the car, not requiring paperwork to exit the lot.

5. Proactively address the customer's gnawing sense of anxiety. Eliminate questions in the customer's mind. Hertz did this by having each customer listed on the electronic manifest when he boards the shuttle bus

and by proactively monitoring flight arrivals and delays to ensure that the customer's car is ready when he actually arrives.

6. Make it easy for the customer to *use* your product or service. Hertz does this by offering customers two different ways to get driving directions: by using the self-service Computerized Driving Directions terminals and kiosks or by opting for an in-car NeverLost GPS system.

7. Use a single set of back-end systems for a variety of customer interaction channels. In Hertz's case, whether the customer deals with Hertz directly by phone, uses the Web for self-service, and/or goes through a travel agent, the reservation information, and the customer experience, is identical.

OWN THE CUSTOMER'S TOTAL EXPERIENCE
(IN THE VIRTUAL WORLD)

Amazon.com
www.amazon.com

Executive Summary

Amazon.com is much more than the "Earth's Biggest Bookstore." It's one of the most comprehensive retail experiences on the Web. Amazon.com continues to refine both the retail experience it offers customers and its business model, always managing to keep a step ahead of its competition. The company has more than 3.1 million fanatically loyal customers, because management keeps its eye on the most important ingredient for success: ensuring that a customer's total experience of doing business with it is so satisfying that customers don't bother to switch.

Critical Success Factors in the Amazon.com Story	
Target the right customers	✓ Let customers help themselves
✷ Own the customer's total experience	Help customers do their jobs
✷ Streamline business processes that impact the customer	✓ Deliver personalized service
✓ Provide a 360-degree view of the customer relationship	✓ Foster community
✷ = Featured in this discussion	✓ = Touched on in this discussion

Amazon.com Sets the Standard for On-line Retailing

AMAZON.COM WAS the first virtual bookstore to emerge on the Web. It certainly wasn't the last. The company's early popularity and the fanatical loyalty of its growing customer base attracted lots of competitors. Some of these, like Barnes & Noble and Borders, were book retailers in the physical world that wanted to add the Web as a marketing and distribution channel. Others, like Cendant's BookStack, were also virtual retailers—companies with no physical sales outlets. What Amazon.com has done that none of its competitors have been able to overtake has been to set the standard for the on-line retail experience and then continually raise the bar. Just as quickly as others imitate Amazon.com's Web site and business model, the company moves on to the next level. As long as the company doesn't run out of money, this learning game will continue. The company that continues to learn the fastest what its customers want and need and implements that the fastest will prevail. That's how the "new economy" works.

Focusing on the Customer's Experience

JEFF BEZOS, AMAZON.COM'S founder, understood that the battle between physical and virtual bookstores would be waged not on price but rather on convenience. He knew that, as a virtual bookstore, Amazon.com would have one huge advantage over its physical competitors: its inventory. There is no theoretical limit to the number of books a virtual store can carry. (By the end of 1997, Amazon.com had 2.5 million titles listed, and the company was reaching out to the thousands of smaller, independent publishers whose books never make it into bookstores. By mid-1998, Amazon.com offered 3 million book titles and 125,000 CD titles.) However, the *experience* of shopping in a good book and music store is hard to beat. You can browse to your heart's content, picking up and sampling books as you roam through the shelves. The best bookstores have coffee shops, comfy couches, and roaring fires. Knowledgeable employees will recommend books to you or help you find something when you can't remember the author or the title, but you know something about the plot. With these tactile and interpersonal advantages, how could a virtual bookstore ever hope to compete with the experience of going to a really good physical bookstore? The best way was to make the *experience* of shopping at Amazon.com as rich and fulfilling as those described above, yet in other ways. A virtual bookstore can't yet offer the smell of freshly roasted coffee, the heat and smell of a crackling fire, or the feel of leather and paper in your hands via the Web. But it can offer an equally satisfying experience. And that's what Bezos set out to do. He analyzed the entire book-buying process and broke it down into discrete sets of tasks. Then his team set out to optimize each set of tasks and to try out scenarios across tasks. In 1998, when Amazon expanded to carry music as well as books, the team embarked on a similar analysis and implementation effort.

Shopping On-line

Amazon.com's designers understood that bookstore customers are usually in one of two moods: browsing or hunting (for a particular book). To satisfy the browsers, the merchandisers at Amazon.com organized the on-line bookstore much like a physical bookstore. There are "tables" at the front of the store featuring new releases, specials, and gift ideas. After checking out the items on display, you can go to a particular section: cooking, architecture, computers, and so on. There, browsers will find recommendations made by experts in that topic. Or you may choose to look at the books recommended by particular critics, like *The New York Times Book Review* or Oprah Winfrey's book club. By contrast, hunters can find the particular book they want simply by typing in whatever they know or remember about the book (author's name, words in the title, or words in the topic). Amazon.com's quick search engine provides a list of books that match the information provided.

Once you've found a book you're interested in, you can read a synopsis or reviews from other readers. Amazon was the first retailer to feature the "readers who bought [this book] also bought. . ." device, listing three other titles in the same subject area or books by the same author. Personally, I find these "other readers who bought this book also bought . . ." recommendations to be extremely valuable, and I often order a second book from the list. And I'm not the only "impulse buyer" in Amazon.com's customer base. After conducting an informal poll among other Amazon.com shoppers, I estimate that at least 10 percent of Amazon's orders probably include such an upsell.

Each book Amazon carries also lists the anticipated delivery time, ranging from twenty-four hours to a month or more if the book hasn't been published yet. Bezos understood that customers wouldn't place an order if they didn't know how long it would take to receive the book in question. After all, they did have an alternative—they could go to a physical bookstore in their neighborhood.

What can a virtual bookstore do that a physical bookstore can't? Besides carrying much more inventory, that is. One service that many buyers appreciate is being able to order books that are slated for publication but that haven't yet hit the bookstores. They can order the book and then forget about it, knowing that it will be sent to them as soon as it's available. For books from smaller, independent publishers that choose to join Amazon's Publisher's Advantage program, Amazon.com stocks five copies of each book and reorders as they're sold, so that customers ordering these harder-to-find books won't have to wait several weeks for them to arrive.

Purchasing On-line

Amazon.com was the first retail Web site to get the actual purchasing process just right. The company followed the twin principles of convenience and peace of mind. First, it reassured customers about the security of their purchases. Amazon was among the first Web sites to take credit card purchases over the Internet. In a section on security, it carefully explains how the credit card number is encrypted and how it is stored securely. And for customers who are still leery, it offers e-mail or fax as an alternative method for supplying credit card information. Then it walks the customer through a five-step purchasing process. (Amazon.com was the first on-line company to explicitly number each step in the purchasing process and to walk customers through each one.) After you've placed all the items you want in your shopping cart, you identify yourself to the system (if you're a returning customer, all your information is kept on file), indicate whether your purchases are gifts (if so, you can select gift wrap and write a card), select or enter the shipping address, select from a variety of shipping options, check your final bill, and confirm the order. At any point, you can go back and make changes, add more books, delete books, or even abandon the buying process. If you do, the next time you come back to the site, your shopping cart will still be there waiting for you, containing all the books you've already selected.

Once you've purchased once from Amazon.com, you have a customer profile. It contains all the information you entered for your first purchase. If everything is the same (shipping address, credit card number), you can breeze through the purchasing process by verifying the information and pressing the "purchase now" button. If you want to make a change, say, ship to someone at a different address, that new address will be added to your profile. The next time you order, you can select from among the shipping addresses Amazon.com has on file for you.

To streamline the purchasing process even more, Amazon introduced the 1-Click option. This lets you select a single credit card and a single shipping address from the ones listed in your customer profile, and a particular shipping method (standard, two-day, or overnight, for example), and designate it as the operant profile for all 1-Click transactions. You just find the books you want, press the 1-Click key, and the purchase is complete based on the information you've selected from your profile.

Fulfillment

Within a few minutes (literally) of placing your order, you'll receive an e-mail confirmation from Amazon.com. (Amazon.com was the first on-line company to initiate proactive order confirmation.) Then, as soon as Amazon.com ships any of your books (you can opt to have them shipped together or separately, as soon as each is available), it sends you another e-mail telling you what it just shipped and which books are still on order. My own experience with Amazon.com fulfillment has been very satisfying. I almost always receive books earlier than they were promised, with upgraded delivery service. Even if I select standard service, Amazon.com upgrades me to priority shipping. I'm not really sure why. I guess being a loyal customer gets me a few unadvertised benefits!

I suspect that when Amazon.com's founder, Jeff Bezos, conceived the business model for a virtual bookstore, he probably thought he could dispense with inventory. His original plan was to use the Web site as a substitute for retail outlets and to have books shipped directly to the customer from distributors. Yet it quickly became apparent that to offer the kind of total customer service Bezos had in mind, Amazon.com would need to warehouse and ship the books itself. Customers weren't willing to wait more than two days to receive a popular best-seller they knew they could find on the shelf in any bookstore. So Amazon.com leased a 50,000-square-foot warehouse in Seattle from which it could pack and ship books to customers as soon as orders were placed. It stocked enough copies of the best-sellers so it could fulfill those orders quickly. Bezos convinced his two major distributors, Ingram Books and Baker & Taylor, to ship books to Amazon.com on demand, using rapid fulfillment, so he could keep inventory and storage costs down. In November 1997, Amazon doubled its Seattle distribution facility and opened a new 200,000-square-foot distribution center in New Castle, Delaware, enlarging its stocking and shipping capacity sixfold, so that the company could reach customers on both sides of the United States much faster. "Now with distribution centers on both coasts, we can dramatically reduce order-to-mailbox time for Amazon.com customers everywhere," Bezos explained. With 300,000 square feet of space to house inventory and $116 million in sales for the second quarter of 1998, Amazon.com is close to achieving $1,547 in annualized revenues per square foot of inventory space. Of course, the cost of that inventory is simply the cost of warehousing it, since Amazon.com doesn't pay for any books until they are sold.

Account Maintenance

My own experience with Amazon.com has been so informative and reliable that I rarely have occasion to check my account maintenance file. It contains a record of every book I ever ordered from Amazon, to whom it was shipped, and when it was shipped. So although I've never had to track down a book on order (since Amazon's proactive notifications are so reassuring), I do consult my account information in order to see whether I already have a particular book or whether, for example, I already sent a favorite book to my father. Besides customer convenience, however, this account maintenance function serves another purpose. The profile information Amazon.com keeps about each customer includes not only the information the customer maintains about his billing and shipping addresses and credit card information, but also the list of every book he has ever bought. Apart from the company, only the customer himself has access to this information, so it's not a violation of his privacy. On the other hand, this is the information that Amazon uses to recommend other books you might like, so it serves a useful purpose.

Notifications

Amazon.com was the first company on the Web to realize that customers would welcome proactive e-mail notifications about things they are looking for. You can sign up to receive notifications by topic or by author, or based on certain other criteria (for example, new books reviewed by *The New York Times*). You'll then begin receiving e-mail from Amazon.com's Eyes service. I find this service very valuable. Every time a new book is published on the topic of "customers," for example, I get an e-mail from Amazon.com notifying me. Some real bibliophiles sign up to receive notifications of every new book listed each day!

Personalized Service

Amazon.com is doing a great job of personalizing the book-buying experience. Returning customers are greeted by name and offered a set of recommended titles based on the books they've bought in the recent past. Or, if you visit Amazon's Recommendation Center, you'll see an even longer list of titles handpicked for you based on your past purchases. These notifications also make customers feel connected to Amazon.com in a special way. The 1-Click purchase option, the ability to add or change your profile at any time, and the ability to see everything you've ever ordered are all great ways for Amazon.com to cement its relationship with the buyer. The more you purchase from Amazon, the more useful you'll find its personalized recommendations. Since I tend to buy books for a variety of people with different needs and tastes, I'll often find a new title that's just right for that special person (the latest Java programming guide for my son, the newest, seminal nonfiction work for my husband, the latest John Grisham novel for myself).

A less successful experiment, in my opinion, has been Amazon.com's use of "intelligent agents" to suggest books to you based not on what you or others have actually purchased, but on which books and authors you say you like. To participate in this BookMatcher game, you go through a series of multiple-choice options, ranking titles and authors within categories (fiction, nonfiction, and so forth). The intelligent agent continues to make suggestions to you based on your answers, by comparing your choices to those others have selected. So, for example, if thirty people who like to read Michael Crichton novels also enjoy Tom Clancy novels, the agent will recommend Tom Clancy to you once you've selected Michael Crichton. Why is this a less successful approach? For two reasons. It requires a fair investment of the customer's valuable time to make these choices and to iterate through successive approximations a few times. So it's not saving the customer time. Second, working from a sample subset of authors and titles is much less precise than tracking what you've actually bought and comparing each title, topic, and author to the database of those purchased by others.

Building Community

How has Amazon.com gone about building a community? Very carefully. While competitors have jumped in with both feet, offering on-line chat rooms, real-time interviews, and discussion forums, Amazon.com has proceeded more slowly. You become part of the Amazon.com community by contributing book reviews. These reviews are carefully vetted by Amazon's staff to make sure that they're relevant and tastefully done. The result is that customers feel that they can trust one another's recommendations and reactions.

Evolving the Technical Infrastructure

When Bezos first launched Amazon.com in mid-1994, he hosted the site on Sun Sparc systems. However, as traffic to Amazon's Web site began to increase exponentially, he decided to switch over to two Digital AlphaServer 2000 systems. These 64-bit processors are joined together in a symmetric multiprocessing configuration with one gigabyte of RAM. This high-powered system gave Amazon.com the breathing room and scalability it needed for the next couple of years. Amazon.com relies on the AlphaServer's memory address space to do high-speed indexing. Amazon keeps its entire list of 3 million–plus titles in RAM, so that customers' queries are answered fast. The underlying database is on Oracle.

For the first three years of operation, Amazon.com wrote all of its own software. In 1997, the company added NetPerceptions intelligent agent software in order to implement the Matchmaker recommendations capability. By late 1997 and early 1998, the company was investigating the possibility of substituting some "off-the-shelf" electronic commerce software modules to replace some of its homegrown code, in order to lower the cost of software maintenance. Like many companies that have written their own software and modified it over the years, Amazon.com discovered that it's difficult to find commercial packages that have all or most of the functionality they had already developed.

Over time, it's likely that Amazon.com will buy and customize third-party software modules as it evolves its Web business functions. In August 1998, Amazon.com purchased Junglee, a company whose core technology expertise is in its use of XML to provide the platform for next-generation electronic commerce.

Streamlining Business Processes for Stakeholders

IN ADDITION TO pioneering and continuously improving the end customer's experience at its Web site, Amazon.com has done a masterful job in recruiting and satisfying stakeholders—publishers, distributors, and other on-line retailers. Because it's so easy for these stakeholders to do business with Amazon, the total customer experience is improved. Publishers like to preview upcoming books because they can get an early indication of interest. They add information to the listings that appear on the Amazon site: reviews, quotes, a table of contents, excerpts, and other marketing information that helps the customer decide whether or not to purchase the book. Publishers also appreciate the detailed information that Amazon provides them about the sales of their titles on a weekly basis. Amazon's large distributors like dealing with the company because of the volume the company does, as well as the efficiency of its streamlined ordering and returns processes. But the most impressive set of stakeholders in Amazon's success is the 100,000 associates the company had recruited by mid-1998.

Any business or organization that has a Web site on a specialty topic can register to become an Amazon.com associate. The associate then selects a group of books from the Amazon.com Web site it would like to feature on its site. The associate can add its own book reviews and commentaries. When its customer clicks on the book to purchase it, the customer is passed directly on to Amazon's Web site. He completes the purchase using Amazon's purchasing process, and the associate receives a commission for the sale of the book.

Amazon makes it as easy for a company to become an associate as it is for an end user to buy books. The description of the program and the legally binding contract are posted on Amazon's Web site, along with detailed instructions on how to actually link your site to Amazon's. You fill in a simple on-line application form, wait for Amazon.com's approval (which takes about twenty-four hours), and you're off and running. Although Barnes & Noble has already imitated Amazon's popular associates program by offering an affiliates program of its own, Amazon has a much larger base of associates and one that's growing all the time.

Results

AMAZON.COM'S SALES HAVE been growing exponentially. The company's revenues in 1997 grew 838 percent over its revenues in 1996! Net sales for 1996 were $15.7 million; in 1997, net sales were $147.8 million. Net sales for the fourth quarter of 1997 were $66 million, compared to $37.9 million in the third quarter. Net sales for the second quarter of 1998 were $116 million, an increase of 316 percent over the second quarter of the previous year. Amazon has over 3.1 million customers. And repeat orders represented close to 65 percent of the company's business in the second quarter of 1998. So Amazon.com is doing an excellent job of keeping its customers loyal and coming back for more—the secret of success in the profitability game.

Yes, it's true that the company is losing money—the accumulated deficit was $64 million by mid-1998. However, the company has been investing heavily in marketing and advertising. And Amazon.com keeps appreciating in value—to its shareholders, its customers, and the industry. As of mid-August 1998, the company was valued at $5.9 billion (more than ten times revenues)!

Once an on-line company is attracting 1 million–plus repeat visitors to its site, that property becomes very hot. It attracts partners, advertisers, and more customers, simply by word of mouth. As of mid-1998, Amazon.com did not accept advertising at its Web site, although most of its competitors, including Barnes & Noble, did. If the company really needs to increase its revenues quickly, selling advertising will be a no-brainer.

In 1998, Amazon.com branched out into other related areas of retailing—in particular, music. Bezos wanted to offer its 3.1 million–and–growing customer base a one-stop-shopping experience for like products. The companies that are already in the on-line music business—CDNow and N2K—were openly skeptical that Amazon.com could do as good a job with music retailing as it does with books. But we know from experience in the physical world that books and music retailing are very complimentary—witness the success of Borders Books and Music in the physical world. As a loyal Amazon.com customer, I was offered an opportunity to test-drive Amazon.com's music retailing. As I had expected, it was a satisfying experience. I searched for a little-known jazz musician, found the titles I was seeking, and was able to see what tracks were on each CD and to read reviews and comments. I could use the same 1-Click purchasing I have come to rely upon, and I received my CDs in the usual timely fashion. Now, when I go to Amazon.com to order books, I often browse and buy in the music section as well. Amazon.com lets me easily upsell and cross-sell myself. I suspect I'm not alone.

I must admit that I was puzzled by one aspect of Bezos's business model. Why did a virtual book retailer need to invest in so much physical warehousing space? Why couldn't the distributors provide the shipping service that Amazon.com needs? At least one of Amazon's competitors in the book world—Cendant's BookStack—and most of the on-line music retailers do not stock inventory, but rely instead on distributors to fulfill their orders. I suspected that the answer to this question lay with the customer's total experience.

In February 1998, I placed three orders for the same book simultaneously at Amazon.com, Barnes & Noble, and BookStack. Amazon's order confirmation arrived first—about five minutes before Barnes & Noble's—not a material difference. BookStack's confirmation arrived two days later! Amazon's books arrived first, Barnes & Noble's second, and BookStack's lagged by a week. I guess that experience answered my questions.

Today's book distributors aren't organized to fulfill onesy-twosy orders quickly. Their processes and systems were designed to serve bookstores, which typically order hundreds of books at a time. Until a distributor steps in to fill this service need cost-effectively, Amazon.com will have to continue to invest in leasing warehouse space.

Patty's Rx for Amazon.com

One of the smartest moves I think Amazon.com could make would be to capitalize on its branded experience with in-bookstore kiosks. Physical bookstores have limited real estate and, thus, have to restrict their stock on hand. They also typically have a bottleneck at the information counter, where employees try to help customers with all their questions. By signing up to be Amazon.com associates, these bookstores could place an Internet terminal in their store, use their own brand name, and let customers help themselves by searching the database to find books they'd like. This database would need to be linked to the in-store inventory systems so that if the customer selects a book that's in stock, the system could display a map to the correct shelf. But if a customer selected books that weren't in the store, she could simply order them then and there and have them shipped directly to her home (or her friends' homes). The bookstore would receive its commission without doing any of the work. And the customer would go home satisfied.

In mid-1998, Amazon.com purchased two companies, Junglee and PlanetAll. Junglee provides an XML-technology platform for broad-based electronic commerce. What does PlanetAll bring to the table? In addition it its 1.5 million members, PlanetAll has provided a "breakthrough in doing something as fundamental and important as staying in touch," Jeff Bezos explains. Bezos appreciates simple business models that work. And PlanetAll has one. You sign up for free, list your own contact information, and add the names of any friends or contacts you'd like to keep track of or reconnect with. You can streamline this process by listing all of your alumni groups and other associations and affiliations. All of the folks who are maintained by your college alumni association, for example, will be listed, and you can select the people you want to keep in touch with. Each of the friends or contacts you've listed will be asked if it's okay to give you *their* contact information and to notify you of any future changes. From now on, your contacts will maintain their own information in your personal organizer. Your personal database on PlanetAll will synchronize with the contact manager in your PC or your handheld Personal Digital Assistant through Puma Technology's Mobile Data Exchange software. You'll never have out-of-date information or be out of touch again!

Combine your automatically updated contact manager with a calendar that keeps track of important dates—birthdays, anniversaries, or any gift-giving occasion—and you have a retailer's dream come true. Your personal organizer beeps, or you receive a reminder e-mail, in time to select from a list of suggested gift items and specials that are specifically tailored to your tastes and habits, based on your past buying behaviors (as tracked by Amazon.com).

I think that Bezos may be gearing up to turn Amazon.com from a destination shopping site for books, CDs, and soon, videos, into "your personal store." What if there were a single Web destination you could go to no matter what you needed to purchase? This personal store would save you lots of time (the most precious commodity of all). All of your (and your family's) personal profile information would already be stored on this site as a result of your earlier shopping expeditions—favorite authors and musicians, types of clothing, sizes, colors, and so on. Your most frequently used credit cards for personal and business use would already be on file (securely, of course). The addresses to which you typically need things shipped for yourself, family, and friends would already be there. If a friend or relative moved, you'd be notified of their new address. All of your friends and relatives' birthdays and anniversaries would be maintained there. If friends were getting married, the bridal registry of the gifts they wanted would be posted there. With a single click, you'd be able to see a list of everything you'd ever ordered from your personal store and to whom it was sent. Anytime you wanted something, you'd just go to your store, enter the parameters you needed, and, voilà, you'd quickly get a list of all the items that were in inventory (anywhere in the world), with up-to-date prices. For more information, you could click and browse the provider's Web site, but as soon as you'd want to actually place the order, all of the relevant information would be automatically filled in; you'd just check the information, make any changes, and be done with it. Personalized, one-stop shopping! Why not? And who better to provide it than Amazon.com, the world's most popular on-line retailer?

"Take-Aways" from the Amazon.com Story

1. Focus on the customer's total experience of doing business with you. Identify each step or business event in the customer's most likely interactions with your firm, and streamline each of those steps.
2. Reassure customers at each step, with features like near-real-time order confirmations and shipping notifications.
3. Capture customers' profile information and offer them the opportunity both to change their profiles at any time and to select a set of profile defaults for "fast-path" dealings with your firm (like Amazon.com's 1-Click purchasing).
4. Give customers access to their entire transaction history with your firm.
5. Let customers specify what, if anything, they'd like to receive proactive notifications about.

6. Recruit thousands of business partners who can represent your firm to their customers by making it *really* easy for them to sell your products and receive commissions.

7. Make it so easy for your suppliers to deal with you that they're eager to do so. Help them present their products to your customers in the most effective way.

8. Focus on excellence in the customer experience and in execution of customer service to keep your customers loyal and to stimulate referrals. Combine that with aggressive marketing to bring in new customers who will be seduced by the customer experience as well as the products you offer.

Own the Customer's Total Experience: Lessons Learned

This critical success factor may be one of the more elusive ones to master. It's tightly interwoven with the next one: Streamline business processes that impact the customer. In other words, you can't really take control of a customer's total experience unless you've streamlined most of the scenarios related to how that customer interacts with you. Yet it's useful to understand the big picture—what the customer's total experience is—before you get down to the issue of picking specific business processes to work on. Both the Hertz and Amazon.com examples bring home to me how complete your thinking needs to be if you really want to take responsibility for the customer's total experience of doing business with you.

Here's another example: Bill Finkelstein, who's the chief technical architect behind Wells Fargo's on-line banking initiatives, commented to me that Wells is very concerned about its customers' experience of accessing Wells Fargo via the Internet: Will the customer be able to get through quickly? Will the connection stay up? While Wells Fargo can design its Web site to offer high performance and good response times and ensure that the site is open twenty four hours a day, the company has no control over the broader Internet infrastructure that customers are using. What Wells Fargo and all Internet commerce players can't control are factors such as: How good is the quality of the customer's phone line? Is his Internet service provider experiencing problems? Has his session been routed through a node in the network that is failing? Yet Wells Fargo worries about this issue constantly and is even taking steps to try to tell when customers are likely to encounter problems. That kind of thinking is a good example of owning the customer's total experience in the e-business world.

Use Customer Profiles as the Focal Point for Your Applications

WHAT HAVE WE learned from going behind the scenes at Hertz and Amazon.com? Both companies' experiences show us that having good, complete customer profiles at the core of your system is key. Hertz asks customers to update theirs on paper, over the phone, or at the Web site. Amazon.com invites its customers to modify their profiles at any time via the Web, which seems natural, since all customer interactions with Amazon take place on the Web. But notice that, in both cases, there are some subtleties in the way that profiles are used and managed. Hertz has run into problems in the past by letting customers change their profiles on the fly, while they're making reservations. Amazon.com makes it easy for customers to change or add profile information at any time and to select a subset of that information to be their current active 1-Click setting. In both cases, the customer profile information acts both as a launching point for each business process and as a grounding mechanism. As various business events occur, you need to keep checking back with the customer's profile, to see what actions to take.

Make It Really Easy for Business Partners to Deal with You

NOTICE THAT BOTH Hertz and Amazon.com go out of their way to streamline operations for their business partners as well. Hertz wants to make it as easy as possible for travel agents to book Hertz cars by giving them access to customer profile information as well as more detailed information about the different cars on offer via the Web. Amazon.com makes it really easy for publishers to promote their books, even before they're available, and gives them detailed weekly reports about what customers are buying. And Amazon has recruited a vast new set of channel partners through its associates program, by making it really easy for these special-interest Web sites both to sign up as associates and to implement the linkages.

From the customer's standpoint, these streamlined partner relationships translate into a win. Hertz car rental customers can easily switch between helping themselves on the Web site and asking for help from a travel agent. Amazon.com customers get the same, superior service whether they buy from Amazon directly or from one of its associates—since they are one and the same.

Focus on Peace of Mind

WHAT'S REALLY AT the core of "owning the customer's total experience" is an appreciation of what makes a customer nervous. You need to deal with the unarticulated gnawing sense of anxiety the customer experiences whenever he doesn't know exactly what's going on. That's why Hertz bus drivers have your name on an electronic clipboard in front of them. If your name's not there, they immediately radio in to alert the operations crew that you're en route. By the time you arrive at your car, it's ready for you, even if there was a change in your flight plans. Amazon's five-step shopping process and the notifications that the company pioneered—every time an order is placed or a book is shipped—go a long way toward reducing customers' unspoken fears.

Give the Customer Control over the Experience

WITH HERTZ, THE customer controls most of his experience through his profile information. Hertz's NeverLost option gives customers all the information they need at their fingertips to find the way to their destination in a timely fashion. With Amazon.com, letting the customer control his 1-Click purchase settings, giving him lots of different shipping options, and letting him tell you when and why he wants you to tap him on the shoulder with an e-mail are all great examples of giving the customer control over his experience of doing business with you.

CSF 3:

Streamline Business Processes That Impact the Customer

I love the convenient service American Express offers its customers over the Web. As a frequent business traveler, I have two fairly common problems. First, I need to submit my expense reports as soon as I return from a trip so that my company can process payment in time for me to pay my AmEx bill. And second, although I always get and keep the receipts from the hotels and restaurants I frequent, when traveling internationally, I never know exactly what exchange rate was used to pay the bill. I could take the time to guesstimate it, based on the interest rate published in the local paper on the day of the transaction, but I usually don't remember to check the paper. So what do I do? I log on to American Express's Web site within a day or two of my return and enter my account number and password. There I can see every charge that's been made to my credit card since the last bill and know the exact amount that was actually charged, in U.S. dollars. This is a great example of streamlining a business process that impacts me, the customer. By giving me the information I need to take care of business, American Express makes it easy for me to pay my bill on time.

How do you go about streamlining all the various business processes that impact your customers? How do you decide what's important and what's not? What are the actual steps you should be taking? I propose that you follow these guidelines:

- Start by identifying the end customer.
- Streamline the process from the end customer's point of view.
- Streamline the process for key stakeholders.
- Continuously improve the process based on customer feedback.
- Give everyone involved a clear view of the process.

Start by Identifying the End Customer

EVEN IF YOU don't deal directly with end customers, you'll want to begin your business process streamlining from their point of view. This will ensure that you get the priorities right. Do you remember how National Semiconductor targeted its end customers, the design engineers? As you'll recall, this led it to streamline all of the processes that impacted the design engineer's ability to get his job done. When the engineer has completed a design, he needs to build small quantities of his end product for market-testing purposes. In the past, the engineer called his purchasing agent and asked him to order small quantities—say, 100 chips—and to get them within a week. Keeping the design engineer's needs for quick turnaround in mind, National Semiconductor worked with its catalog distributors to link them to its Web site. Now when it's time to place a small quantity/fast turnaround order, the engineer or his purchasing agent can place the order from National's Web site and have it fulfilled within two days by one of the company's distributors who specialize in stocking and supplying these small quantities.

Brooklyn Union Gas is a hundred-year-old utility company that provides heating and cooking gas to a large population in metropolitan New York. In the early 1980s, the company's executives realized that it needed to know a lot more about the end customers for its products and services. So led by Tom Morgan, a visionary technologist, the company revamped its customer information system so that end-customers were the focal point. The end customers—the people who actually consumed the heating and appliance services—often lived in apartment buildings that were maintained by management companies. Often the gas bills were paid by a third party and maintenance work was requested through a building supervisor. Brooklyn Union Gas captured all these relationships in its customer database and equipped its field service personnel with handheld terminals that could tap into the company's information systems. Now any question the end customer has from "When will they be back to read the meter?" to "Has my gas bill been paid?" to "What's happening with the heating in this building?" can be answered by any of the company's employees.

So if your goal is to satisfy end customers with the products and services they need, at the time and in the way they need them, you need to begin by identifying those end customers and putting yourself into their shoes.

Streamline the Process from the End Customer's Point of View

ONCE YOU'VE IDENTIFIED the end customer, the next step is to re-think your process from that person's point of view. Virtual Vineyards did just that. It actually had two sets of customers in mind when it streamlined its shipping and delivery process: the customer who purchased wines and the prospective customer, who was often the recipient of the purchased wines. Virtual Vineyards realized that the purchaser needed to know when the person to whom the wine was shipped had actually received it. And sometimes the end customer for whom the wine was intended also needed to know that it had arrived at his office. If you send a case of California wines to a colleague in Japan, you want to know that it has been received. And if you are in Japan waiting for a case of wine to arrive, it's great to get an e-mail telling you that your secretary has just signed for it.

As you read the two case studies that follow, notice that when Babson College's reengineering team set out to make it easier for its end customers, the students, to register for classes, the team designed a scenario—of how the new process would function—from the student's point of view. Then they tested the scenario by having actual students try it.

Streamline the Process for Key Stakeholders

OFTEN IT'S EASIER to streamline business processes for key stakehold-ers—such as agents, dealers, other channel partners, purchasing agents, or comptrollers—than it is to streamline the business process for the end cus-tomer. Sometimes this is the best place to focus your efforts, especially when doing so makes it easier for your channel partners to serve your end customers. Ingram Micro is the world's leading wholesale distributor of computers and peripherals. The company doesn't deal with end customers at all. Yet over the past four years, Ingram Micro has totally transformed the buying and selling of PCs in a way that is directly benefiting end cus-tomers. Ingram Micro has taken the lead in creating XML-based standards for specifying and describing the characteristics of every component a computer user ever uses: type of part, dimensions, properties, price, and so on. All the major computer and peripheral manufacturers and most of In-gram Micro's competitors have agreed to use the same conventions. They like this idea because it makes it easier for them to market, procure, ship, and deliver products cost-effectively. What benefit does the end customer receive? It means that you'll soon be able to search the Web looking for the "least expensive memory chips that are compatible with my Dell Latitude LM laptop that are available within 24 hours." Because the back end of the computer industry has streamlined its business processes, the end customer at the front end of the value chain will find it easier to do business with any supplier.

Sometimes the stakeholders you need to take into account are people who work in the same company as your end customer but whose jobs are in different departments and whose needs are different. In the ensuing case study describing the National Science Foundation's FastLane, you'll see how NSF recruited a cross section of the stakeholders involved in the grant submission, approval, and administration process—both employees within NSF itself and representatives from all the university departments that interacted with NSF on a regular basis. These stakeholders then redesigned their own business processes and prioritized their implementation. The end customers—the researchers themselves—were not actively represented on the design team. Nevertheless, many of the improvements that have been made to the NSF grant process directly impact the researchers' interactions with the funding agency.

Continuously Improve the Process Based on Customer Feedback

OFTEN, FIGURING OUT how to really make things easy from the end customer's point of view is a matter of trial and error. You start out by surveying customers, asking them what they want, and doing your best to accommodate those needs. But then you have to be patient and sit back and watch and listen and see what really happens. And that's exactly what National Semiconductor did to satisfy design engineers. National Semi took its marching orders from the engineers it talked with, designing the Web site to match the customers' wish list. But then they watched what these customers did on the site, noting how many steps it took them to get where they were trying to go, and, using this feedback, eliminated all the unnecessary steps.

All the people responsible for designing, improving, and maintaining their companies' interactive Web sites will tell you the same thing. There is no magic to getting it right. You simply do the best you can to anticipate customers' needs and interests, then monitor the site every minute of every day (actually, you buy software that will do that for you). You analyze this information, and you look for ways to improve the navigation through your site. At the same time, you make it really easy for customers to give you their reactions by providing a feedback form on every single Web page. You pay attention to what they tell you, gather all the results, and then use them to prioritize your Web redesign efforts. There's really no guesswork involved. Customers will tell you exactly what they want and need.

In cyberspace, process improvement can be pretty straightforward. When you're dealing in the real world, on the other hand, continuously improving the process can be somewhat more of an inexact science. A single customer feedback form doesn't really do it. How many of us have seen these in hotel rooms and restaurants and simply ignored them? What you are really after is tracking the customer's experience on an event-by-event basis. Each time your company touches the customer, you want to give him an opportunity to give feedback about that particular encounter.

BC Transit is the municipal organization responsible for the bus and ferry service in Vancouver, British Columbia. Once content to publish paper bus and ferry schedules and to post these on signs around the city, it soon realized the need to provide telephone access to the same information. Seeking to keep costs down, it offers personal assistance during peak hours and Touch-Tone-accessible schedule information twenty-four hours a day. In 1996, BC Transit opened a Web site and began publishing all the bus and ferry schedules and routes on-line. It supplemented this information with a lot more—maps, information on which buses offered handicapped access and which routes had bicycle- and pet-friendly buses, and so on. Customers were glad to have the additional information, but they wanted more. They wanted to know whether *their* bus or ferry was running on time. They wanted real-time schedule information available to them over the Web and via Touch-Tone phone. So BC Transit linked its real-time scheduling systems into its customer information systems. Now you can find out if the bus will arrive at your corner within the next fifteen minutes before you walk out the door.

Give Everyone Involved a Clear View of the Process

YOU'LL NOTICE IN reading the two case studies that follow that, in both instances, all those involved in the business process has access to all the information they need. Each stakeholder, including the end customer, can actually "see into" the process. Nothing just disappears from sight. All the elements of the process are clearly visible to all concerned.

This may seem like a subtle point, but it's an extremely powerful one. Notice that there are entire industries that have been completely transformed by the process transparency resulting from electronic commerce. The freight industry is the most obvious example. It used to be that we were content to ship packages off to their destination and trust that they'd arrive. If the package was really important, we'd insure it or send it certified delivery so we'd know when it arrived. Federal Express changed all of that when it began tracking every air freight shipment and making that information available to its customers—the people who shipped packages. This was such a successful differentiator for FedEx that the company has continued to build on this strength. Federal Express was the first to post its package-tracking information on the Web. Not only did this give customers the ability to see this information for themselves, it also gave them an easy way to design programs that would automatically grab this information off of FedEx's Web site and supply it to their own customers. Then FedEx began to encourage its customers—catalog shippers such as Lands' End—to post the status information for the packages they shipped on their own Web sites. So, if you order a product from Lands' End and specify FedEx delivery, you can go back and check to see if your package has been delivered yet and who signed for it. And, Federal Express now offers an e-mail service that lets a sender notify the recipient that a package is en route.

Although Federal Express pioneered giving shippers and their clients a view into the shipping process, all the other carriers have followed suit. UPS does an equally exquisite job of tracking packages, but on a much larger scale than Federal Express. In 1997, Federal Express was typically tracking 2 million packages per day; UPS was tracking 18 million packages per day. UPS scans each package at least three times during transit. And, like Federal Express, UPS makes this tracking information available from its Web site and through the software that large customers use to interact with UPS. What new capabilities does this transparency in the shipping process enable? For example, a company that is shipping shirts manufactured in Hong Kong to different retail outlets in the United States could change the routing of all or some of the shipment while the boxes are in transit. Or a bride who is getting married on Saturday, upon discovering that her wedding dress was shipped using three-day air service on Wednesday, could intercept the package and ask to have it delivered overnight instead.

In the National Science Foundation case study, you'll see that making the grant submission and proposal approval process transparent to everyone involved has greatly improved the quality of life for both the researchers and all the university departments that depend on the grant monies. Instead of submitting a grant proposal and waiting six months to hear if a grant will be awarded, all the parties involved can see exactly where their application stands in the process.

STREAMLINE BUSINESS PROCESSES
THAT IMPACT THE CUSTOMER:

Babson College
www.babson.edu

Executive Summary

Students liked the business education they received at Babson's undergraduate and graduate schools, but they were critical of its administrative processes. Students and their parents found it time-consuming to do business with the school. Babson spent three years redesigning its customer-facing business processes and implementing a Web-based environment that handles everything from applying for admission to course registration to class discussions. At the core of the new systems is a single customer profile database that students are responsible for keeping up to date.

Critical Success Factors in the Babson Story

✓ Target the right customers	✓ Let customers help themselves
Own the customer's total experience	Help customers do their jobs
★ Streamline business processes that impact the customer	✓ Deliver personalized service
✓ Provide a 360-degree view of the customer relationship	✓ Foster community

★ = Featured in this discussion	✓ = Touched on in this discussion

Babson College: Improving the Quality of Student Services

WILLIAM GLAVIN, BABSON College's president, wanted the school, well known for its leadership in business management education, to practice what it preached. Babson, a private college in Wellesley, Massachusetts, offers both undergraduate and graduate programs. Babson's graduate program had been rated the number one MBA program in entrepreneurship in the country. And U.S. *News and World Report* had named Babson's undergraduate program the best business specialty school for over six years. Yet Glavin wasn't satisfied with these external ratings. He was concerned about how his students—his real customers—rated the college.

In student surveys, the academic program received rave reviews. However, in the early 1990s, these same student surveys pinpointed general dissatisfaction with the administrative support services offered by the college. The school was hard to do business with. In particular, students complained about:

- Admission processing
- Registration
- Financial aid packaging
- Student billing
- Student loan processing
- Lack of communication across administrative departments

So in late 1993, Glavin appointed a task force of senior administrators, faculty, and reengineering experts to examine the potential of reengineering the administrative processes at Babson and to make specific recommendations on how to proceed. As a result of the task force's recommendations, Glavin appointed a Reengineering Design Team, chaired by CIO Richard Kesner. The team was charged with developing a detailed plan for the renewed delivery of student administrative services. This plan was to include scenarios for desired results, a game plan for attaining the results, and computer systems prototypes.

Desired Results: A Sample Scenario from the Student's Perspective

IN FEBRUARY 1994, when the reengineering team began the redesign work, the typical process for registering for classes each semester was baroque. Students had to stand in long registration lines to select the classes they wanted. Then they had to wait around to meet financial aid officers. Then they would find out that the classes they requested were overbooked, so they wound up having to run around to professors' offices to plead for an exception or to sign up for a different class, all the while juggling a set of prerequisites and conflicting requirements. In the same time period, they had to register for housing, negotiate for the room they wanted, and renegotiate if it wasn't available. It was a very stressful process! The new scenario the design team came up with was much simpler, and all of it could be done from the student's computer from home or campus.

This is what the proposed process of registering for classes and housing would look and feel like to the students:

- You can schedule courses—and because the transaction is in real time, you will know immediately what courses are full and what alternatives are available. For assistance, you can access course syllabi, faculty biographies, and student evaluations of faculty. You can also view your records and the academic requirements for your major so that you can choose the courses most appropriate and desirable for you.
- You can pick your residence hall room and dining plan.
- You can figure out what your bill will be and arrange for payment. You can also apply for financial aid and/or bank loans. Work-study jobs are posted so that you can apply for a job electronically.
- This system would include intelligent agents to make sure that all transactions are "legal" and to remind you about submission deadlines.

This scenario certainly seems impressive compared to the time-honored method of running yourself ragged before the semester even begins. And of course, this was just one piece of Babson College's vision of electronically supported student administrative services.

Setting Up the Structure for the Process Redesign Work

How was the reengineering work done? The design team narrowed the focus of the project to five key areas they deemed to be essential to the satisfaction of the college's primary customers and stakeholders—students (the end customers), parents, and employers (both key stakeholders in the process). These areas were:

- Admission
- Academic records and registration
- Advocacy (academic, administrative, and student life advising)
- Student financial services
- Field-based learning and career services (corporate internships and job placement)

Cross-functional teams were formed to redesign the business processes in each area. The teams included students, administrators, and faculty, as well as IT staff.

The teams went to work completing scenarios, designing prototypes, and testing the proposed prototypes and scenarios with target groups of students and administrative staff. As the prototypes and scenarios came together, it became clear that Babson would need to do some major rework on its information technology infrastructure.

The IT team decided to leverage the college's existing robust wide-area network. They would expand Babson's use of Lotus Notes to support the streamlined business processes. They elected to design a single, consolidated student information database. This database would then become the "database of record" for all student-related information. Instead of keeping bits of information about each student in each of the separate systems on campus, student profile informaton would be stored in one place, and each of the other applications would have to come and get the particular information it needed. The IT team chose to contract out the work required to integrate all of the college's existing systems into this new framework.

E v o l v i n g   t h e   T e c h n i c a l   I n f r a s t r u c t u r e

In 1992, Babson had begun an implementation of a new client/server network, which the college called GlobeNet. GlobeNet employs a fiber-optic backbone that connects all buildings on campus and runs Banyan VINES. By 1994, all of the college's desktop PCs had been replaced or upgraded to 486 PCs running Microsoft Windows and Microsoft Office personal productivity applications. Students typically arrived on campus with their own 486 or better machines.

Consolidating Information in a Single Customer Data Warehouse

The information technology team proposed developing a single, integrated information database to capture all relevant customer profile information. They called this the "Person Master" database. The idea was a capture-once, use-in-many-ways design. This customer database was designed using Microsoft SQL Server. The Person Master database would be the source of all the students' profile information (name, address, phone number, ID numbers, and so on) for all existing legacy systems as well as for new client/server applications that were being built or purchased to replace the existing transaction systems.

Adding Workflow and a Groupware Platform

The Babson design team realized, however, that having a common data warehouse and client/server networking capabilities was not enough to ensure that the information would be easily accessed in a usable and seamless way. The college, therefore, decided to investigate workflow solutions to assist users as they go through the administrative processes. Babson selected the ActionWorkflow suite of products from Action Technologies as its workflow platform, with the workflow applications deployed in Lotus Notes. In retrospect, Kesner admits that this was probably a mistake.

Evolving a Universal Front End to Student Administration Services

Kesner did not plan, however, to use Lotus Notes as the front end for the student administrative services. Rather, the IT team at Babson first built a graphical point-and-click, forms-based front end to these services using Visual Basic. Each reengineered system would provide a front end with the same look and feel, making it easy to train users across systems. They called this front end (and the underlying applications) View It & Do It Online, or VIDIO.

By the spring of 1997, it had become clear that using a Visual Basic forms-based front end to Notes-based applications that were talking, in turn, to operational applications was too complex and not universal enough. The unexpected popularity and ubiquity of the World Wide Web intersected Babson's VIDIO project. It was obvious that both the front end and the workflows needed to migrate to the Web. Richard Mickool, who succeeded Kesner as

Babson's CIO and who had worked on the redesign teams, took stock of the situation and decided to focus all development on a single platform: Lotus Domino. This allowed Mickool's development team to capitalize on their knowledge of Notes, yet provide a universal browser-user interface to all VIDIO applications. They were also able to jettison the complex and costly separate workflow development environments they had been trying. As Mickool explained, "We could do everything we needed to do in native Domino." And all the back-end application integration work that Babson had done, as well as the student data warehouse, plugged right into the new Web-based Domino infrastructure. Once the college moved over to the Domino platform, Mickool reported, application development went much faster.

Linking to Operational Data

For the course registration application, Mickool's team decided not to link directly to the college's VAX-based course scheduling system. For one thing, the VAX-based application was being phased out. For another, they didn't want to impact the performance of the production system. Instead, they created a second SQL Server database—this one an operational data store. Each night, they pull an image off the VAX scheduling system. The Web-based registration and course-scheduling application interacts with the operational data store. In late 1997, Babson replaced the VAX application with a new scheduling program that runs on Microsoft SQL Server. Now instead of creating a nightly image of the operational data, they simply create a separate view for use by the Web applications.

Designing and Launching the New Applications

ABOUT NINE MONTHS into the reengineering work, it became evident that someone needed to take full-time responsibility for overseeing and building the technology infrastructure for the redesigned business processes. Rick Mickool, who had been involved with the IT team on the reengineering project from the start, took on the responsibility of overseeing the implementation, giving up his previous job as director of user services. When Kesner left Babson in the spring of 1997, Mickool stepped into the CIO position.

By September 1997, Mickool's team began deploying the applications that had been designed and piloted over the past couple of years. The first applications to be rolled out were designed for students, although faculty members and administrative staff, with the appropriate privileges, could access much of the same information. Applications designed for parents, alumni, and other stakeholder constituencies would come later.

Applying for Admission

For students applying to Babson, the college now offers a variety of Web-based approaches. The student can visit the Babson Web site (www.babson.edu), get information about the college, and fill in his or her application form on-line. The application does not have to be completed in a single sitting. The applicant can return to complete different portions of it. Only when he presses the "submit" button will the application be processed by the college. This on-line application flows directly into Babson's admissions system. Or students may choose instead to fill in a generic Web-based application form—one that is shared among several different business schools, including Stanford University. Again, the student fills his or her application out on the Web and submits it, and it flows directly into Babson's admissions system (and into those of its cooperating competitors). This makes it easier for students to apply to a number of business schools without having to complete multiple applications.

Getting Ready to Attend

Once a student has been accepted by Babson, the college sends out a formal acceptance letter (by regular mail) and includes a log-in ID and password for a special Web site designed for entering students. Part of the reason for this is to ensure that students who haven't yet sent in their tuition deposits don't change their mind about attending the college. This welcome Web site helps cement the accepted student's relationship with the college. This Web site includes all the information a student will need to prepare for arrival on campus: travel to the college, housing, courses, the greater Boston area, and so forth. The new students' Web site also includes answers to frequently asked questions and discussion forums. And students can pose questions and determine whom they'd like to have answer them: a current student, a faculty member, an alumnus, and so on. These e-mails are posted in a database, and volunteers in each category are notified that there is a question in the database waiting to be answered.

They can log on and answer the question, and the new student will receive his answer by e-mail. (The question and answer are also retained in the database so the most useful or frequently asked ones can be posted for others.)

Streamlining the Process of Doing Business with the College

Once they've been admitted to the college and paid their tuition, Babson students gain access to their personal profiles. The information in these profiles drives all the applications that touch the student, from housing to library access to bookstore charges to course scheduling and billing. Each student is also issued a Babson One card, which contains a digitized photo and a magnetic stripe. This card identifies him to all the physical systems (building access, cafeteria meals, bookstore, library, and so on). The card is linked to the student's profile information.

Students maintain their own profile information by logging in via the Web. They can specify several different mailing addresses, phone numbers, and e-mail addresses and indicate which ones they prefer to have used for official communications. Students can also check off what part of their profile may be shown to others. Will they allow their digital photo (the same one that's on their student ID card) to be published? Will they permit their parents to see their grades? Will they let their parents see their phone bills or only their tuition bills? Which address information do they want published in the campus directory? And so on.

From the same Web-based environment, students can also view their grades, register for courses, see their class schedules, review their bills, request transcripts, and petition for graduation (fill in a form specifying how they want their diploma to read, how their name should be pronounced, and so on). In short, most of the administrivia that clutters up a student's life has been streamlined.

The most complex application is the course registration application. In the fall of 1997, Mickool's team rolled out the first version of that application. It lets students get information about course requirements and register for their first and second choices. However, this initial version was not a real-time application. Instead, the electronic forms were submitted to the registration application, and as soon as the application had generated the results, the students were notified by e-mail. Or they could log on, look up their schedules, and see what courses they'd been assigned.

Mickool reported that the students really liked this application. One

Venezuelan student told him how happy he had been to be able to sign up for his next semester's courses from an Internet café in Caracas. Babson staggers course registration, giving preference to certain groups of students, such as graduating seniors or those who didn't receive their first choices the previous semester. Each time a new group is ready for scheduling, an e-mail is sent out to each student with a link to the course registration Web page, telling them that they are now entitled to register and that registration will close in two weeks.

The next version of the application, rolled out in the fall of 1998, enables students to register in real time. So they can make new choices quickly based on the availability of the courses remaining.

Entering the Electronic Classroom

As soon as a student is registered for a course, a set of automated processes spring into action, registering her on Babson's electronic campus and in the appropriate electronic classrooms. (Each class has an electronic classroom.) The student's profile, or that portion of her profile she chooses to make available, is automatically posted. The professor's syllabus, reading list, and course schedule are all posted, along with homework assignments. Each electronic classroom includes discussion forums where students can continue discussions with one another and with their professor.

Hurdles in Implementing the New Business Processes

THE COMBINED REENGINEERING and information technology efforts have taken about three years to bear fruit. A number of iterations of technology platforms were tried and discarded (see above). And there were a number of thorny organizational issues that have continued to plague the groups.

Letting Customers Maintain Their Profiles

The biggest organizational obstacle Mickool has encountered has to do with giving ownership and maintenance of students' profile information to the students themselves. From the outset, the reengineering team realized that the obvious people to maintain the name, address, and other profile information in the Person Master database that sits at the core of the new applications were the students themselves. They also recognized that some percentage of the students wouldn't bother to keep their records up to date. And they agreed that that would be okay. If students didn't receive their grades or their bills in the mail, they would eventually notice and would take the necessary steps to correct the address that Babson was using to contact them. This issue keeps coming up in department meetings. "We don't have clean data, because the students aren't maintaining their profiles" is a recurring refrain. Yet when Mickool points out that this is the choice that the college has made and that it is much more cost-effective to have a single source for customer information that is maintained by the customer him- or herself, everyone agrees in principle. What they don't like is the reality of the situation. Before, each department maintained its own duplicate student information, but each department was more comfortable about the integrity of the data it maintained.

As Mickool points out, "It's one thing for people to be involved in visioning and brainstorming new business processes; it's another thing entirely when they see the new applications and they don't look or act the way they're used to."

Results

AFTER THREE YEARS of continuous design and improvement, Babson has made major strides in the redesign of most of its business processes from the students' point of view. From the time a prospect applies for admission to the time she graduates from Babson, she is part of a well-oiled but highly personalized electronic support environment. This streamlined electronic environment is particularly attractive to Babson's many international students and their parents. For many years, Babson has been a magnet for Latin American students seeking an American business education. Now these students and alumni can interact much more easily with the school, since all the administrative and financial functions, as well as much of the background required for their academic work, are available to them on-line.

Now that the infrastructure is in place and many of the cultural changes are under way, Babson is well ahead of many competitive institutions. The student profile, the first set of streamlined business processes, and the electronic campus environment are only the start of an impressive set of offerings Babson will be able to create quickly and easily for all of its stakeholders at little additional cost. In fact, by having a customer database at the core of all of its administrative and academic systems, Babson has been able to eliminate redundancies and errors across all of its systems.

And by letting students maintain their own profile information, Babson can keep its administrative costs down, while gradually improving the quality of that information over time as students begin to realize that they really have control.

Patty's Rx for Babson College

The next step for Babson is to continue streamlining and enhancing all of the academic and administrative processes that impact its students. Second, the college should come up with a "belt-and-suspender" approach to maintaining its student profile information. Although, ideally each student (or alumnus or faculty member) should maintain his or her own profile, it sounds as if there should be a backup data integrity guarantee. Each record in the Person Master database should probably have two owners: the person him- or herself and someone whose job it is to ensure that this particular constituent's data is accurate. The second person or department could be considered the "shadow owner." Any updates on the part of the real owner would take precedence. But the shadow owner would be empowered to make informed updates in the absence of the actual owner's doing it for him- or herself. This seems to me to be a more realistic solution to the data ownership problem that Babson is facing. Note that I am not suggesting that *several* different departments become "shadow owners" of the same information. That would take Babson back to where it was before, with different departments maintaining sometimes conflicting profile information. Alumni affairs could "shadow own" the alumni records, the admissions department could "shadow own" the profiles of students applying for admission, and so on. Once a student is admitted, ownership would be turned over to the administrative department responsible for each entering class, for example.

Next, Babson needs to continue its plan to design context-dependent business processes for each of its other core constituencies: parents, alumni, faculty, administrative staff. Today, the faculty and staff can gain access to student information and status information by logging on as aliases (assuming they have the authority to do so). So they can get a complete picture of a given student's profile. Yet much of the detail information is still contained within the functional "stovepipe" systems used by each department. Ideally, this detail information should be accessible to other authorized administrative or academic pesonnel, using the same Web-based point-and-click interface that the students can now use.

In 1998, Babson's alumni affairs group is focusing on the design of applications specifically for its alumni. These will include the ability for alumni to maintain their own profiles, to join affinity groups—for example, Arthur Andersen employees, investment bankers, Latin American entrepreneurs—to enter into discussion forums, and to get information about college events.

I think parents will turn out to be an equally vital stakeholder community for Babson. And I encourage the college to accelerate its streamlining of business processes and provision of contextual information and relevant discussion groups for parents. One of the things that is slowing down the implementation of a set of applications targeted for parents is the privacy issue involved. Students are very particular about what they want their parents to know. For example, in the original scenario design, the plan was to provide students and parents with a single billing application that would consolidate all the students' bills into one place: tuition, housing, library, bookstore, telephone, and so on. However, students reviewing the prototype complained that they didn't want their parents seeing the details of their telephone bills. So that application was never developed. Yet in the student's profile, he or she can check off exactly what information he wants his parents to be able to access: grades, tuition bills, library fines, telephone bills, course schedules, and so forth. I would encourage Babson to complete the development of the applications that would give parents access to information and the ability to perform transactions, based on the permissions established for them in their student's profile.

"Take-Aways" from the Babson College Story

1. Focus first on the end customers for your product. Babson focused on the students who consume the education it provides.
2. Note that a good product isn't sufficient to keep customers happy and generating referrals. If your organization isn't easy to do business with, no matter how good its products and services are, you're going to lose business. Babson's president averted this trend before it happened by noticing customers' dissatisfaction and dealing with it head-on.
3. Use a cross-functional team approach for identifying and streamlining core business processes. Include end customers, stakeholders, and IT staff. In Babson's case, students participated actively on the design teams together with stakeholders from the relevant administrative departments and the faculty, along with IT professionals who could take the requirements and turn them into a technology architecture.

4. Create a single, central customer information database to act as the hub for all of the systems and processes that impact customers.

5. Avoid using too many layers of technology. Babson's original idea of using "intelligent agents" and workflow was appealing. But the idea broke down when they tried to build it using add-on tools. By focusing on a single development platform—Lotus Domino—for Web design and workflow, the team was able to break the logjam and move forward.

6. Use the Web as your infrastructure for giving customers and stakeholders access to their profiles and to all the applications and information with which they need to interact.

7. Once you've optimized the business processes for your end customers and are continuously improving them, focus next on improving processes for key stakeholder groups. Babson focused next on employees (administrative and faculty) and alumni. Now they need to target parents.

8. Although it's a great idea for the end customers to maintain their own profiles, there also needs to be an internal "owner" for each customer's profile information to ensure that it is accurate and up to date.

STREAMLINE BUSINESS PROCESSES
THAT IMPACT THE CUSTOMER:

National Science Foundation
www.nsf.gov

Executive Summary

Intent on reducing the amount of red tape involved in procuring and administering grants, the National Science Foundation created FastLane. FastLane is a Web-based environment that was designed in collaboration with NSF's key stakeholders—the different departments at the universities and research institutions that apply for grants. It has turned out to be easier to streamline the administrative and financial processes than it has been to streamline the grant creation and submission process. More than $2 billion per year in grant monies is disbursed automatically via

FastLane. The biggest benefit to researchers to date is that Fast-Lane has created a much more transparent grant proposal process. Grant applicants can always see exactly where their proposals stand.

Critical Success Factors in the National Science Foundation Story

Target the right customers	✓ Let customers help themselves
✓ Own the customer's total experience	✓ Help customers do their jobs
☆ Streamline business processes that impact the customer	☆ Deliver personalized service
✓ Provide a 360-degree view of the customer relationship	✓ Foster community
☆ = Featured in this discussion	★ = Touched on in this discussion

The National Science Foundation's FastLane: Cutting Through Layers of Bureaucracy

The National Science Foundation (NSF) is an independent U.S. government agency with a budget of more than $3 billion used to fund 20,000 research and educational projects initiated and performed by U.S. educational and research institutions. Among the best-known breakthroughs that can be attributed to NSF support are the Internet, the Mosaic browser (which launched the World Wide Web), and the gene-splicing start-up Genentech.

One of the key concerns of the NSF and its customers is that the process of deciding who gets these grants each year needs to be absolutely fair, impartial, objective, and very visible to anyone who cares to scrutinize the decisions.

Who Are the Customers and Stakeholders?

THE NSF's CUSTOMERS are the thousands of scientists and researchers in the United States who are looking for funding to support their research. Approximately 40,000 of them apply for grants each year. The majority of these scientists work for colleges, universities, and other institutions that depend in large part on these grants to help defray the costs of supporting their scientific research. So the deans, professors, department heads, development officers, university presidents, finance officers, and human resources professionals at these institutions are also key stakeholders in the grant procurement process.

Because there's so much at stake for most of the institutions that apply for grants, quite a few review cycles are typically put into place before a grant proposal is even submitted to the NSF. A researcher puts together the original grant proposal (which is an elaborate document including technical documentation, budgets, résumés, and so on) and sends it to his department head, who in turn makes suggestions. The modified proposal may then be resubmitted to the chair of the department, who will also have modifications and suggestions, and so on. Eventually, the proposal wends its way to the administrative side of the institution, where the grants office, the finance department, and the administrative overseers of the institution will each add their two cents' worth. There is, in fact, no typical pattern in which these activities take place. The business process varies significantly from institution to institution.

While the complexity on the customer side of the equation seems bad enough, it's compounded by the fact that each of these players typically uses a different type of computer, running a different operating system and using different technical applications, word processing, and spreadsheet programs. So the simple handoff of files from one person to another within the same institution becomes a time-consuming task involving file conversion and reformatting.

The biggest obstacles to streamlining this process, however, are the patterns and departmental politics ingrained in the universities and research institutions themselves. Resistance to change is deeply rooted in academia; technology-led initiatives take a long time to come to fruition. Business process redesign is an uphill battle that tends to need high-level support and major, long-term financial commitment in order to take effect in many university settings.

The Genesis of the FastLane Program

THE IDEA OF designing applications on the Web to support the entire grant submission, review, and fulfillment process was the result of the gradual evolution of a series of projects and attempts to streamline different aspects of the NSF's work. It all started in 1990, when NSF launched a project to help researchers and investigators. It wanted to reduce the amount of time and effort it took the customers—researchers—to submit proposals. NSF program directors felt that by helping researchers surmount the interoperability problems among all the different computer systems that were used to review and modify their original proposal submissions within their own institutions, they could shave months off the submission process. This was a brilliant idea: make it easy for the end customer—the researchers—to slash through some of the arbitrary obstacles at their end of the process. Unfortunately, this first attempt was unsuccessful. It just added another layer of complexity to the proposal submission process. So the project was scrapped.

In 1993, the NSF formed a new cross-functional team to revisit the idea of streamlining the grant proposal submission process. This group recommended that the NSF look not only at the proposal process but at all the different ways in which both its customers—university researchers—and all the other key stakeholders—department heads, grant officers, administrative staff, financial officers—interacted with the agency.

Fred Wendling, the NSF's director of information systems, took this expanded charter seriously. Wendling requested and received a budget of $800,000 to design and implement a series of streamlined business processes. Just as he was gearing up to begin work on the project in the fall of 1993, Wendling became aware of the first Web browser. One of the NSF's funded agencies, the National Center for Supercomputing Applications (NCSA) at the University of Illinois, had rolled out the first version of its Mosaic browser. Of course Wendling already knew about the Internet. The NSF had already been using the Internet to disseminate information to the scientific and technical communities it served. But the advent of the Mosaic browser, with its easy-to-use graphical user interface and its cross-platform support, looked as if it might make the Internet in general, and the World Wide Web in particular, much more accessible to people who were not computer scientists. Wendling realized that it might be possible to develop his suite of applications using a single computing environment: the World Wide Web and the Mosaic browser.

A Calculated Risk That Paid Off

This was a very risky strategy at the time. First, in the fall of 1993, the version of Mosaic that was available was not even a fully released software program. Second, the Web was not in widespread use at the time. Many of the people who worked in universities, particularly on the administrative side, didn't have direct Internet access. So only about 50 percent of the NSF's customer base would have access to the Internet and the NSF applications. Nevertheless, the NSF was used to placing bets on technology. NSF director Neal Lane made the final judgment call. He felt that it was indeed a risky proposition to count on Mosaic and the Web becoming ubiquitous, but it was a risk he felt the agency should take. Obviously, Lane's bet paid off when Marc Andreesen left the University of Illinois, founded Netscape, and spawned the Web industry.

Getting Internal Stakeholders Involved in the Design Process

THE FIRST THING Wendling's FastLane project team did in late 1993 was to form a FastLane internal review committee. This was made up of senior representatives from different departments within the agency. The head of the finance division, the head of the grants and agreements division, the deputy assistant director of the NSF, and three program managers (the people who actually process the proposals) all participated actively on this committee.

"Review" may be somewhat of a misnomer. For this committee was actually very proactive in the design and development of FastLane. They identified each of the projects that should be addressed. In fact, they targeted twenty-eight different areas that needed to be streamlined, and they prioritized these.

This oversight committee met every other week. However, in between meetings, they were usually involved in detailed design work. Each prioritized initiative was assigned to a member of the committee. That person (and the people he or she would recruit from his or her own organization) then became the lead designers from the NSF side of the house. They worked with the programmers on the prototyping and design of the actual applications.

Getting Customers Involved

By EARLY 1994, the FastLane team began soliciting customer input. They recruited key players from sixteen universities to form a customer advisory group. They made sure that the group included a good cross section of representatives from both large and small educational institutions. This group has convened on a regular basis since early 1994. The FastLane advisory group quickly became a prestigious and influential group. The current FastLane project director, Carolyn Miller, reports that every time she went to an academic conference, people would approach her and beg to join the FastLane advisory group. She quickly realized that Fast-Lane was considered a hot and eagerly awaited project within academic circles.

Key Stakeholders Prioritized the Projects and Reviewed Work in Progress

The members of the university advisory group took the list of initiatives that the NSF review committee had created, added a few of their own, reprioritized them, and shifted the scope of many of the items on the list. Here's one example: the NSF had planned a module targeted for the research administration offices at the universities. The research administrator would be able to view the status of each proposal his or her institution had submitted. The advisory group's feedback was "We want to see the status of *all* the proposals we have in to you, not view them one at a time. In fact, we'd like to look at the entire portfolio of grants in one sitting— grants we've been awarded, as well as those still being considered. And there are many other people in our organizations who will also need and want to see that information, such as the researchers themselves."

One of the biggest stumbling blocks in the design and development of any application is getting end customers to see and appreciate the benefits the new way of doing things will have for them. As the FastLane modules were being developed, Miller's team would put them up on the NSF's development server and invite the advisory group members to log on, try them out, and give feedback. Miller was very proactive in calling and soliciting feedback from each of the advisory group members. Miller described the gradual conversion process that she saw taking place among the advisory board members: as members logged in to look at the prototypes of the applications under development, "they realized that the information we're able to provide them will be a big benefit to them. They'll have much more control over the entire process and access to a lot of data they didn't previously have. . . . They began to take real pride of ownership in the system."

The one real difficulty the NSF had at the outset was getting input from the *real* end customers: researchers themselves. These people are very busy. In general, they aren't interested in investing time to improve their institutions' overall business processes; they are focused on doing the research they are passionate about doing. The only real feedback the NSF has been able to garner from actual researchers has been from those few who have actually submitted their own complete electronic proposals. And, of course, the researchers who have been willing to prepare their own submissions electronically are the "early adopters" of technology. They aren't representative of the entire customer base. Getting these end customers on board and gaining their participation in the redesign of the FastLane modules is a high priority for the NSF and its institutional stakeholders.

Evolving the Technical Infrastructure

FastLane runs on a Sun Solaris server with a Sybase SQL Server relational database. The Sybase database is, in turn, interfaced to NSF's mainframe computers through a gateway that sends requests to the mainframe and receives back authorizations and information. The Sybase database holds all the customer information that is used in populating the NSF's "smart forms." It also holds tables of information with valid university codes and program identification numbers. Any time a user is asked to supply information, he or she is presented with a list of valid choices. This greatly reduces the amount of error checking that the NSF employees have to do.

The NSF is constrained in terms of the browsers and the programming technology it can use. It is vital to the success of the program that everyone, not just those researchers with the latest and greatest software, be able to access the applications. The NSF awards grants not only to large, well-funded institutions, like MIT, but also to smaller, lesser-endowed colleges like Santa Rosa Community College. Therefore, the NSF sticks to the lowest common denominator in terms of the browsers it supports. FastLane applications are equally accessible from Mosaic, Netscape, and Microsoft browsers.

The FastLane development team has consisted of six programmers over the course of three years. The programming has been done in C and in Perl. Interfaces have been built to all of the NSF's pre-existing systems: financial, accounting, program management, and so on. All of the Web application modules are forms-driven. They use "smart forms": as soon as the form "knows" who is filling it in, it will access the database and pre-populate any information that has been previously supplied: name, address, title, university codes, and so on.

Ensuring Security

The FastLane project team knew that it needed to ensure secure access and privacy, both for the proposals that were being submitted and were in the review process, and for all the financial transactions. It was vitally important to the success of FastLane that no one be able to impersonate a researcher or a university official.

At the time the NSF was being implemented, digital certificate technology was not available. The NSF opted for a system of encrypted personal identification numbers (PINs). They chose BSafe as the encryption system for the PINs. Each university issues its own PINs to those people whom it wants to have access to the NSF FastLane applications. If a small institution hasn't done business with the NSF in the past and doesn't have a mechanism for issuing and maintaining the PINs, they are issued by the NSF directly.

The financial transactions that take place are protected in two ways. First, only the authorized users are able to request funds or view the financial reports. Second, all of the payments are made directly into the universities' preapproved bank accounts. So even if an unauthorized person were able to request funds, the funds would wind up in the university's bank account earmarked as NSF disbursements and would show up on that university's cash request history report.

Streamlining Business Processes with FastLane

When it went live in 1995, FastLane had six different applications, each one corresponding to a different business process. The most successful and popular FastLane applications were the ones that made it easier for the research institutions' different stakeholders to gain visibility into the grant awards process (giving them peace of mind) and the ones that made it easier for administrators to interact with the NSF (making it easy for them to do business). The application that has been the most difficult to get right (in order to meet all the needs of all the stakeholders) has been the actual proposal submission application.

Of course, FastLane has both secure and open areas. All of the research institutions' dealings with the NSF are secure. Other areas—such as what grants have been awarded and the summary reports—are open to the public. Here are some of the highlights.

Making Life Easier for Researchers and Reviewers

The scientists and researchers who are the end customers for FastLane appreciate the fact that all the aspects of the proposal submission and review process have been implemented on the Web. They now have an easy-to-access, end-to-end view of the entire grant process.

1. **Checking grant proposal status.** Principal investigators—the NSF's real ends customers—love the ability to see the status of their proposals. In the past, once they submitted a proposal, they had to wait up to six months to find out whether or not they were going to get an award. Their proposal went into a "black box" and came out again, accepted or denied. Now, the proposal status module immediately lets them see exactly where in the review process their proposal stands. They can see that the proposal was received and logged, when it was assigned to a particular program manager (and that person's e-mail address), when it goes out for review, whether or not it's been scheduled to go before a review panel, and, if so, when that panel will meet. Although it may still take six months for a grant to be awarded, the researcher knows exactly where her proposal is in the process.

2. **Filing research status reports.** The principal investigator has to file annual reports and a final report within ninety days after a project is completed. FastLane makes this process much easier by giving the

principal investigator a series of forms that are already filled in with the pertinent information from the original grant proposal. So the researcher simply fills in new information and answers the questions in the on-line questionnaire to comply with this requirement.

3. **REVIEWING GRANT PROPOSALS.** Peer reviewers love FastLane as well. The scientists and engineers who are asked to review NSF proposals can now do this on-line, and many prefer to do so, since it saves them time. Reviewers can print out copies of the submissions, review them in hard-copy form, annotate them, and then submit their reviews by filling in an electronic form and pasting in their own comments. This has been a popular application with the reviewers. In 1997, more than 13,000 reviews were submitted through FastLane.

Streamlining Administrative and Financial Processes

What about the rest of the stakeholders who deal with the NSF on a regular basis? What has FastLane done for them? A lot. In fact, FastLane's biggest successes have been in streamlining the administrative burden for universities of doing business with the government.

1. **ELECTRONIC CASH REQUESTS.** Now, instead of sending paper statements in to the NSF on a biweekly basis, universities that have received grants can issue their cash requests on-line. This is a straightforward procedure that vastly reduces the paperwork, gives both sides much more accurate reporting on a project-by-project basis, and results in much faster disbursal of funds. The cash requests flow automatically into the NSF's accounting system, where the budgeted funds are approved. The next day, the funds are released from the U.S. Treasury directly into the research institution's bank account. In 1997, 80 percent of all cash requests were filled electronically.

2. **FEDERAL CASH REPORTING.** Any organization that receives federal funds has to file quarterly reports with the government. FastLane provides a simple form that financial officers can use to submit this report. FastLane provides a list of all awards for the organization, and the business officer simply enters the amount spent on each award.

3. **ADMINISTRATIVE REPORTS.** Virtually all of the requests and notifications that the principal investigator or the administrative office has had to do in the past by making phone calls and filling in paper forms can now be done with a simple point and click. FastLane has on-line forms that correspond to virtually all of the issues that arise during the

course of a project: leaves of absence, vacations, changes in project methodology, and so on. It is now fast and easy to go on-line, open up the form, fill in the request, send it off, and get an on-line approval back again in a matter of hours or, at the most, days. These everyday administrative details are handled quickly and easily on both sides.

Making Information Available to the Public

1. **REVIEWING THE AWARDS.** The most popular publicly accessible Fast-Lane application is the NSF awards module. Anyone, anywhere in the world, can see all the NSF awards that have been made. These can be searched in a variety of ways: most recently, by NSF program, by institution, or by state, or using a full text search.
2. **PROPOSAL SUBMISSION INFORMATION.** Second in popularity are the lists of all the funding categories and programs as well as the deadlines for submission of grant proposals.
3. **NOMINATING SCIENTISTS.** There is also a FastLane module that anyone can use to submit a nomination for National Medal of Science awards. These prestigious awards are given out each year to people who have made significant scientific contributions.

Streamlining the Proposal Submission Process

FastLane makes the proposal submission process reasonably painless. Each person involved has a password that gives him or her permission to enter information, change it, and/or submit it. (Only the institution's sponsored research office may submit the final proposal, for example.) But grant proposals are still very complex documents requiring input from a variety of stakeholders in a variety of forms. For example, the principal investigator's technical submission has to be submitted as a PDF (portable data format) file. This is done to ensure that the scientific part of the proposal looks exactly, word for word and line for line, the way it did when the researcher signed off on it. So all of the preparation and review of the scientific portion of the proposal takes place off-line. Only when the submission is letter-perfect is it loaded into FastLane (often by an administrative assistant, rather than by the researcher him- or herself). The budget portion of the proposal, on the other hand, is in the form of an Excel spreadsheet, which the researcher, the department head, and the finance office can pass back and forth, iterating as necessary until they reach a consensus. Other aspects of the proposal are simply filled in using FastLane's on-line forms.

Once information has been entered once—the research team's names and contact information, for example—that same information will reappear in the appropriate places in all subsequent forms.

Results

IN EARLY 1995, FastLane was used primarily by the sixteen advisory institutions that were asked to test and evaluate the initial FastLane functions. By fall 1995, FastLane was up and running for production use both by the sixteen institutions and by reviewers (who could access proposals and submit their reviews electronically). By the end of 1995, just over 100 universities and research institutions were using FastLane and only two proposals had been submitted electronically. By the end of fiscal year 1997, there were 52,000 users at 580 institutions; 3,000 proposals had been submitted electronically (out of a total of 35,000); and 13,000 proposal reviews had been submitted electronically (out of a total of 100,000). Also in fiscal year 1997, 80 percent of the NSF's $3 billion–plus grant monies was being distributed electronically.

By all measures, FastLane has made life much easier for the NSF's customers and stakeholders. The grant proposal and submission process has gone from being a "black box" to being a completely transparent process. All those who have a legitimate need to know where they stand can get immediate access to that information. Administrative and financial processes that had been mired in paperwork and delays are now quick and painless. And as more and more proposals are submitted and reviewed electronically, the researchers and the reviewers involved will be saving even more time and effort.

Patty's Rx for the National Science Foundation

Any set of applications that changes the way people work as dramatically as FastLane does for university departments requires a lot of proselytizing and training. Carolyn Miller and her small staff have been very proactive in reaching out and educating their constituents. But Miller is very conscious of the fact that her staff will never be able to train and support all of the people who use FastLane. She is therefore really excited about the various grassroots support initiatives that have emerged. For example, "Fast-West" is a FastLane users' group that has sprung up on the West Coast. Members get together periodically to compare notes, and they correspond with the rest of the group via e-mail whenever they have a question or a problem. The obvious next step would be for the NSF to support these user groups right on the FastLane Web site, giving them a place to post their questions and answers where others could benefit from them. The NSF can go even further than it has in building community to support its customers.

Of course, the NSF is only one of many sources of funding for educational institutions. It has been very active in working together with other government agencies to ensure that they are all working in concert to make life easier for the customers they have in common. They evolve standards together. And they share information with one another so that two agencies aren't working on the same application.

A logical next step would be for these agencies to join together (along with a customer-stakeholder advisory group) to prototype a consolidated grant proposal, submission, and tracking framework. This wouldn't be a single consolidated application, because, as we've seen, each institution's workflows are different. But it could definitely be more than just a set of common interfaces. It could consist of a set of customizable business objects and business rules that could be deployed on each college's internal computer network. Then each institution could customize the behavior of these objects and specify the workflow rules it wanted to use for different processes or for different granting agencies. This grant process framework could be continuously refined and improved by all the different players involved.

"Take-Aways" from the National Science Foundation Story

1. When you're streamlining business processes in a business-to-business environment, you may discover, as the NSF did, that the front end of the process—the part end customers and their stakeholders engage in—needs streamlining as well.

2. By involving a cross section of stakeholders from many different kinds of institutions in the actual process redesign, the NSF was able to streamline many of the institutions' cross-departmental processes by making it much easier for people within different departments to share information and to gain access to the whole picture of the work in progress.

3. By not involving the actual end customers—the research scientists—in the process redesign, the NSF still has the furthest to go in redesigning the actual proposal creation and submission process so that it is

really easy for scientists to create, edit, and submit their grant proposals with complete confidence.

4. By involving a cross section of internal stakeholders in the process re-design from the start, the NSF was able to make substantial changes in how it operates, eliminating many steps. For example, financial trans-actions that used to flow through several departments and computer systems every two weeks before payments could be issued are now sub-mitted electronically and checked electronically against the institu-tion's grant award, and the payments are then issued electronically.

5. One of the NSF's most impressive accomplishments has been its ability to create a vibrant sense of community around the FastLane applica-tion. People who interact with FastLane in institutions across the country get together in face-to-face meetings and on-line forums to share tips and give advice to one another about how best to use the ap-plication and how to overcome internal organizational barriers to suc-cess.

6. The NSF's FastLane took a series of business processes that had been secretive and difficult and transformed them into a set of streamlined electronic forms and business events that are visible to all of the legiti-mate parties involved, across organizational and departmental bound-aries.

7. The NSF's decision to use the Internet and the Web as its develop-ment platform seems an obvious one in retrospect, but at the time the decision was made, in 1993, it was a bold move that paid off hand-somely. The moral of the story: If you're in a position to know what the default technical standards are most likely to become, you can place that sort of bet.

Streamline Business Processes That Impact the Customer: Lessons Learned

One of the most interesting things about both of these stories is the num-ber of stakeholders who are involved in the business processes. At Babson College, although students were the primary target audience, the affected stakeholders included virtually every administrative department, the fac-ulty, alumni, and parents. At the National Science Foundation, although researchers were the primary target audience, the affected stakeholders in-cluded not only every department within the NSF—on both the program management and the administrative sides of the house—but also a large number of departments within each of the researchers' sponsoring institutions. The moral of this story is that to do business process design right, you need to involve all these stakeholders in the design effort from the very beginning.

Use Cross-Functional Design Teams

BOTH BABSON AND the NSF excelled in involving all the different stakeholders at every step in their design processes. Notice that these were not "quick fixes," either. These design projects took almost two years to really bear fruit. The teams included a cross section of people from the different departments whose procedures would be affected. In both cases, the "doers" as well as the policy makers were involved on the teams. In both cases, too, the information technology group was well represented. By being involved at the outset of the business process design work and being integral parts of the design teams, IT staff were able to translate the evolving requirements into system requirements and architectural choices.

Prototype As You Go

BOTH GROUPS DEVELOPED business process scenarios and then prototyped them so that team members could see, touch, and interact with the proposed applications. Having the IT members on staff made this much easier. Instead of throwing a specification "over the wall" to the developers, team members were able to take what they'd heard, in context, and translate it into screens and process flows. In both cases, the members of the target audience—the real end customers and stakeholders—were repeatedly invited to try out the prototypes and react to them. It's often easiest for end customers to visualize how a new, streamlined process will impact their way of doing business when they can touch it, feel it, and begin to interact with it.

Use the Web as Your Development Platform

THE NATIONAL SCIENCE Foundation figured out right away that the Web was the right platform to use for an application that needed to reach across hundreds of organizational boundaries. It took the Babson group longer to come to that realization, in part because they were already making widespread use of Lotus Notes. Babson was lucky that IBM/Lotus's migration plan from Notes to its Web-native counterpart, Domino, was an easy migration. The advantage of using the Web for business process design is that you can design quickly, get prototypes up quickly, and gauge reactions quickly. Working in "Web time" is ideal for the iterative nature of business process redesign. The other benefit the Web brings to the party is the fact that it is rapidly becoming a ubiquitous platform. Therefore you can include all the different groups of stakeholders you'll need to interact with, without requiring any of them to change their existing computing infrastructure.

Getting End Customers to Play an Active Role

BOTH ORGANIZATIONS HAVE had difficulty getting the end customer to play as active a role as they'd like. In Babson's case, although students were actively involved in the design work, it has been hard to get the entire student body to take responsibility for keeping their profiles up to date and accurate. In the NSF's case, no actual grant-submitting researchers participated on the original design team, and getting feedback from them has been problematic. The NSF is now taking the carrot-and-stick approach: several categories of grants can be applied for only by using FastLane's electronic grant submission module. Over time, the percentage will increase. Soon, if you want to receive a grant, you're going to have to make your submission electronically.

So, although the goal is to start from the end customer and work back through the process, the reality is that sometimes the end customer is a reluctant participant. Time, patience, and incentives will be required to lure your end customers on-line. Obviously, there has to be enough in it for them to make it worthwhile for them to change their behavior. In National Semiconductor's case, giving design engineers instant access to the information they needed to do their jobs seems to have provided the necessary incentive. Babson and NSF still have work to do to seduce their end customers into changing some of their behaviors. In Babson's case, I suspect that real-time course registration will help tip the balance. If you can't register for courses without updating your profile, those profiles will get updated at least once a semester, because students are motivated to register for the courses they want. In NSF's case, making electronic grant submission and review a requirement for awarding the grants will go a long way toward luring end customers on-line.

Provide a 360-Degree View of the Customer Relationship

In order to be successful in electronic commerce, everyone who touches the customer needs to be able to see the total picture—a 360-degree view—of that customer's relationship with your firm. Many organizations are currently embarked on relationship management initiatives. Yet when you examine these efforts closely, you usually find that they are addressing only one or two aspects of the customer's relationship with the organization. For example, companies typically streamline and automate the sales process. Or they focus on help desk processes. Occasionally, an insightful organization might combine the two processes and their underlying systems and data. In that case, a salesperson can be made aware of an outstanding service issue with the customer he's wooing, or a service rep would know just how valuable this particular customer is to the firm.

But even this doesn't go far enough. There are still any number of customer interactions not addressed by salespeople or help desks. For example, exactly who does a customer call with questions about a bill, when a delivery hasn't taken place, or when he has an idea for a new product or feature he could use?

Here's an example: I mentioned the evolution of Microsoft's customer database strategy earlier. Now let's look at how Microsoft is instilling this 360-degree approach for everyone who works with its enterprise accounts. Today, Microsoft provides each of its very large "enterprise" customers with its own set of Web pages. This is where Microsoft consolidates everything it knows about the account, not only in terms of software and systems installed and on order, but also regarding competitive situations (where the customer might be considering solutions from another vendor), possible strategic or tactical initiatives that the customer is considering implementing, and the customer's up-to-the-minute service records.

While the customer's account manager "owns" this customer Web site, key executives, such as Bill Gates and Steve Ballmer, will consult this database before they interact with any accounts. Key consulting partners may be offered access to this information in exchange for entering their client engagement notes on the site (providing rewards on both sides for sharing the information). The benefit to customers is that they feel they are being served by "one Microsoft," even though there may be hundreds of different interactions with the company each month.

The enterprise customer and her team of professionals also have access to their own view of this customized Web site. They can view and modify their own contact profiles as well as update the records on their information systems infrastructure, and they can ask for assistance. This account-centric Web site is where key members of the customer's team can go to check on the delivery status of products ordered, request technical support, check on the status of a service call, or ask for background information on new products. It's the customers' window into their relationship with Microsoft.

What should you be thinking about in planning your own "customer-surround" strategy? To truly provide a complete 360-degree view of your relationship with your customers, you'll want to:

- Provide one-stop shopping for the customer.
- "Remember" everything your company knows about the customer.
- Ensure that everyone in the company has access to the complete customer picture.
- Put an underlying technical infrastructure into place to provide a 360-degree view.

Provide One-Stop Shopping for the Customer

WE'RE ALL TOO busy as consumers and as businesspeople to learn our way around your company's departments, divisions, and switchboard extensions. As customers, we're going to gravitate to the organizations that offer us one-stop shopping. In the past, most companies have handled this by having account managers who can take care of all the customer's needs. In electronic commerce terms, one-stop shopping means that the customer should be able to access information, perform transactions, and request services across all the product lines from your organization, with or without the help of a person.

One-stop shopping doesn't obviate the need for personal relationships with our favorite salespeople, account managers, or service technicians.

But it reduces the friction that we find as customers when we just want to take care of business quickly and efficiently.

As you'll see from the Wells Fargo case study that follows, Wells Fargo has redesigned its information systems to give the customer one-stop shopping across its consumer product lines. Customers can conduct transactions seamlessly across all of Wells Fargo's products and services. That's great. However, if I am both a consumer banking customer and the owner of a small business that banks with Wells Fargo, those two relationships are not yet explicitly connected by the bank's information systems. Ideally, they should be. As a customer, I'd like Wells Fargo to know that it has two separate banking relationships with me and that any dissatisfaction with the way I'm treated as a consumer might impact my business banking relationship.

Bell Atlantic has also segmented its products, customers, and markets between residential and business accounts. Yet, according to Gary Weisenborn, former vice president of information systems, the company is trying to figure out how to link the households in its customer database to the small-business owners or key influencers. "We want to know who the economic buyer is, both in businesses and in households, and to know when they're the same person."

Telecommunications suppliers and financial services companies tend to be leading the way in providing customers with the ability to take care of multiple transactions across product lines. Telcos understand that the customer should be able to add a phone line at home, sign up for Internet service, and purchase cell phone service in a single interaction. Banks understand that a customer should be able to transfer funds from her checking account to her money market account, pay her bills, and invest in a mutual fund in a single session on the Web.

Implementing this cross-product-line transparency can be pretty challenging, from a technical perspective as well as from an organizational perspective. Who in your company "owns" the customer who purchases multiple services across product lines? Will they be willing to let others see "their" information about that customer? What if someone else wants to add or change information about that customer? How will you change your incentive or commission structure so that the customer receives the same quality of end-to-end service no matter whom they contact?

Customers' requirements don't stop with the need to buy from different departments or divisions of your firm. Customers also need to interact with different functional groups within your organization. For example, I may need to report a problem with static on my local phone line, find out if voice mail services are offered on my exchange, and question an item on last month's phone bill before I pay it. Each of these requests touches a completely different service organization within your company. How are you going to make it possible for me to take care of business with a single interaction?

"Remember" Everything Your Company Knows About the Customer

WHAT ELSE DOES it take to make the customer feel that you value his or her business? From the customer's standpoint, the most important thing is for your company to have a single, comprehensive view of all of the transactions and interactions he's had with your firm. Nothing turns off a customer more than having to remind the supplier about past communications. And to the customer, your organization is one entity. So if sales knows something, the customer expects customer service also to know it. You don't want to try to sell a customer on the latest and greatest you have to offer the day after that customer has called to complain that the current version of the product has blown every circuit on his shop floor!

How are companies addressing this issue? They do it by consolidating all the information about each customer's account and relationship in one single, easily accessible place. Whether you're handling a complaint, processing payment for an invoice, closing a multimillion-dollar deal, or following up on a delivery to check that it was received when expected and in good order, that interaction needs to flow into a common, well-organized repository that can be accessed by anyone else who may be dealing with the customer.

However, consolidating information isn't enough. Companies must also foster business practices that support and encourage the sharing of information. Each of these systems—customer accounting, help desk, sales, and so on—is managed and maintained by different groups within an organization. Not only are there technological challenges surrounding the integration of data from the disparate systems, there are also issues of ownership. Having a technical infrastructure for making information available to all appropriate personnel doesn't work unless the business also puts into practice methods and processes that reward employees for using the shared information. And this isn't always easy, especially in sales-focused organizations, which have typically organized around territories. Or where competition rather than collaboration has been rewarded.

Here's an example from the health care industry: Health Alliance Plan is the largest health maintenance organization in Michigan, with 540,000 members. The company's membership system keeps detailed records about each insured individual over time. In the database, each family member is a separate customer. All correspondence relating to each customer is digitized and immediately available to customer service representatives, who can answer customers' inquiries about claims, payments, and coverage over the phone. Every encounter the customer has with a health care provider or pharmacy is also logged in an encounter database, along with the outcomes of the treatment. Both customers and their health care providers have access to the information in these systems by phone, integrated voice response systems, e-mail, fax, and, most recently, through a secure Web connection.

Ensure That Everyone in the Company Has Access to the Complete Customer Picture

WHILE IT'S IMPORTANT for customers to have one-stop shopping and to feel that everyone they interact with knows who they are and what they need, it's equally important for your employees and your key business partners to have access to the complete customer picture. As mentioned earlier, this is not always easy or comfortable for an organization. This idea of open access to information scares a lot of middle managers and executives. They instinctively feel that employees and partners should be given customer information only on a "need to know" basis. Yet CEOs understand the value of knowledge of customers to the smooth functioning of an organization.

I remember complimenting a CFO on the wonderful customer profitability database his bank had. I wondered, however, why it was accessed by only two hundred people within the bank. Wouldn't it be useful for everyone to know how profitable each customer was and how that profitability picture might be improved? He recoiled at the idea that salespeople, account representatives, or customer service people would have access to this information. He was afraid that one of them would leave and take this knowledge along.

About two weeks later, in interviewing the CEO, I brought up this situation and asked his opinion. It turned out that he was frustrated that so few people in the bank had access to this valuable information. He wanted everyone to have it as soon as possible. What about the security of the information? I asked. He replied that the bank's information privacy and security policies were well ingrained in every employee. He felt they should have better information about customer profitability in order to inform their day-to-day priorities and decision making.

Example: Norwest Bank Minnesota's Twin Cities Banking Group

Norwest Bank Minnesota's Twin Cities Banking Group embarked on this path in the late 1980s by building and deploying a customer relationship management system. The Twin Cities Banking Group manages both the commercial business and retail banking for the Twin Cities region (Minneapolis and St. Paul). It has $12 billion in assets and is the single largest Norwest business unit. Starting in 1988, the Twin Cities Banking Group spearheaded an initiative to focus on relationship management with its commercial customers. All of the different product line managers, account representatives, and sales and service personnel who have any contact with customers, along with accountants, loan processors, and credit officers, share the use of a common customer database. In this database they measure the profitability of each business customer's relationship, every contact that customer has had with anyone from the bank, and the status of all of his accounts and banking relationships. Employees' compensation is based, in part, on the profitability of the accounts they work on as a team.

The results for Norwest were dramatic. When it launched the relationship management initiative in 1988, 60 percent of Twin Cities Banking revenues were derived from interest earned and 40 percent were the result of more profitable fee-based services. After four years, the ratio had reversed: by 1992, 60 percent of Twin Cities Banking revenues were derived from its more profitable, fee-based businesses. And the fee-based business continued to grow at nearly double digits every year! Profitability for the bank as a whole improved as the use of the customer relationship system spread throughout the bank.

Put an Underlying Technical Infrastructure into Place to Provide a 360-degree View

WHAT'S INVOLVED IN beginning to build these kinds of solutions? In the case studies that follow, you'll discover a number of steps that two companies—Bell Atlantic and Wells Fargo—have taken to move toward the goal of having a 360-degree view of their customers. The thorniest issues typically revolve around how customer-related information is currently stored and accessed across product lines, functions, and jurisdictions. Most organizations are not starting from a clean slate. We all have existing information systems, most of which have been organized by product line or by departmental function.

FIGURE 5

ISSUE: NONINTEGRATED INFORMATION AND APPLICATIONS

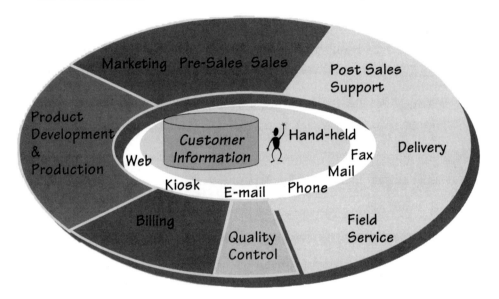

The problem most companies face: there are multiple information systems in different departments or divisions, each of which contains some piece of information about the customer's relationship with the firm.

Redesign Systems So the Customer Is at the Center

First and foremost, you need to start with the customer at the core of your systems. You may be lucky and already have a good, robust customer database you can build upon. You may discover, as Community Playthings did, that the people you have in your database aren't in fact the actual customers. Its direct-mail marketing database contained a list of schools and day care centers and its accounting system had information about the people who had paid the bills. But the company didn't have any information about the people who actually selected their equipment! Or, if you're like Bell Atlantic, it may take you three or four years to redesign your customer information systems from being product line–centric to being customer-centric.

FIGURE 6

GOAL: INTEGRATED APPLICATIONS, INFORMATION, AND CONNECTIONS

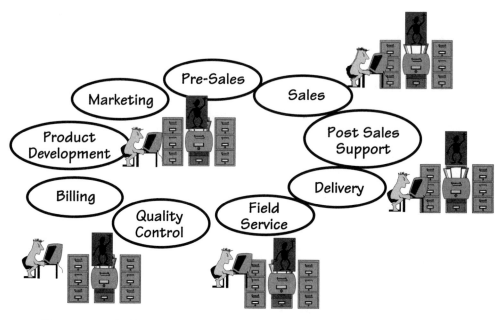

The conceptual solution looks like this. Consolidated customer information forms the core of the company's information systems. Customers can access this information and perform transactions using a variety of channels: phone, fax, e-mail, World Wide Web, kiosk, or face-to-face. Each of the employees in every department that touches or impacts the customer also has access to a comprehensive view of the customer's relationship with the firm.

Redesign Business Processes from the Outside In

In order to deliver one-stop shopping across products and functions, you'll need to redesign your core business processes from the customer's perspective (from the outside in, rather than from the inside out). Then you'll probably need automated workflow and middleware to enable customers or customer service reps to actually perform transactions, access and approve bills for payment, and procure new services. Bell Atlantic and Wells Fargo began their initiatives by streamlining business processes for the customer who interacts with the company by phone. In each case, streamlining these customer-facing business processes required doing a fair amount of "plumbing" to interconnect all the applications and databases that were required to service the customer. Wells Fargo was the first of the two to offer customers the ability to interact via the Web as well as by phone, using the same business processes and infrastructure that had been put into place for their call centers.

Create a Repository of Customer Events, History, and Profitability

In order to give everyone in your company an accurate picture of your dealings with each customer, you'll need to pull all the key business events out of the systems in which they take place and publish those events in a common customer repository, along with whatever information you have about the profitability and retention history of that customer's account. In Bell Atlantic's case, separate data warehouses are used to gather information about customers' profitability and call patterns. These data warehouses are then "mined" by marketing specialists to alert the company to new target marketing opportunities.

Shift Your Culture to Share Customer Information

Most important, you'll need to change everyone's attitudes about sharing and contributing customer-related information. Gone are the days when sales reps or agents "owned" their customers. In order for a company to be profitable in today's competitive economy, everyone needs to own the customer relationships.

PROVIDE A 360-DEGREE VIEW OF THE CUSTOMER RELATIONSHIP:

Bell Atlantic
www.bellatlantic.com

Executive Summary

Recognizing the need to provide exquisite customer service in the face of new competition, Bell Atlantic consolidated its customer information, built customer profiles, defined business rules, and streamlined all its customer-facing business processes. The result is that Bell Atlantic's customer service and sales personnel now have a 360-degree view of all of the different interactions that impact the customer. And the company now has an infrastructure in place that will let customers enjoy one-stop service, whether they are talking to a sales or service representative, using an integrated voice response system, or interacting via the Web.

Critical Success Factors in the Bell Atlantic Story

✓ Target the right customers	✓ Let customers help themselves
✓ Own the customer's total experience	Help customers do their jobs
✓ Streamline business processes that impact the customer	✓ Deliver personalized service
✷ Provide a 360-degree view of the customer relationship	Foster community

✷ = Featured in this discussion   ✓ = Touched on in this discussion

Bell Atlantic Puts Customers First

IN THE EARLY 1990s, Bell Atlantic was still enjoying a monopoly in providing local telephone service for 16 million customers in the mid-Atlantic region of the United States. The company not only had had no real competition, it had also been guaranteed a profit margin for the services it provided. But once competition was unleashed in the mid-1990s, it had to scramble to defend its territory and sustain its profit margins against long-distance telephone companies, cable companies, and cellular service providers. As they felt the hot breath of competition on their necks in 1991, the telco's executives decided to focus on improving customers' experiences of doing business with them. If they could keep customers happy, they reasoned, customers would be much less likely to switch when offered alternatives.

Problem: Too Hard to Order or Change Service

BRUCE GORDON WAS the executive in charge of the 6,500 telesales consultants who sold phone service to both consumers and small businesses for Bell Atlantic. As a twenty-three-year veteran of the old Bell system, Gordon was painfully familiar with the tortuous process required to take a customer's order over the phone. The process often took up to forty-five minutes. It involved looking up products, codes, pricing, and availability in three-ring binders, checking customer information in a number of different computer systems, and checking the customer's credit history with an outside service.

Not only was this order entry process a lengthy one, it was fraught with error. More often than not, the customer would call back later to complain that the service or equipment hadn't been properly provisioned. Unhappy customers were prime targets for any competitor who could offer competitive rates and better service.

Streamlining the Sales and Order Entry Processes

TO ADDRESS THIS critical customer satisfaction problem, in 1991 Gordon commissioned a new system from Bell Atlantic's corporate information systems group to support his sales consultants. The basic goals of the system were to reduce the amount of time customers had to spend on the phone and to minimize order entry errors. Gordon also realized that if order entry could be streamlined, the sales consultants could turn their attention to cross-selling and upselling of additional products and services, thus increasing the profitability for each account. The system, dubbed the SalesService Negotiation System (SSNS), became the platform upon which Bell Atlantic's future e-business initiatives would be based.

The SSNS project began with a complete redesign of the sales and service process by the business process redesign team, which included sales consultants who spent all day every day on the phone with customers.

Capturing Clues About the Customer's Situation

The design team realized that they needed to capture, in the initial dialogue with the customer, as many "clues" as possible about the customer's circumstances, creating a customer profile. They identified a number of facts about the customer that sales consultants might be able to deduce: hearing a baby crying in the background would indicate small children in the household, loud rock music might suggest teenagers lived there, and so on. Further, sales reps could often elicit relevant information during the phone call, such as whether there are grandparents living at home or if the customer ran a home business, whether she needed Internet usage, had an answering machine, and so on. The designers specified that the SSNS user interface needed to have a way for these clues to appear on the screen and be easily checked off by the telesales consultant as the customer volunteered information or as the sales rep deduced or elicited it. Thus, the salesperson simply clicked on the "small children" clue button when he heard children crying, "Mommy, mommy," in the background.

Using Business Rules to Trigger the
Sales/Order Entry Process

A fundamental information architecture decision was triggered by the decision to use this clues-based approach. The design team quickly realized that they could develop a group of different scenarios that could be used depending on the customer's situation. If the customer did have teenagers at home, for example, the sales consultant could be prompted to offer Bell Atlantic's Call Waiting service or to suggest a second phone line. The technologists on the design team realized that they could use business rules to set up an *"If there are teenagers, offer a second phone line"* logic for each of these situations. These business rules could be easily changed by the marketing department or by product managers. And because they would be maintained separately from the rest of the computer programs, a change in a business rule wouldn't require a rewrite of any of the application logic.

Once the design team had stumbled upon the business rules approach, they realized how useful it would be for solving a number of other thorny problems. For example, there are different regulations governing how phone service can be sold in different states. In addition, certain products are available only in certain locations based on the infrastructure Bell Atlantic has in place. The design team decided it could load all of its product availability tables into a business rules engine as well: *"If customer is in Region A, we can offer the following products."* This fundamental architectural decision gave Bell Atlantic a great deal of flexibility, supporting rules on pricing, taxes, product configurations, and even credit approval.

SalesService Negotiation System Rollout

THE INITIAL SSNS system was developed in two years and rolled out to the field starting in 1993. The rollout itself was a big challenge, according to Gary Weisenborn, who joined Bell Atlantic as vice president of information systems, responsible for Bell Atlantic's business systems, just before the rollout. His team had to install servers, workstations, networks, and software for 6,700 consultants in 51 residential service centers and 18 small business centers.

Dealing with Cultural and Organizational Issues

From a business process redesign perspective, the toughest challenges had to do with legal and regulatory issues. Most of the team members, who were longtime Bell Atlantic employees, didn't want to challenge the assumptions underlying how things had been done in the past. They assumed that many of these decisions had been mandated by law. It took outsiders, like Majid Naderkhani, Bell Atlantic's CIO, to challenge these assumptions and to press the design teams into working on breakthrough process design instead of simply replicating what had been done in the past.

According to Weisenborn, the biggest difficulties with the rollout were not technical (although, of course, there were some hiccups); the hardest part was overcoming the resistance of the most seasoned sales consultants. These people prided themselves on their knowledge of all the arcane codes that Bell Atlantic's back-end systems required. Much of their job satisfaction had been derived from being experts in the appropriate use of these esoteric and difficult-to-learn commands. Now new consultants coming in off the street could be trained much faster to use the system. The other issue was that despite their job description, most of these employees had never really been asked to actively sell anything. They had been taking and fulfilling orders by entering the information into these complex systems. Now the order entry complexity was removed and replaced by the need for a new set of skills: consultative listening and proactive cross-selling and upselling. Although training was provided, a number of the staff either opted out or had difficulty making this transition.

Streamlining Provisioning and Service

IN LATE 1993, the next major systems redesign effort Bell Atlantic undertook was a new integrated network trouble management system called

LiveWire. There were two important components to LiveWire. The first, dubbed the Ready-to-Serve application, was designed to switch on or alter telephone service for customers within a few minutes after they called. The second application was a maintenance case management system that enabled service representatives to quickly diagnose and repair service problems, tracking the status of each problem until it was resolved.

LiveWire's Ready-to-Serve capabilities were then integrated directly into SSNS, so the sales consultant could not only order new service but also assign a new phone number on the spot and verify that service could be turned on at the customer's service address (home or business). LiveWire has improved provisioning of service with its centralized repository for assigning telephone numbers and its service address database.

Migrating from Phone Lines to Customers: Building the Customer Database

LIKE ALL PHONE companies, Bell Atlantic's information systems were designed around phone (or access) lines and the services offered on each line. The records kept for each access line included its physical location—the exact location at which a service person could locate the end of the line on the customer's premises—and a billing address. The "customer" was probably, but not necessarily, the person who paid the bill each month.

So Bell Atlantic knew how many phone lines it had. It knew how to maintain and provision service on these lines. And it knew who paid the bills for each phone line. But there was no notion of an actual "customer"—someone who might be using three different phone lines, a cell phone, an Internet service, and a pager, all provided by Bell Atlantic.

Therefore, in order to support the SSNS effort, Bell Atlantic's information technology group launched a massive customer database project. It took several years to transform the information from 20 million–plus phone lines and cellular accounts into 16 million households and businesses and to link these records to the profiles of the individuals responsible for ordering service and for paying the bills. But once the customer database was complete, it became the centerpiece of all of the surrounding sales, service, provisioning, and billing applications.

Redesigning Billing

BILLING WAS ANOTHER hot issue for Bruce Gordon. Neither his business nor his residential customers were satisfied with the number of bills they were receiving for different services and with the formats of those bills.

The goal was to provide customers with a single consolidated bill for all the different services they procured, including local, cellular, paging, and Internet service. As a stopgap solution, Bell Atlantic chose to outsource this requirement to International Billing Services, a company that specializes in bill consolidation. Bell Atlantic piloted the consolidated billing approach for a targeted group of high-value customers. These customers now receive attractive-looking bills that pull all their different services together, total the monthly charges, and calculate the appropriate discounts.

Not content with this cosmetic solution to its baroque billing infrastructure, however, Bell Atlantic's CIO, Majid Naderkhani, also embarked on an entire billing systems redesign effort, focusing first on Bell Atlantic's largest business customers, since they have the most complex needs and requirements. Traditionally, telephone billing systems have been designed around particular geographic regions, product sets (for example, residential or cellular), and network architectures. Instead, this comprehensive new billing program is based on customers and their accounts. Products can be grouped together flexibly. For the first time, Bell Atlantic will be able to easily pull together account and billing information in whatever configuration makes the most sense to each customer. Using expressTRAK billing, business customers will be able to organize their bills by division, by product line, or by geography. Residential customers will be able to choose between combining all their services on a single bill or separating out family and home business lines on two separate bills, for example.

Piloting the Sales of Bundled Services to Customers

IN JULY 1997, Bell Atlantic opened a brand-new call center, staffed with three hundred highly trained outbound telesales professionals, designed to pilot the sales of bundled services. By late 1996 and early 1997, using the new consolidated customer database, Gary Weisenborn's group had designed and deployed a massive customer data warehouse. This took customer profile information from the customer database, combined it with customers' calling records, and enabled Bell Atlantic's marketeers to mine the data to discern promising patterns of usage that would pinpoint customers who were good candidates for particular service bundles.

Evolving the Technical Infrastructure

In 1991, Bell Atlantic's Information Systems (BAIS) group made the bold move to a TCP/IP-based backbone network, a technology that had not yet hit most people's radar screens. The next architectural decision BAIS made was equally precocious. Instead of designing SSNS to run on networked PCs, Bell Atlantic decided to design and deploy on a three-tier Unix-based system. They chose Sun Sparc servers for the back-end and middle tiers and decided to use X-Windows terminals for the sales consultants' workstations. Not only was this a less expensive architecture to deploy, since X-terminals cost half as much as PCs, but it would be much cheaper to maintain. Software upgrades could be loaded once, on the server, instead of having to be reinstalled on each of thousands of PCs every time a new software release was delivered to the field.

The next innovative architectural decision was the decision to use a business rules engine in the design of the SSNS application. By separating the business rules from the rest of the program logic, BAIS kept the parts of the application that would be subject to constant change and customization in an environment that was easy to change and maintain.

The Technical Details

BAIS selected the ART/IM rule-based knowledge system. The product databases used for the SSNS application were implemented in Sybase. The core customer database is housed in a DB2 in Bell Atlantic's two mainframe data centers. The middleware selected for initial application integration was Peerlogic PIPES.

The original SSNS application was written in C. In later versions, BAIS switched over to C++ but was able to reuse many of the original software modules. By 1997, BAIS was using Java to deliver Web-based versions of the software to the dealers and partners who sold Bell Atlantic products to the small-business market.

In each regional customer service center, BAIS deployed Sun

symmetric multiprocessing servers to house the regional product configuration databases, the rules engine for that region, and the application logic. Servers and workstations were connected on Ethernet LANs using 180 Sun network servers and interconnected by a TCP/IP wide-area network. Customer profile information captured by the sales consultants was first entered into a Sybase database and then uploaded into the DB2 customer database over Bell Atlantic's high-speed wide-area network.

The Largest Effort: Building a Customer Database

By far the largest and most time-consuming part of this set of interlocking initiatives was the customer database migration. It took the company four years to migrate the information into a comprehensive customer database organized by household for consumers, and by business for small and large business customers. The information was cleaned, transformed, and migrated into a large DB2 database housed on an IBM mainframe. As you can imagine, a lot of human effort was involved to make judgment calls about each step in this consolidation effort and to verify the information. But by 1995, Bell Atlantic had all 16 million customers identified and updated in a centrally maintained DB2 database that was backed up in a second data center.

Evolving the Three-Tier Architecture

As mentioned earler, the original SSNS system was designed using Unix servers with X-terminal "thin clients." Business rules were housed in a separate rules engine. Product information was stored in regional databases, while customer information was maintained centrally. Over time, SSNS has evolved to use thin PCs as clients instead of X-terminals. Much of the shared product information is stored on a central Web server. Consultants bookmark the areas in the knowledge base to which they need frequent recourse.

The next complex customer care and order entry system was designed to support Bell Atlantic's direct sales operation as part of the expressTRAK project. This system was implemented using object-oriented programming on NT client and server platforms. The integrated billing portion of expressTRAK is a "buy and integrate" solution from a variety of suppliers. Once completed and

rolled out, it will consolidate five legacy billing systems into one comprehensive billing process. Its flexibilty to bill a variety of products comes from its rules-based approach.

Adding Electronic Commerce: Letting Customers Serve Themselves

THE NEXT STEP was to begin giving customers the ability to help themselves using automated technologies. First, Bell Atlantic redesigned its integrated voice response systems to allow customers to report service problems, add phone lines, check to see if their bill had been paid, and get current pricing and service options—all from a Touch-Tone phone. By late 1998, the integrated voice response system will be integrated into SSNS. So, at any point in the interaction, if a customer becomes confused and presses the "O" for operator, her call will be routed to a telesales specialist who will have her record open on the screen in front of him and who will know exactly how far she has gotten in the interactive telephone dialogue.

The second electronic commerce initiative was implemented on the Web for a target group of customers: college students. Each year in September and May, thousands of college students call the phone company to start and stop phone service. Gary Weisenborn reports that it was very straightforward to design a Web front end that lets students apply for new phone service or turn off their service. The initial implementation simply captured the new orders and cancellations. Once these orders were received via the Internet, they were then manually transferred into Bell Atlantic's order entry systems. This student services application has been running for more than two years, reducing Bell Atlantic's costs to serve these customers and moderating the seasonal peaks in the customer service centers.

The company built on the experience with student accounts to expand the services it offers all its residential customers via the Web. By late 1998, the company had designed a more robust order entry capability for the Web. This second-generation Web order entry system hooks directly into Bell Atlantic's streamlined back-end systems to check the customer's account information, check her credit, and arrange to provision service. So any residential customer who wants to add a new phone line, order new services, or check, pay, or adjust her bills will be able to do so from the Web.

Bell Atlantic Merges with NYNEX

IN AUGUST 1997, Bell Atlantic merged with NYNEX, the regional Bell operating company that served the northeast region of the United States. By combining forces, the two companies' territories now covered the most populous two thirds of the eastern United States, with a combined total of approximately 30 million customers.

While the top executives of both companies were jumping over regulatory hurdles, the information technology executives of both firms compared notes on their systems. A systems task force made up of executives from both companies realized that Bell Atlantic's customer-facing systems—the customer database, the LiveWire service application, the new billing systems, and the sales and service systems—were more advanced and more widely deployed than NYNEX's systems.

As a former NYNEX customer, I breathed a sigh of relief when I heard that Bell Atlantic had won the privilege of designing the systems that would serve me and my company. I'm looking forward to the day when I will no longer receive nine separate phone bills for my family's phone service! And I'm eager to see what special offers will come my way based on my family's telecommunications patterns.

The one downside of the Bell Atlantic/NYNEX merger is that Bell Atlantic/NYNEX has its proverbial hands full just migrating and integrating their systems. So although Bell Atlantic has a head start over much of its competition in laying the foundation for electronic commerce, others may be able to catch up by the time Bell Atlantic's executives find the time to think about next steps in electronic commerce. Meeting the requirements of the Telecom Act of 1996 and moving into long-distance service are currently the top priorities for Bell Atlantic's management team. In August 1998, Bell Atlantic announced a second big merger, this time with GTE. What interests me about the GTE acquisition is that GTE was the first large U.S. Telco to redesign its customer-facing business processes using a business rules–based approach. So, Bell Atlantic and GTE share a common view of e-business architecture.

Results

BELL ATLANTIC SERVES about a quarter of the total U.S. telecom market, with close to 40 million access lines and one third of the country's Fortune 500 company headquarters. As of September 1997, Bell Atlantic's residential customers had 25.1 million phone lines. In its first three years of operation, SSNS increased Bell Atlantic's residential sales consultants' revenues per hour by 84 percent and decreased order errors by 98 percent. Training time for new sales reps was reduced by 66 percent and the cost of distributing product and training information dropped to nearly zero. Weisenborn estimates that by 1999, Bell Atlantic will have invested $124 million in SSNS and have saved nearly $567 million. And that's not even counting the savings from customer *self*-service.

Patty's Rx for Bell Atlantic

It's pretty clear that Bell Atlantic now needs to assimilate NYNEX's customers—and soon, GTE's—into its massive customer database and customer data warehouses. It needs to extend the LiveWire service system, the new billing system, and the next generation of SSNS north throughout the former NYNEX territory. According to Gary Weisenborn, that process will probably take another four or five years.

In the meantime, however, I would recommend that Bell Atlantic continue to streamline and combine all the applications that touch its customers. The company needs to get much more aggressive in its use of the Web to enable customers to help themselves. There is no real impediment that I can see to delivering all of the functionality sales and service representatives enjoy directly to customers over the Internet. Bell Atlantic has used the Web effectively to reach out to other markets, such as its wholesale market, but lags in its use of the Web to make it easy for residential customers to do business with it.

"Take-Aways" from the Bell Atlantic Story

1. Streamline the processes required for customers to get information about products and services, make a decision about what they want, configure a valid offering, complete the order (including credit checking and account maintenance), and receive the product or service.
2. Begin by pulling together all the information required for customer support and sales personnel to take orders, configure products and services, upsell and cross-sell appropriate products and services, and complete the sales, order, and service delivery process.
3. Build customer profiles based on what you already know (that is, have somewhere in your system) about each customer. Add to the customer's profile each time you interact with the customer.

4. Define a series of easily modifiable "if . . . then" business rules for marketing, pricing, and configuration that will match against customer profiles and product information to propose new offers, constrain the choices offered, and/or trigger the appropriate set of processes for this type of customer.

5. Pull all customer information together into a global customer database organized in ways that are meaningful to the company. Have all other applications get their customer information from that central repository.

6. Consolidate all product and marketing information into an easily searchable knowledge base on the Web. Organize that information for decision making and problem solving.

7. Once you've streamlined the first layer of customer-facing applications—marketing, sales, order entry—move on to the next layer—service/product delivery, repair, and billing. Consolidate all these applications into an integrated modular architecture that can be evolved over time. Keep customer information at the hub of the system. Give employees access to all the information about each customer.

8. Let customers serve themselves using Touch-Tone phones, via the Web, and so on, by giving them access to streamlined versions of the same processes and information used by your customer representatives.

9. Redesign your billing systems so that customers can customize their bills to better serve their own needs.

PROVIDE A 360-DEGREE VIEW OF THE CUSTOMER RELATIONSHIP:

Wells Fargo
www.wellsfargo.com

Executive Summary

Focusing first on serving its high-net-worth customers better, Wells Fargo pulled together all customer information and applications so that customer sales and service representatives could provide one-stop shopping for any banking service or transaction.

> **Then Wells quickly leveraged that infrastructure to provide one-stop shopping via the Web for all of its customers. Wells Fargo's on-line banking services are the fastest-growing part of its business.**

Critical Success Factors in the Wells Fargo Story

✓ Target the right customers	✓ Let customers help themselves
✓ Own the customer's total experience	Help customers do their jobs
✪ Streamline business processes that impact the customer	✓ Deliver personalized service
✪ Provide a 360-degree view of the customer relationship	✓ Foster community
✪ = Featured in this discussion	✓ = Touched on in this discussion

Wells Fargo Focuses on Convenience

SAN FRANCISCO–BASED WELLS Fargo prides itself on leading the pack in customer service. Wells Fargo's middle name is convenience. In 1988, Wells Fargo was one of the first banks to offer twenty-four-hour person-to-person telephone banking to its customers. In September 1989, Wells introduced guaranteed service in five minutes or less at its branch banks (if the wait is more than five minutes, the customer receives $5!).

As part of its focus on convenience, Wells Fargo also believes in one-stop shopping. Wells Fargo introduced supermarket banking in 1990. By the end of 1997, nearly half of Wells Fargo's 1,918 staffed branches were located in supermarkets and at other in-store locations. In October 1997, Wells Fargo joined forces with Starbucks Coffee Company to offer convienence and one-stop shopping with a mix of services under one roof. A first of its kind in the banking industry, these retail centers feature Wells Fargo and Starbucks, plus a variety of retail businesses such as postal and copying services, sandwich cafés, and dry cleaning outlets.

For Wells Fargo, this move is consistent with its ongoing strategy of providing customers with more points of access to do their banking as well as offering more services at these locations. Since 1991, all of Wells Fargo's ATMs have offered instructions in Braille, and since 1993, customers have been able to access their Wells Fargo investment accounts and pay their bills via ATM or Touch-Tone phone. Wells Fargo began dispensing postage stamps at its ATMs in 1994. It has offered on-line banking since 1989 and Internet banking since May 1995. Wells Fargo is one of the leaders in Internet banking today. Let's take a look at how it got there.

First Step: Build a Customer Relationship System

IN 1993, DUDLEY Nigg, who headed up Wells Fargo's savings and investment group, was looking for a solution to a customer service problem. He wanted to design products and services that would build and maintain relationships with Wells Fargo's high-net-worth customers, yet there was no way for the people serving these customers over the phone to get a picture of each client's total relationship with the bank. All of the customers' accounts were organized by account numbers. And each was maintained in a separate system. Checking and savings accounts were handled in one system; mutual funds were tracked in a different system; brokerage accounts were handled by yet another. So whenever a customer called to transfer money or to get information about the balance in his accounts, the customer service agent had to ask the customer for his account numbers and access a variety of systems to fulfill the requests. This took too much of a customer's valuable time. Obviously there had to be a better way!

Wanted: Pilot Project to Try Out New Information Technology Approaches

Serendipitously, in about the same time frame, a group of the bank's technologists were looking for a pilot project. In the spring of 1993, a small team of Wells Fargo's technology and business managers had attended an evangelical workshop hosted by popular technology guru John Donovan. They learned how they could use the latest techniques (rapid application development) and technologies (three-tier architectures) to develop complex applications very rapidly. They were looking for a project they could use to test these new concepts. Eric Castain offered to tackle the design and implementation of an integrated customer relationship system—a system that would bring together customer information from a variety of different applications so that a single customer service agent could help a customer with any transactions he or she needed. By October, Castain had put together a team to begin the design and implementation work for the first pilot of Wells Fargo's new Customer Relationship System.

The Wells Direct team decided to focus first on Nigg's high-net-worth clients, since they were an important subset of the bank's retail customers. These clients typically had multiple accounts and a number of different banking relationships with Wells Fargo. They wanted to be treated like customers, not account numbers. And the agents who served this customer segment were the most senior call center agents. They were likely to welcome the changes in their work process and to be willing to contribute to the design of an integrated solution.

Pilot Project Completed in Record Time

The pilot phase of the Customer Relationship System was developed and deployed in just over three months! Now a customer service agent could enter the client's Social Security number and see all the information about each of the client's accounts, culled in real time from a variety of systems and applications. And from that same PC, the customer service agent could enter transactions for any of these accounts directly into the appropriate systems. The confirmation that the transaction had been successfully completed would appear on the representative's screen—a vast improvement over the old process.

The new Customer Relationship System went live on December 27, 1993, with twenty agents in Wells Fargo's Concord, California, office (25 miles east of San Francisco). For the first time, customer service agents could easily assist customers in performing transactions involving most of the accounts in their portfolios. The agents were so pleased with this improved system, they traveled to San Francisco to take the developers out to lunch and present them with an award.

Once Wells Fargo's technical team knew how to integrate its back-end systems so that all of a customer's accounts could be viewed and accessed from a single point, they were able to add an interactive voice response unit as an additional channel that customers could use to access their account information.

Second Step: Lay Additional Groundwork

In 1993 the bank supported additional initiatives that turned out to be critical to quickly implementing an Internet strategy the next year. First, it adopted the Internet protocol, TCP/IP, for its new bankwide network. Second, it installed the first fire wall as part of bank security when external e-mail was launched. So all of the building blocks were now set for Web-based banking: customer accounts could be systematically accessed on a relationship basis, the network was designed based on Internet protocols, and the fire wall was in place.

Third Step: Build a Web Site as a New Channel

Back in 1989, Wells Fargo had tried to anticipate its customers needs for added convenience by offering them access to their bank accounts through both proprietary Wells Fargo software and Prodigy's on-line service. Yet six years later, only 20,000 of Wells Fargo's customers had opted to use these services. In the meantime, consumer software packages like Intuit's Quicken and Microsoft Money had become a popular way for customers to manage their money.

By 1994, when Dudley Nigg took over as executive vice president of direct distribution for Wells Fargo, he knew that a massive change was afoot among Wells Fargo's customers. First, the use of PCs in the home had mushroomed. Second, more and more consumers were jumping onto services such as America Online and the World Wide Web. Third, more and more customers were using the company's convenient automated telephone banking service. Nigg realized that customers wanted the convenience of anytime, anywhere banking and that they were increasingly willing to use technology to have that convenience.

To get the ball rolling, the bank began to explore the PC as an electronic commerce solution. A team was formed to build a new PC-based client/server solution, utilizing the technology used in the Customer Relationship System. This team was headed by company vice president Bill Finkelstein, who formerly headed Corporate Systems Planning. In his prior role, Finkelstein had joined CommerceNet to tap into the latest research in electronic commerce. In his new role, he developed a simple informational internal Web site to test the Internet waters and to educate executives. Soon, the Web-site idea caught on. Wells Fargo's corporate communications group took responsibility for the informational site during 1994, launching it to the public on December 12 and using it to strengthen the bank's brand and to showcase much of Wells Fargo's colorful history—Wells Fargo began as a stagecoach company transporting mail, passengers, and gold.

By March 1995, Nigg had decided that Wells Fargo should offer on-line banking via the Internet. He asked Finkelstein how long it would take to develop an Internet-based banking solution. "We can have the basics—the ability for customers to access their accounts—in around thirty days" was the response. That was the answer Nigg was looking for. It actually took sixty days before the Web site was ready. On May 18, 1995, Wells Fargo became one of the world's first banks to open its doors on the Internet.

Because Castain's team had already designed an integration applications infrastructure for the call center, it was a relatively simple job for Finkelstein's six-person team to build a Web front end to deliver an Internet banking solution. There were many issues, however. Finkelstein remembers that most of them had to do with how to display customer information in the new medium. It was imperative that the customer get exactly the same numbers whether he came in across the Internet, checked the ATM, used the Touch-Tone phone system, or came in through the Prodigy or direct dial links. So team members tested the software using their own live bank accounts. Not until they were satisfied that customers would see exactly the same information about all their accounts no matter how they accessed the system were they ready to go live.

Customers Flocked to the Net

ONCE INTERNET BANKING was launched, Castain left for a well-deserved vacation. He expected that about ten people might call in and sign up for on-line banking the first day and perhaps a hundred within the first week. When he called the office to check, he was told that more than 1,500 people had registered for on-line banking the first day! And the momentum was continuing. Luckily, Wells Fargo had the foresight to engineer the Web site to be robust enough to accommodate the surge in traffic. So Eric was able to complete his vacation.

Signing Up Customers

What process did Wells Fargo use to enable customers to sign up for on-line banking? It asked customers to call a toll-free number and provide enrollment information. The fulfillment process was labor-intensive and time-consuming. Today, all that has changed. Customers can register and select their password on-line, without making a phone call. They can begin on-line banking and bill payment immediately.

Dealing with Security Issues

How did Wells Fargo make customers feel secure? Back in 1994, the encryption offered by Netscape in its browsers was not very robust, so at first, Wells Fargo worked with Netscape to ensure that its browser incorporated features appropriate for banking. Most importantly, the bank worked with Netscape to be sure that no personal account information would reside on the customer's hard drive after an on-line banking session ended. Later, when Microsoft launched Internet Explorer, Wells Fargo also worked with Microsoft to ensure that appropriate security and privacy measures were also incorporated into its new browser.

Other security features? All customer information transmitted over the Internet is encrypted—40-bit encryption is required to check bank balances and history and to transfer funds between a customer's own accounts. The bank waited until July 1996 to launch bill payment in order to require the more stringent 128-bit encryption.

A banking session is launched only by use of a personal password selected by the customer. And a customer's banking session "times out" after 10 minutes of inactivity in order to protect privacy in case the customer leaves the computer with an active session on the screen. There are some behind-the-scenes protections as well. The bank believes that it uses some of the strongest fire-wall technology in the industry, and it monitors systems for any unusual activity.

And just in case that isn't enough to persuade a customer to bank on-line, the bank promises its customers that they will never suffer a fraud loss simply because they bank over the Web. The bank believes that Internet banking with Wells Fargo is every bit as secure as banking over the phone, at an ATM, or in a branch, and it stands behind the integrity of on-line banking just as it does all of its other delivery channels.

Evolving the Functionality of the Web Site

In the eighteen months between the initial customer relationship pilot and its evolution to a full-blown production system, Wells Fargo had learned a great deal more about how best to interconnect the back-end applications for maximum performance. By February 1996, Wells Fargo development teams had reworked the infrastructure so the on-line banking team was able to offer customers the ability to perform transactions via the Web. Customers could transfer funds from one account to another and pay their credit card bills. Within a few months, Wells added access to more types of accounts, such as home equity lines and unsecured lines of credit. Later that year, when Netscape and Microsoft both offered browsers with the more bullet-proof, 128-bit encryption, Wells introduced on-line bill payment—customers can schedule the payment of all their bills, both one-time and recurring, from their bank account. Customers can use the service to pay anyone—their landlord, their phone company, their baby-sitter, or their friends—not just a limited list of approved payees. Wells Fargo added other conveniences, such as the ability to use financial planners; apply for accounts on-line; order traveler's checks, cashier's checks, and foreign exchange; change their address; and reorder checks. Since its launch in 1995, the bank has worked constantly to update and improve the site, with new functions added regularly.

By mid 1997, Wells Fargo announced that customers using WebTV and Nokia 9000 cellular telephones could also perform secure Internet banking transactions. The company had worked closely with both companies to test their implementation of the Secure Sockets Layer (SSL) security.

In 1998, Wells offered its on-line banking customers the ability to apply for a line of credit based on the equity in their homes and to receive preliminary approval in seconds, not days! This capability was so popular that in the first three months the amount of equity-line business that was booked on Wells' Web site was the equivalent of 200 bank branches' worth.

Automatic Bill Presentment: A Strategic Weapon

WHEN YOU PAY your bills electronically, by using a software package like Quicken or Money or asking your bank to automatically enable direct withdrawal from your account by a preauthorized payee, very little information is actually exchanged electronically between the merchant and its customer. As a customer, you still receive the detailed transaction records of your phone bill or your electric bill in paper form, although you may have authorized the phone company or the electric utility to debit your account each month.

Dudley Nigg feels that the next step in on-line banking is bill presentment. He feels that bill presentment will give both customers and billers much more convenience and satisfaction. Wells Fargo piloted a bill presentment in 1998. Here's how it works: a biller establishes a relationship with a bill presentment consolidator like CheckFree or MSFDC. Then the consolidator links to the bank. When a customer goes into an on-line banking session, the customer receives an indication that bills are waiting. The customer then opens her bills and sees all the detailed transaction information, any disclosures that the biller wants to make, and any additional marketing materials that the biller wants to send. The bill is branded as if it came directly from the biller. If a customer's bank is linked to a number of different bill presentment consolidators, the customer will seamlessly receive most of her bills through her on-line banking session, without regard to who the consolidator is.

Nigg believes that bill presentment provides the ultimate in convenience for customers. They pick up most of their bills in one place, receive all of the billing information they need on-line, and in the same banking session, authorize all or partial payment, schedule payment to be made whenever they want, and e-mail the biller if they have questions about their bill. No more opening envelopes, writing checks, remembering to mail payments on time, and waiting for business hours to contact a customer service representative with a question. The value? The customer receives and pays bills in the most convenient and efficient manner. And the cost for the biller of creating and sending bills, receiving payment, and providing customer service using electronic presentment and payment is significantly lower than with paper transactions.

Evolving the Technical Infrastructure

Back in 1993, when Castain's group tackled the first Customer Relationship System (CRS) as a pilot project, they knew they needed some form of middleware that would link the PCs being used by the customer service representatives directly to all the applications that serviced the customers' different accounts. They chose Digital's Object Broker middleware and worked with Digital's consultants as well as with consultants from the Cushing Group as mentors for this first project. This mentoring approach worked well. And the technology didn't let them down. Five years later, Wells Fargo is still very happy with the approach it took.

How does distributed object middleware work? Basically, you decide what services you need to request from each application (for example, "Transfer money into an account" or "Debit an account"). Then you write the programs to request these services from the back-end applications. The middleware acts as a broker, translating requests from front-end applications to the back-end data sources and servers. Each application may be running on a different platform and may be written using a different programming language, but the object request broker interface enables it to accept requests for services and to respond to those requests. By using this middle layer of software (middleware) to broker requests for services, you make it much easier to change both the back-end systems and the front-end user interfaces without having to rewrite a lot of code. Over the last five years, Wells Fargo has taken advantage of the flexibility of this approach to manage the impact of changes in each of the three layers. At the same time, it has had the opportunity to greatly refine the way it described Wells Fargo's business to its computer systems by continuously improving the company's business object model.

When Wells Fargo's team wrote the first set of distributed object applications for the CRS and the first user interface for the Web, they were new to the concepts of object-oriented programming. As it turned out, with the help of their mentors and consultants, they made a pretty good first stab at defining the bank's key business objects (customers, accounts, products). However, by the time they had extended the infrastructure to interconnect lots of different systems, they realized that it was time to go back and rethink their design from the ground up.

So in 1995, the Wells Fargo team began a second iteration of the business process redesign effort. What they discovered was that each of their systems had different interpretations of basic concepts such as "customer," "account balance," "account profile," and "transfer." Each system was using a different set of implicit rules to define these basic concepts. Teams of technologists worked together with teams of businesspeople to rethink each of the core concepts of the business: What do we really mean by "account"? Is the definition the same for an FDIC-insured account as it is for a noninsured investment account? When we transfer funds from one account to the other, what are all the rules that have to be met for the transfer to be valid? These are the kinds of questions they had to review and answer. As they did so, they refined the conceptual (business object) model they were using to design new applications and services.

Using this refined object model, a team of developers was chartered to improve the CRS. By the fall of 1996, the original CRS had been replaced by an entirely new front-end system known as the Customer Information View (CIV) system. This second-generation call center environment offered several improvements. First, the goal was to eventually replace all the different terminal interfaces of each of the different back-end systems that the agents were currently using. They simply filled in forms that popped up on their screens. These forms, in turn, verified the information and transferred it in real time to the appropriate back-end systems using a new version of the original object request broker middleware. Second, the user interface was much more streamlined. Instead of using graphical icons, the agent could quickly tab to different types of accounts. Finally, the CIV system was optimized for high performance so that 1,500 representatives could be servicing customers simultaneously with excellent response times.

At the same time, a separate business and development team continued to evolve and maintain Wells Fargo's Web site. Another group was responsible for the transactional interfaces to Quicken and Money. And still another group evolved the interactive voice response system. All of these initiatives rely on the same underlying object model and services, which are being continuously improved and extended by Castain's team.

The decision Wells Fargo made in 1993 to move to a three-tier architecture using object broker middleware was probably one of the smartest technical investments the company has made (next to deciding, in 1992, to rewire all its systems using TCP/IP, the standard Internet protocol). The bank's continued commitment to and evolution of this architecture has enabled it to streamline and to continuously improve its customer-facing business processes. Although the user interfaces and client-side applications are quite different for the Web, the interactive voice response system, and the call center system, they all rely on the same common set of services. Therefore, customers are offered a consistent set of options, with predictable results, no matter which way they happen to choose to interact with the bank.

Another benefit Wells Fargo will reap from its investment in advanced middleware technology will be in its ability to easily integrate other banking systems. This will come in handy as the company completes its merger with Norwest. Nigg's team expects to be able to link all of Norwest's back-end retail banking systems into Wells Fargo's on-line-banking and telephone-banking systems as soon as the final merger is approved in the fall of 1998.

Strategic Next Steps: Move Customers from Credit Cards to Smart Cards

WELLS FARGO IS one of the primary investors—along with Chase Manhattan, NBD First Chicago, AT&T, Citibank, and others—in Mondex U.S.A., a company that has been chartered to develop and deploy stored value multiple-application smart cards. What's the business driver behind smart cards? They offer lower costs for the merchant, greater convenience for the customer, and a platform on which the bank can build strategic business partnerships.

How does the Mondex card work? Unlike an ordinary ATM card, it can be programmed to perform a variety of services. For example, your Mondex card could contain your digital certificate. When combined with your PIN number or some other form of authorization (such as a fingerprint or iris scan), your digital certificate could be used to conduct absolutely secure transactions over the Internet. You could also store monetary value on the same card. So you could use it to make phone calls, to ride the bus or subway, or to buy a newspaper. And you could use it to track loyalty programs. It could store your frequent-flyer account numbers and mileage earned, as well as the electronic ticket information for your next flight.

Smart Cards Enhance Security and Reduce Processing Costs

Wells Fargo believes the Mondex smart card will be successful because of the relatively low cost of processing a transaction using Mondex technology compared to the transaction fee imposed on merchants when their customers use a credit or debit card, which can range, on average, between 1 and 3 percent. Why the difference in cost? When a customer presents a credit or debit card to a merchant for approval, the information on the card has to be transmitted across a network to a central processing system that can verify that the customer has a valid account and, in the case of a debit card, that there are sufficient funds in the account to cover the transaction. Once the transaction has been completed, a second step takes place to actually debit the customer's account. All this network transmission and processing time costs the banks and merchants money. However, if the merchant can transfer funds directly from the consumer's card to the merchant's card, there is no need to transmit information over the network or to process the transaction on an expensive computer.

Mondex is also well suited as a payment mechanism for transactions over the Internet. Since processing costs are so low, on-line merchants will be able to generate revenues from delivering research, music, information, game playing, and other small-ticket items for which it might otherwise be economically impractical to charge for because of the high cost of processing credit card transactions. Much of this value is given away for free today.

Dudley Nigg sees the opportunity to use the Mondex multiapplication smart card as another platform on which to build business relationships that would benefit the customer while increasing the bank's mind share and market share.

Becoming a Destination Site

WHEN DOES A task-based site become a destination site? In 1998, there was a great deal of Internet-merger and acqusition activity as portal sites—Yahoo!, Lycos, and Excite—scrambled to become destination sites. Portals are the Web sites you go *through* to get somewhere else. Usually, they provide the search engine you use to find your way to your destination. Destination sites, like America Online, are the places you go to and hang out in. These offer all the services you need in a single location. Most of today's portal sites are scrambling to become destinations. Why? Because advertisers will pay more if they know the same customer will be sticking around for a while and not just passing through.

These portals cum destination sites will be competing with task-based sites, like Wells Fargo, Travelocity, and others that you go to to perform a task—pay your bills, or book reservations for your next trip. While you're there, you'll be offered the opportunity to handle other time-saving tasks. For example, in early May, Wells Fargo offered its on-line banking customers the opportunity to purchase flowers for Mother's Day by partnering with Flowers USA. Many of Wells Fargo's customers took advantage of this time-saving offer. In fact, the promotion was so successful that it increased Flowers USA's Mother's Day business by 200 percent!

Dudley Nigg sees a big opportunity for Wells Fargo to continue its tradition of convenience by offering on-line banking customers ancillary, time-saving services. The hard part is figuring out what other services customers will value while they're banking. In the physical world, Wells positions its retail branches in supermarkets and drugstores. In the virtual world, it's unlikely that a customer who goes on-line to pay her bills will come to the banking site with her shopping list in hand! On the other hand, context-sensitive offers, like flowers for Mother's Day, candy for Valentine's Day, or the offer of a home equity loan when your bank account is overdrawn and your credit card is maxed out, may all be welcome offers.

Building Community Around Banking Services

DUDLEY NIGG IS convinced that his customers are now ripe for the next step in cementing relationships. Wells Fargo will continue to add value to its Web site by creating a community of interest. Since all visitors to the Wells Fargo Internet site share something in common—an interest in managing their money—Nigg feels that by providing them with more information and services about financial planning, money management, and investment, Wells can begin to build a sense of community. Nigg might partner with a variety of players ranging from financial information services to tax advisors and from insurance companies to booksellers, like Amazon.com. Each partner could add value by offering information and services to members of the Wells Fargo community. Wells Fargo's customers would benefit from the increased richness of the offerings provided, the enhanced one-stop shopping, and possibly the opportunity to interact both with these service providers and with one another.

The first prerequisite for building community is to have a trusted relationship with the customer. Wells Fargo feels that it already has accomplished this first step. The second prerequisite is to offer information and services that will appeal to these individuals, engage them, and keep them coming back for more. Wells Fargo has begun this process with its on-line banking and bill payment services. Already, 1998 has seen the addition of financial planners and tools. But there should be more in store. Another step in community building might be allowing customers to interact with one another, answering one another's questions, and sharing common concerns. Only time will tell whether people will be willing to create a community around their on-line banking services in the same way they enjoy bumping into neighbors in the lobby of a physical branch bank.

What I like about Nigg's vision is that he realizes that, in order to be successful, Wells Fargo will need to consider offering its customers services that are competitive with the bank's own offerings, including investments, credit cards, and related products and services such as car and life insurance. He knows that his customers will value one-stop shopping and will be more likely to give their loyalty to a financial services provider that doesn't try to lock them in but offers them choices.

Results

ONE OF WELLS FARGO'S key strategies is to reduce the costs of its extensive branch banking network by augmenting its existing branch network with much smaller, more convenient banking locations in supermarkets and other in-store locations. "Why make the customer make two stops?" Wells Fargo's convenience-minded executives reason. If the customer has to go to a supermarket to purchase his everyday necessities or to Starbucks to pick up a cup of coffee, that's where his bank should be. These new convenience outlets vary from a simple ATM to a small, full-service branch. But they share real estate costs with their partners—Safeway, Vons, Albergson's, Kmart, Starbucks, and other retail establishments.

In addition to co-locating with retail outlets, Wells Fargo offers customers telephone banking and the Internet. This is a winner for both the customer and the bank. Customers gain the convenience of banking from their home or office, anytime they want. And the bank has a lower cost structure when customers transact their business by telephone or Internet.

On-line Banking Gains Momentum

Remember that Wells Fargo first offered customers on-line banking in 1989 using its own PC software. In the six-year period from 1989 to 1995, a total of 20,000 customers took advantage of this offer. But in 1995, when Wells Fargo delivered a more convenient form of on-line banking over the Internet, the floodgates opened. By the end of 1996 Wells Fargo had more than 300,000 on-line banking customers. While 170,000 customers used the Internet directly, the remainder interfaced with their Wells Fargo accounts through Quicken or Microsoft Money. By the second quarter of 1998, Wells had more than 470,000 on-line banking customers.

On-line Banking Customers Are More Profitable

Nigg estimates that it costs Wells Fargo $1 per call to serve a self-service telephone banking customer and about half that to serve an on-line banking customer. More significant than the cost-savings, however, are the increased profits that stem from the economics of customer loyalty (discussed in Step Five: Foster Customer Loyalty). You'll recall that, according to Frederick Reicheld's model, loyal customers are more profitable because:

- The longer you retain them, the more money you make.
- They cost you less to serve.
- They invest more in your products.
- They cross-sell and upsell themselves.
- They generate referrals.

Wells Fargo's experience with its on-line banking customers maps nicely to Reicheld's principles:

1. On-line customers have a 50 percent lower attrition rate than customers of the bank as a whole. Why? One theory is that when customers move away, they change banks. With on-line banking, customers do not have to switch banks when they move. Another is that once customers have consolidated their relationship on-line, they are less likely to want to give up the convenience of banking on-line to move to a new institution. And a third theory, which is relevant for bill payment customers, is that the pain of setting up a new bill payment relationship (which would require entering all of their merchants, their merchants' addresses, and their account numbers) is a big disincentive to moving their accounts to a new institution.
2. Wells Fargo's average cost per customer is steadily decreasing. According to Dudley Nigg, every time the bank adds more functions that customers can do themselves, Wells Fargo's cost of doing business with those customers decreases.
3. On-line banking customers carry higher balances with the bank than they did before they went on-line. This is not surprising, according to Nigg. "Customers like being able to see everything in a single spot. Customers naturally want to do what makes life easy."
4. On-line customers use more Wells Fargo products than the average customer in the bank. Once they come to the Web site to pay their

bills or check their account balance, they tend to explore on their own, learning about, and signing up for, other products.

5. Wells Fargo's on-line banking customers tell their friends. These referrals come to the bank's Web site to see for themselves and sign up.

Patty's Rx for Wells Fargo

What I like about the Wells Fargo story is how well the company leveraged one investment in back-end integration to reach out to customers using a variety of channels: call center, interactive voice response, and the Web.

What seemed to me to be missing on Wells Fargo's Web site, however (as of mid-1998), is the ability for me to really manage my money. Although I could pay my bills, see all my accounts, and transfer funds, I couldn't categorize expenses and compare actual versus budgeted expenses unless I downloaded the data to Microsoft Money or Quicken. The reason many people choose to use PC money management packages like Quicken and Money is that these programs enable you to categorize all your expenses the way you want to and then to better control how and where you spend your money. Shouldn't an on-line banking solution offer the same functionality? Why should I need a third-party software package? Why can't Wells Fargo offer me all the same features from its Web site? Granted, if I'm already hooked on Quicken, I'm not going to change my ways. But if I'm not a loyal Quicken user, I'd probably enjoy reaping more of the benefits of money management without having to load and learn a separate software program.

I do believe that Wells Fargo is well on its way to offering its customers complete one-stop shopping for their financial management needs. The innovative approach to electronic bill payment is a good case in point. What the bank needs to do next is to let the customer categorize payments, create family budgets, and do other forms of financial planning on-line. Next, Wells Fargo should let me keep my entire investment portfolio and insurance records on their site as well, updating the value of my portfolio each day. The financial services world will be one of the most highly competitive markets over the next several years, and one-stop shopping is likely to be the most critical beachhead.

Finally, I need to be able to conduct seamless interactions with other financial institutions from the Wells Fargo site. I want to be able to transfer funds from my Wells Fargo account to accounts at other financial institutions and to schedule these fund transfers in much the same way I would schedule the payment of my bills.

"Take-Aways" from the Wells Fargo Story

1. Lay the groundwork: Make sure your company has an Internet infrastructure in place. Update your company's information security policies and implementation to take current Internet technologies and behavior into account.
2. Start by focusing on convenience for your end customers.
3. Target your most profitable customers first.
4. You can pull customers' account information together in real time using middleware; you don't have to create a central customer database to put everything into.
5. Use the same middleware infrastructure to support your call centers, your interactive voice response systems, your Web interface, and any other devices that customers use to interact with you—in Wells Fargo's case, these include ATMs, PC software packages like Quicken, and other on-line services like Prodigy and AOL.
6. Make sure that the answers and information that customers receive are identical, no matter which channels of interaction they are using.
7. Don't let current technology capabilities limit your vision. Once Wells Fargo had implemented automated bill payment via the Web, ATMs, and interactive voice response, Dudley Nigg didn't stop there but continued to pursue his dream of offering bill presentment to customers.
8. Once you make it easy for customers to help themselves to information and transactions, they'll upsell and cross-sell themselves.
9. Begin by offering information, then transactions. Then evolve to a one-stop-shopping environment; include relevant services and offerings from third parties, even competitors.

Provide a 360-Degree View of Your Customer's Relationship: Lessons Learned

As we can see from the two very different approaches taken by Bell Atlantic and Wells Fargo, there are many different ways to skin this cat! Basically what you're trying to do is to pull together all the information about customers across product lines, accounts, and functions and make it available to the people in your firm who interact with customers as well as to customers themselves. You do this by consolidating all of your customer profile information, account details, and service history and making this information available in easy-to-grasp form. You may need to pull all the information together first in a customer database, then add the real-time details "on the fly." Or you may simply pull everything together dynamically at the time it's requested by a customer service agent or the customer himself. In either case, this is a major systems integration task and one not to be taken lightly, as you can tell by the time and money both Bell Atlantic and Wells Fargo have invested. On the other hand, if you haven't already embarked on the kind of major systems integration and redesign efforts described in these pages, you're already hopelessly behind. A new competitor starting from scratch with customer-centric systems could blow you out of the water. Or an old competitor who's been chipping away at this problem for years may well beat you to market.

Focus on Business Objects, Business Events, and Business Rules

NOTE THAT THE technical and business teams in these two different companies (on two different sides of the country, in two different industries) chose the same basic underlying architectural principles. To build these large, complex, highly integrated systems, both found that it made the most sense to come up with a set of business objects: customers, accounts, households. Both used the concept of business events to plan the interactions they'd need across systems. In Wells Fargo's case, a business event might be "Transfer funds from checking to savings." Such events translate into a series of transactions (debit checking account; credit savings account). In Bell Atlantic's case, a business event might be "Open a new account." This would trigger a series of actions that need to take place across a variety of systems (check customer database for duplicates; create new-customer record; check credit; and so on). Bell Atlantic used business rules very explicitly (by opting for a business rules engine) in the design of its original SSNS system. Wells Fargo used them implicitly in its business object model. Both companies opted to develop their systems using object-oriented design techniques. The payoff has been that as these systems have evolved over time, it's been relatively straightforward to create new functions and services without rewriting entire systems.

Integrate Information for Your Call Centers First

BOTH WELLS FARGO and Bell Atlantic focused on integrating all their back-end applications and information, pulling that information together and presenting it first to customer service agents. This is not a bad first step. Customer service representatives are usually able to deal with more of the "seams" between systems than you'd want your end customers to see. You may find it easiest and most cost-effective to build this 360-degree infrastructure for your sales and service representatives first, then move on to customer self-service. However, as you do so, you don't want the call center to be the end focus of your design efforts. Instead, you want it to be a step on the path to a complete 360-degree approach, supporting multiple customer support functions and, eventually, multiple channels of interaction.

Build Customer Self-Service Front Ends on the Same Integration Framework

ONCE YOU HAVE this integrated infrastructure in place, it becomes much easier to develop and/or plug into lots of different channels of interaction. Wells Fargo added integrated voice response (IVR), ATM access, Web-direct access, and access via PC money management software packages. Bell Atlantic added IVR and Web access. But remember, as you extend your integration framework out to these different self-service channels, you need to pay close attention to the end customer's experience. Remember the work Wells Fargo had to do to ensure that customers got exactly the same information at the same time of day from each account, no matter which interaction channel they used.

Use the Internet as Infrastructure

THERE'S ANOTHER INTERESTING similarity between the two companies. Both had been early adopters of the Internet as their corporate backbone for wide-area networks. Both companies had large investments in other networks, yet in the early 1990s they were both forward-thinking enough to realize that they should evolve their internal networks to sit on top of the protocols that were going to be widely used for global networks. Both companies also began migrating their knowledge bases of product information to the Web, so that employees could easily access product, marketing, and technical information. This made it much more straightforward to give end customers and key business partners access to that information, either by allowing them to dial in to retrieve it or by making the information available to them for their own internal networks (intranets).

If you were to follow in these companies' footsteps, you'd want to use the Internet as your corporate networking backbone. You'd pull together all of your customer-related information into applications that can easily be accessed by a variety of different sets of employees—sales, service, logistics—who interact with your customers over the phone and face-to-face. You'd pull together all the product, pricing, and technical information people need in easy-to-navigate Web pages. And you'd leverage the same back-end infrastructure to design Web self-service, Touch-Tone phone self-service, and kiosk self-service options for your end customers and business partners.

Let Customers Help Themselves

Today's customers value their time above all. They want to be able to conduct business at the time that's most convenient to them. And they want to do it in the way that's most convenient at that time. Your customers want more than a good Web site; they want a seamless web of interactive applications that will let them help themselves to information, perform transactions, check on the status of things, make inquiries, and get information that's relevant to their particular situation. They'll want to be able to perform all of these functions more or less interchangeably, by phone, fax, or e-mail or via the Web. And when appropriate, they want a person integrated into the process.

However, letting customers help themselves is not always smooth sailing. Here's an example of what can go wrong.

The U.S. Social Security Administration (SSA) provides social insurance coverage to more than 142 million workers and their families. For years, the agency has practiced service to the citizen by disseminating information to the public in printed form, by mail, and by taking requests for information—in person at the agency's 1,300 field offices or by telephone—and then sending the information out to those requesting it. Since 1987, the SSA has offered Personal Earnings and Benefit Estimate Statements (PEBESs) by mail. These statements provide a year-by-year listing of your Social Security and Medicare earnings and taxes paid, an estimate of what your retirement benefits will be at various ages—62, 65, and 70—and other information useful for financial planning. As you can imagine, producing these benefits statements is a labor-intensive process. For each request submitted, a computer program is run and a benefits statement issued and mailed. In 1996, the SSA produced more than 3.4 million of these custom-generated reports.

Letting customers help themselves to this information via the Web and letting them play "what-if games" on-line—"What if I retire at age 55?"

"What if I earn more money for the next ten years?"—seemed like an obvious win/win situation. So by the spring of 1997, the agency was quietly testing a secure Web application that let citizens make these inquiries online. The initial results were positive. Those who came to the Web site to try it out were amazed and delighted by how easy it was to fill in the form and get the results right back. But just as the SSA was preparing its public announcement of this new service, a newspaper reporter got wind of it and published an inflammatory article in *USA Today*. He claimed that anyone armed with a person's Social Security number and a few other bits of authenticating information could tap into the system and retrieve a person's earnings, employment history, employer, home address, and so on. This raised a furor! In fact, the authenticating information you must provide is not easy to come by, and the only information that's provided on-line is the benefits information—not earnings, employment history, address information, or anything else. Nevertheless, the damage was done. The SSA stopped the project and embarked on a road show across the country to gather feedback and to educate the public. A revised version of the offering was ready to be rolled out about twelve months later—this time, customers would be able to apply on-line, but a private access code would be e-mailed to them. This seemed to satisfy critics' concerns.

The SSA's story is a good example of what can go wrong with the best of intentions. John Sabo, a senior manager in the SSA's Office of Programs and Policy, says that the most important lesson he learned is that you have to understand the concerns of all of your stakeholders. The one thing he would do differently if he had it to do all over again is that he would have involved privacy advocates from the beginning in the design of the application. If you can involve the people who have informed, legitimate concerns in your planning process and strike a good balance among those often conflicting points of view, you'll save yourself a lot of grief in the long run!

Yet successful customer self-help stories abound as well. Charles Schwab is one of them. Since March 1996, when Schwab launched its Internet-based interactive trading site, which provided clients and their financial advisers access to their accounts, market data, financial planning, and portfolio management tools, along with stock-trading capabilities, Schwab's on-line brokerage business has skyrocketed. As of mid-1998, Schwab's on-line services boasted 1.2 million active customers, with more than $80 billion in assets. That's two thirds of the estimated $120 billion in the entire electronic brokerage industry! Schwab provides customers transparent access to their account information and the ability to make trades, whether they do it by automated phone system, by talking with an account rep, by working through a financial planner who uses Schwab's back-end services, or by doing it themselves over the Web or via America Online.

So what are the important points to bear in mind when designing customer self-help solutions?

- Let customers help themselves to information and perform transactions on-line.
- Let customers check on the status of orders, pay or adjust bills, and access service.
- Let customers interact using whatever media they choose.
- Give customers the ability to design their own products.

Let Customers Help Themselves to Information and Perform Transactions On-line

ONE OF THE first mistakes most companies make as they venture out onto the Web is to assume that their products can't be sold on-line. On Web site after Web site, you find vast amounts of product information—often enough information, in fact, to help the customer make a purchasing decision. Yet instead of closing the sale on-line, the Web site offers a phone number to call or a list of stores or dealerships. This is incredibly off-putting! The customer has just invested a fair amount of time educating himself about your product, and he's ready to buy. Why stop him dead in his tracks now?

Oh, I've heard plenty of excuses: "Our products are too complex to be purchased over the Web." "Our products are too high-priced. It's one thing to sell a $25 book or a $15 bottle of wine, but we sell $50,000 products!" "We don't sell directly; we sell through dealers; we don't want to cut them out of the loop." In my experience, none of these reasons—alone or in combination—is adequate for not giving customers a seamless opportunity to research and buy your products, or at least to get as far down that path as *they* choose to go on their own. Cisco Systems and Dell Computer are good counterexamples for the first two objections. Both companies sell products valued in the tens (in Dell's case) and hundreds (in Cisco's case) of thousands of dollars directly from their Web sites. Both companies offer products that are very complex to configure correctly. Yet both offer automated configuration programs that let the customer design his or her own manufacturable system. The third objection—the fear of upsetting your channel partners by enabling the customer to buy direct—simply doesn't hold water. You can, for example, let the customer research, configure, and purchase directly from your Web site. Then, if you want to keep the dealer in the loop, you let the dealer configure and ship the product to the customer; or you ship the product and give the dealer some credit for the sale into his territory; and/or you give the dealer the follow-on installation, maintenance, and support business. This is the model Hewlett-Packard and others are now beginning to use for many of their system sales.

One of the amazing benefits of allowing your customers not only to research but also to configure, order, and pay for products on-line is that they can now have a true one-stop-shopping environment, and you never have to involve a salesperson. Amazon.com works this way, letting people browse the virtual stacks or search for specific books, then walking them through a comprehensive yet easy-to-navigate ordering system. This is actually very similar to the traditional bookstore model, where most people help themselves and, only after making their selections, march up to the register to pay.

But with high-ticket items, such as the Dell's computers, allowing customers to help themselves on-line is a new model. In the past, a telephone salesperson often had to walk the purchaser through all the configuration options, explaining what specific components do, what the price packages are, and how maintenance agreements work. Today, the on-line customer can peruse all this information on the Web site and make educated purchasing choices without taking the time of some telesalesperson. Of course, a real person should be available when the buyer has a question or hits a snag! Still, the cost of making the sale goes down considerably when the customer can drive the purchase himself.

Self-help transactional Web sites are becoming the norm. And they don't always require the customer to deal directly with the supplier. Charles Schwab is obviously an intermediary that excels in providing one-stop shopping to self-service customers. American Express is another great example. As the world's largest travel agent, American Express has a lot to lose if customers begin making their own reservations via the Web through the new agentless intermediaries, such as Travelocity, that are springing up, or by dealing directly with airlines, hotels, and rental car companies over the Web. In 1997, American Express launched American Express Interactive, a comprehensive Web-based offering targeted specifically at large corporate customers. Each corporate account specifies a set of business rules that delineate that company's travel policies for different groups of employees: who can fly first class, which travel providers the company has corporate discounts with, what happens to frequent-flyer miles earned, and so on. These corporate travel rules are combined with each employee's self-maintained customer profile. Employees can book their own travel over the Web, using the service. If they need to, they can call their AmEx corporate travel agent, who will have all the same information in front of him or her and can make whatever changes are necessary. The itinerary appears on the customer's on-line calendar, and the travel expense information flows directly into his or her corporate expense reimbursement workflow.

Let Customers Check on the Status of Orders, Pay or Adjust Bills, and Access Service

OVER AND OVER again, Web marketeers have been surprised by the popularity of many simple customer service applications. Michael Dell, in his keynote speech at Comdex in the fall of 1997, commented that Web-based service and support is one of the most successful applications of electronic commerce. Yet it often goes unnoticed by the press. More than 20,000 Dell customers check the status of their orders on the Web every week! Each of these self-help requests saves Dell $8! Do the math. Pretty impressive, no? And Dell's Web site offers 80,000 pages of detailed service and support information, along with more than a hundred detailed troubleshooting scenarios. This is the same information that Dell's technical support engineers use when they are on the phone with a customer. Many customers are happy to walk through these scenarios themselves to diagnose, and possibly fix, their own problems instead of calling a service technician.

A lot of a customer service representative's time is spent hearing the same complaints over and over. And usually the resolution is the same for each customer. For example, for AT&T, one of the most popular complaints is denying knowledge of 900-number phone calls ("Honest, I never called the Erotic Companions!").

In order to expedite this kind of complaint resolution, AT&T set up some standard business rules. For example, if a customer has never called a 900 number before and doesn't have a teenager in the household, the charge is removed from the bill. However, if the customer regularly has 900-number calls on his or her bill and has called each month to contest these charges, denying all knowledge of these calls, or if there are other household members who might have placed the calls, the adjustment won't be granted automatically; further investigation is undertaken. Once these business rules were in place, it was a simple step to trigger the same rules for customers who choose to check and pay their bills via the Web or to call the self-help integrated voice response system to contest a charge on their bill. The system automatically processes the adjustment request, checking against the defined business rules. If the charge is waived, the customer is notified immediately. If not, the customer is also notified and can switch over to speak to a representative.

Let Customers Interact Using Whatever Media They Choose

NOT ALL CUSTOMERS are ready, willing, or able to jump onto the Web, however. And you have to let customers interact with you in whatever ways they choose, even if that means talking to a human being! Nothing annoys me more than getting an integrated voice response system that doesn't quite ask or answer the questions I have, yet has no mechanism for switching me to a real person!

You also need to provide the same level of information access on all media: phone, e-mail, voice response, Web, correspondence.

Today, most organizations dedicated to sales have some sort of voice response system or call center technology. And many organizations have redesigned customer-facing processes—such as sales and support—for the Web. Now some of these companies are taking the logical next step and experimenting with tightly integrated Web and call center solutions.

The way this works is that a customer gets started in the order process on the Web site. However, if she has any questions or wants something that isn't a standard option, she can click a button that either initiates a call to a call center or requests that a call be made to her (to a separate phone line, if she has two lines). All the information that has been collected so far on the Web is immediately available to the call center person. The technology for making this easy and seamless is about ready for prime time now. In fact, AT&T and MCI both offer this Web integration option to their call center customers. Hewlett-Packard is using this capability for its U.S. customers who would like more information about HP's high-end systems. On the Web pages describing these offerings, there's a "Call me now" button. The customer presses the button and enters the phone number he'd like the customer service agent to use (a second phone line, a cell phone number, or, depending on the phone service he's using, the same line with which he's already accessing the Web). The call request is routed to one of HP's twenty-four-hour customer information centers, and within seconds, the customer receives a call from an agent who knows what he's looking at on the Web site and can answer any questions he may have.

It is vital, however, that all information from each medium be reflected in the other media. American Airlines allows customers to make reservations on-line through either a PC software application or via its Web site. That's good. Unfortunately, even though the reservations go into the same underlying system, the two environments are not yet connected, so if you make a reservation from the PC and then later go to check the Web site, the reservation isn't listed. The same thing happens when you start from the Web—the PC software knows nothing about the reservation.

One of my colleagues was unexpectedly delighted by, of all things, the process of paying parking tickets over the phone. The City of Boston Parking Commission, like many similar governmental departments, allows parking violators with an active credit card to pay by phone. This wasn't what impressed her. What made the experience satisfying is that she wanted to contest several of the tickets and pay for only one individual (earned) violation (parking meters do run out). Not only could she pay the one ticket, but the phone message very clearly indicated how she could contest the tickets and gave her push-button options for the most commonly contested violations (for example, broken meter, "No parking" sign not visible). As it happens, her tickets were not of a common type, but she was told to press a number for "All other" and got a person—who actually could take action—immediately! At no point did she have to wonder what to do next. At no point was she tempted to give up. The seamless interaction between a well-designed integrated voice response system and the customer support representative behind the scenes accomplished what she needed.

Give Customers the Ability to Design Their Own Products

IN THE TWO case studies that follow, you'll notice that customers are able to actually create their own individualized products via the Web site. This is the ultimate form of "helping yourself." In fact, as both the Dell Computer and iPrint experiences show, it's much more cost-effective to let customers "roll their own" customized products via the Web than it is to do it any other way.

There are two kinds of "do-it-yourself" customization that are popular on the Web. One revolves around information-only products, such as *The Wall Street Journal Interactive Edition*. In the case of the interactive *Journal*, the customer can customize the product she receives electronically by selecting the columns and topics that interest her the most. The second type of do-it-yourself customization involves the design and manufacture of physical products to order. Both iPrint and Dell allow customers to design their own physical products on the Web. As you can imagine, neither of these capabilities is one you can "tack onto" existing mass-production processes. In order to let customers design their own physical products, you need to have robust configuration engines and order-to-manufacturing processes in place that will permit the efficient design and production of "one-off" products. However, once these tools and processes are in place, you can't beat the Web for cost-effective delivery of self-customization capabilities.

LET CUSTOMERS HELP THEMSELVES:

Dell Computer
www.dell.com

Executive Summary

Dell Computer's electronic commerce site, www.Dell.com, is so successful precisely because it mirrors Dell's existing business model: sell directly to the end customer; build systems only once an order is placed; keep inventory to a minimum. Yet Dell.com extends that direct business model by giving Dell the opportunity to imbed its marketing, sales, order entry, and service and support capabilities within the customer's own internal network. Dell can now interact not just with a single corporate purchasing department or IT executive but with each one of the thousands of employees who actually use Dell's computers.

Critical Success Factors in the Dell Computer Story

✓ Target the right customers	☆ Let customers help themselves
✓ Own the customer's total experience	✓ Help customers do their jobs
☆ Streamline business processes that impact the customer	✓ Deliver personalized service
✓ Provide a 360-degree view of the customer relationship	Foster community

☆ = Featured in this discussion   ✓ = Touched on in this discussion

Dell OnLine: Maintaining Relationships Through Self-Service

LONG BEFORE THE Web existed, when Michael Dell, the founder of Dell Computer, was building PC-compatibles in his college dorm room, he had a vision of selling computers direct to the end customer. He wanted to bypass the myriad distribution channels that were common in the PC in-dustry—channels he felt often added cost without adding value. Except for a relatively brief foray into the dealer and retail channel, Dell has kept its focus on direct marketing, direct sales, and direct support to end cus-tomers.

This direct relationship with the customer has enabled Dell to become a $13.6 billion company in twelve years. By 1996, Dell had become the third-largest personal computer manufacturer in the world. Dell's profits have often defied Wall Street's predictions, and its service and support have thrilled its customers. Yet despite its phenomenal growth, Dell has re-mained lean. With 17,800 employees, Dell's revenues per employee are a whopping $764,045! How does the company manage this growth? By part-nering closely with suppliers, shippers, and third-party service companies, each of which knows exactly what's going on with Dell's customers. Michael Dell explained how important customer relationships are to his business model in a *Harvard Business Review* interview published in Febru-ary 1998: "You actually get to have a relationship with the customer. And that creates valuable information, which, in turn, allows us to leverage our relationships with both suppliers and customers. Couple that information with technology, and you have infrastructure to revolutionize the fundamental business models of major global corporations."*

Dell's management team recognized very early that electronic commerce on the Web would provide an opportunity to extend its direct-sales model, reaching more customers directly and providing more services at a lower cost. To that end, the company created Dell Online, a division devoted to strategy and to implementation of Dell's internet activities, including electronic commerce and on-line support. The success of that effort has been measurable, with sales attributed to the dell.com Web site at $6 million per day by mid-1998. Equally important are the cost savings the site has created for Dell, reducing the amount of time spent on the telephone with customers without reducing the level of service provided.

Using Computers to Sell and Support Computers

EARLY IN HIS company's history, Michael Dell realized that by integrating his ordering and manufacturing systems, he could assemble and ship computers in a matter of a few days, keeping finished goods inventory near zero and squeezing the most profit from a highly price-competitive industry. He was also quick to recognize that the rapidly changing technology in the PC industry meant that every computer in inventory was potentially obsolete the day it was built. If he didn't build computers until they were ordered, he could eliminate the risk of holding outdated computers in inventory. Dell explains, "In our industry, if you can get people to think about how fast inventory is moving, then you create real value. Why? Because if I've got 11 days of inventory and my competitor has 80, and Intel comes out with a new 450-megahertz chip, that means I'm going to get to market 69 days sooner."†

Dell always takes orders directly from its end customers (rather than channel partners) and builds its computers to order. To support these direct sales activities, the company invested heavily in providing customers with product information so that they could make their own educated decisions about what to buy. And although Dell has third-party service orga-

---

* Joan Magretta, "The Power of Virtual Integration: An Interview with Dell Computer's Michael Dell," *Harvard Business Review*, March–April 1998, pp. 73–74.
† Ibid., p.76.

nizations available for on-site service and repair, telephone support has been central to helping customers troubleshoot their systems. This has required building an extensive infrastructure to aid support engineers who field customer calls with information about customers' past purchases. In addition, they access a comprehensive knowledge-base of known problems and fixes for Dell and third-party hardware and software products, as well as the processes and systems for handling returns, exchanges, and spare parts shipments. All of this infrastructure—customer databases, product information, and help desk knowledge bases—was in place before Dell decided to open up for business on the Web.

The Evolution of Dell's Internet-based Electronic Commerce Channel

LIKE THOSE OF many companies, Dell's first forays onto the Internet were tactical in nature, beginning with customer support. Often, a support call from a customer to a Dell technician would result in the recommendation that the customer obtain a new driver or some other software update from Dell. Customers had the option of having the update sent to them on a diskette, a relatively expensive process that took several days, or of downloading the software themselves. Software downloads were initially available from a Dell bulletin board site on Compuserve. By the late 1980s, Dell had opened up an Internet file transfer protocol (FTP) site as a mechanism for distributing software updates. The FTP site became very popular and provided one of the first lessons to Dell on the potential cost savings the Internet might represent. In fact, some customers could even download a patch while they were on the telephone with the Dell technician, who could then walk them through the installation and configuration of the update. This also allowed the technician to determine whether the update or patch solved the customer's problem. As a result, as many surveys have shown, Dell receives very high marks in customer satisfaction, not only on their products but also on customer support.

The History of Dell's Web Site

In early 1995, Dell launched its Web site as a means of providing marketing and product support information to a group of technologically savvy customers who were early Web adopters. This site was designed and managed by just a few people at Dell who had undertaken the initiative. They took the information that was used to support Dell's sales and support call center activities and coded it for Web access.

Very quickly, Dell's Web effort mushroomed, as the popularity of the Web created substantial customer interest. As customers flocked to the Web site, Dell's various marketing and technical support groups added more and more product descriptions and technical support information to keep up with customer demand. Customers began to help themselves to the information they needed to make purchasing decisions and to troubleshoot their own computer problems.

By October 1995, Dell added the first interactive application—a quote generator—to the Web site. Viewed as a sales support tool, this forms-based application let a customer configure a PC by selecting from a group of options (processor type, amount of memory, amount of disk storage, and so on) and receive a price quotation. Customers could add or remove components and see how doing so affected the system's price. They loved this capability! They stampeded to the site and began asking for the next step: on-line ordering.

By early 1996, the customer mandate was clear: Dell needed to get serious about giving customers the ability to configure and order their PCs via the Web. Scott Eckert, a senior marketing manager, and John Hatchett, a member of Dell's technical staff, began researching and designing an on-line configuration system that would hook directly into Dell's order entry and manufacturing systems.

Creating a Centralized Electronic Commerce Group

Although the logical next step seemed to be to allow customers to order their computers directly via the Web site, there were major organizational hurdles to overcome. You see, Dell isn't simply one homogeneous company; it is divided into several, largely autonomous business unit segments, organized by target market. These markets include federal government, consumer, small business, large corporate, medium corporate, state and local government, and education. A quasi-matrix organization has R&D and manufacturing working with each business unit on product definition and manufacturing. The business units describe the product requirements for their markets to the R&D organization, which is responsible for designing the products necessary to address those requirements. Manufacturing participates directly in this process to ensure that products will be built on time and cost-effectively.

Each of the business segment units has its own profit-and-loss responsibility, its own sales organization, and its own marketing organization. There is also an organizational component that overlies a geographic structure on the business segments, ensuring that the specific requirements and targets for each geographic region are met. The product group is a corporate entity. Manufacturing facilities are globally distributed. Much of the early Dell Web site development had been created and maintained in a fragmented fashion by the marketing groups within each of the different business units.

In early 1996, Dell's corporate management decided that it was extremely important for Internet activities throughout the organization to be coordinated within a central organization. They felt that by centralizing Internet development activities, they could better maintain Dell's standards of performance, availability, and quality. If various business units were allowed to continue to engage in their own efforts, the likely result would be inconsistency across sectors in one or more areas. This could impact more than just graphics and design; different organizations might come up with unique business processes and even customer profiles. Maintaining a consistent brand image for Dell has been a critical part of the Dell model, and maintaining high standards on the Web is a part of this tradition.

When a centralized organization to coordinate and set direction for Dell's Internet activities was first being considered, there was some resistance from various organizational units. The interest level in the Internet was very high throughout most of the Dell business units, and centralizing functions was seen by some as a possible threat to the freedom and flexibility to which the business units were accustomed. There was a very real risk that various groups would head off in different directions with their own Internet strategies, each with different goals, designs, and models for an Internet presence.

Despite this organizational resistance, Dell Online was formed as a new group within Dell in July 1996 as part of a strategic decision to significantly increase the company's investment in the Internet. Eckert was named the director of Dell Online. The formation of Dell Online was one of a short list of corporate initiatives emanating from top management. Internal market research and interviews with many of its customers had shown that the Internet was a potential source of significant growth for Dell, in its sales to both business and consumers. Part of the Internet investment was to take the time to evaluate available technologies and consider how they might be incorporated into Dell's one-to-one marketing effort. The Web was seen as a highly efficient communication medium that would play a significant role in extending the direct customer relationships on which Dell had built its business. At the same time, the move to the Web wasn't a revolution for Dell, just a logical extension to the existing Dell customer model and Dell's already advanced use of the Internet for service and support.

Eckert's charter was to take the fundamental elements of the successful Dell model—one-to-one relationship management, direct sales, and "high-touch" support—and leverage and refine them for the Internet. The primary difference was that the on-line customers would be helping themselves instead of interacting with a courteous, well-trained telephone sales representative or telephone support engineer. That meant that the systems had to be simple, easy to understand, and virtually foolproof.

Dell Online is not part of the core information technology organization at Dell. It was created outside of IT as a separate business group. This new organization was made responsible for worldwide coordination of Internet strategy and execution across the entire company. By the spring of 1997, there were thirty-two people in the organization, half of whom were business and marketing professionals; the other half were technology people actually engaged in building applications. The organization hosts its own servers and maintains its own operations. However, it views the operation of the Web site not as a technology function but as a business function.

The Evolution of Dell's Electronic Commerce Capabilities

FROM 1995 TO the present, Dell has continued to improve and refine its Web site, dell.com. There are two factors that have made Dell's Web business so successful. The first is the fact that Dell's original business model, conceived in 1984, translates superbly to the Web. The second is the company's relentless pursuit of opportunities to improve the buying and support experience for its profitable target market: corporate customers and educated consumers.

Configuration and Ordering

For many first-time purchasers, the core of the site remains the configuration, quoting, and ordering capabilities. Dell's Web site continues to be the industry benchmark in this area. Customers can move quickly and easily from browsing product marketing and technical information about different models of computers to configuring and pricing systems (laptops, desktops, workstations, and/or servers) to placing an order electronically to checking on the status of that order.

Many customers do their shopping and configuration on the Web, yet place their actual order by phone. Why? Often because they have one last question or maybe because they want the reassurance of talking with someone. In my case, it was because I couldn't figure out how to pay by check. Yet Eckert reported that Dell has been able to ascertain that the effort required to close a sale over the phone has been significantly reduced for purchases initiated on the Web site. Although many Web site customers still place a phone call to seal the deal, those that call are 1.5 times more likely to purchase than average callers. As a result, quotas for representatives handling Web calls have been ratcheted upward compared to those of the telephone-only representatives.

Accessing Order Status On-line

Dell.com provides order status for customers who are awaiting delivery of systems. By the first quarter of 1998, more than 40,000 people per week were checking the status of their orders on-line. This saves the customer from having to make a phone call, as well as saving Dell from having to provide call center resources to respond to a large volume of order status inquiries.

Service and Support

Dell has always provided twenty-four-hour technical support over the phone. In 1995, the company supplemented this by giving customers direct access via the Web to much of the information contained in Dell's own technical support knowledge base so that customers could diagnose and solve many of their own problems. In 1997, Dell introduced a much faster and more efficient form of self-service via the Web. Each computer that Dell ships has a service tag number assigned to it. By entering this number at the Web site, the customer is guided through an on-line troubleshooting session that is customized for the particular make and model machine she is using. This is, in fact, the same diagnostic and troubleshooting program that Dell's technical support representatives would walk you through on the phone, but you can do it yourself. If you still need hand-holding, when you call in, you enter your service tag number using a Touch-Tone phone, and the service technician is able to call up the troubleshooting scenario you were in the midst of and pick up from where you got stuck.

Going Global

In March of 1997, Dell launched a European site with seventeen country-specific home pages; much of this information (languages and pricing information) has been localized. By the end of 1997, Dell launched an electronic commerce site in Asia. By the first quarter of 1998, Dell had forty-six country-specific Web sites.

Customer-Specific Web Sites:
Dell Premier Pages Service

In 1997, Dell launched a capability called My Dell. Any customer could create a customized Web page for him- or herself on the Dell site. You could personalize the information you wanted to have appear on that page. For example, if you're interested only in laptops, you will be presented with information that relates to laptops. Or if you're an investor in the company (or a large customer) and you want to track information about the company's latest product announcements and market expansions, you can arrange to see all the latest press releases and investor information on your My Dell page. My Dell was soon replaced by Premier Pages.

Large corporate customers are vitally important to Dell, and by using the Web, Dell discovered that it can provide a set of services that enhance the relationship these customers have with the company. For both large- and small-account customers, Dell offers fully customized, password-protected Web sites, called Premier Pages, which provide one-stop shopping through an extranet application that can be accessed via the customer's own intranet. By the end of Dell's second quarter in fiscal 1999, the company had established more than 5,000 Premier Pages Web sites worldwide.

Each company's Premier Pages site offers a variety of on-line services ranging from the ability to order predetermined configurations negotiated in advance with Dell to up-to-date contact information for the Dell account team. Premier Pages sites also provide access to custom catalogs with pricing based on account-specific customer volume purchase agreements with Dell. Premier Pages sites also provide a custom window into Dell's on-line service and offer purchase history reports. Michael Dell himself is very bullish about Premier Pages. "One of our customers, for example, allows its

50,000 employees to view and select products on-line. They use their Premier Pages as an interactive catalog of all the configurations the company authorizes; employees can then price and order the PC they want. They are happy to have some choice, and Dell and the customer are both happy to eliminate the paperwork and sales time normally associated with corporate purchasing. That frees our salespeople to play a more consultative role." Premier Pages sites also let Dell's multinational customers offer better service to the employees in their international organizations. Michael Dell notes that 40 percent of Dell's multinational customers use the Premier Pages to make it easy for employees oversees to order, service, and maintain their computers.

Dell's customers like the Premier Pages capability because it saves them money. One customer told Michael Dell that he was able to reduce his procurement staff from sixteen people to four, thanks to the customized Premier Pages with his company's terms and conditions built in. Another CIO reported that his company was saving $2 million per year in support costs thanks to its use of Dell Premier Pages for running diagnostics, troubleshooting, and problem solving.

Evolving the Technical Infrastructure

Dell OnLine runs on multiple server farms made up of (what else?) mirrored Dell Poweredge servers. These servers provide Web content, commerce and noncommerce applications, and back-end SQL databases. Behind the production server farms sit testing, prototype, and development servers. The entire site is backed up nightly by a robust group of backup devices. The site's front-end Web servers hold static Web pages and are hosted via multiple mirrored copies of all data. These servers are the gateway to other applications and data behind the Web servers. They are all identically configured with Microsoft Windows NT 4.0, with option pack, Microsoft Internet Information Server (IIS) 4.0, Active Server Pages, and SQL 6.5.

Dell uses many of the capabilities of Microsoft's Site Server 3.0, Commerce Edition, including Site Analyst and Usage Analyst, Search Server, Push Server, Personalization and Membership System, and Commerce Server. Dell's core configuration is **NT 4.0** with option pack, IIS 4.0, Active Server Pages, and SQL 6.5.

One layer of application servers houses Dell's on-line store, which handles over $6 million a day in systems sales through its commerce applications. Another layer houses its service and support applications and its Premier Pages applications aimed at Dell's corporate customers. All these application layers interface with multiple database servers, which allow Dell to deliver dynamic Web pages.

The original Dell configurator was built using NeXT's WebObjects as a front end to an existing Tandem-based configuration system. Configuration information and pricing are stored on the legacy systems. The interface between WebObjects and the Dell legacy systems used Netweave as an integration layer. The ordering process on the Dell site was also a part of the WebObjects/ legacy application. However, Dell replaced the WebObjects configuration engine with a custom component object model (COM)– based application. The result is a home-grown component that fully integrates with the other Microsoft Site Server applications. Michael Dunn, the senior manager of operations and technology for Dell Online, reports that it was very difficult to find developers experienced in using WebObjects, while it has been much easier to attract and retain developers who are experienced in developing for the Microsoft environment.

Evolving the Content and Software Development

Dell follows strict development and staging procedures to constantly modify the core content and applications on its site. An extended authoring community actively participates in the day-to-day publishing of the site. All of Dell's Internet authors develop either HTML pages or applications on numerous servers. Some use Active Server Page (ASP) applications development via Inter-Dev, while some use Visual Basic to develop custom components and JavaScript to add sophistication to basic HTML. Content management is handled via Microsoft Visual Source Safe (VSS). Approved new content is then deployed to Dell's multiple servers and global server farms via Content Deployment Services (CDS).

Hosting and Managing the Site

Managing a site that gets the volume of traffic that Dell OnLine receives is a difficult challenge. Dell does what is called "multi-homing" of its Web site, using multiple Internet service providers, which route into multiple data centers. These house multiple routers, fire walls, intrusion detection systems, domain name servers, Cisco Distributed Director load-balancing units, fast Ethernet switches, real-time twenty-four-hour, seven-day site and application monitoring and alerting software.

Systems for Service and Support

Service and support systems are partly based on call-tracking systems from Edify Corporation and partly developed internally with some commercial tools. The raw data for product information and technical support are now produced and maintained in HTML format. Edify is used for all support-call tracking and recording. These systems have been integrated into the dell.com site wherever possible.

Results

AS OF THE first quarter of 1998, the Dell Web site was receiving an average of 1.5 million customer visits each week! The Dell configurator is being used by one third of those visitors. The resulting revenues were running at $6 million in sales of computers and peripherals per day from the Web site by the second quarter of 1998. Revenue from the site has been growing faster than the number of visitors to the site, reflecting a growing percentage of visitors who become buyers.

Although it is true that a portion of the customers ordering from the Web site would have ordered over the telephone, customer surveys have indicated that nearly a third of the customers who buy computers on the Dell Web site would not have made purchases otherwise. The quality of the site was reflected in the finding that 80 percent of the on-line buyers surveyed would buy on-line from Dell again in the future.

Equally important is the fact that the systems ordered from the Web site generally end up with a higher configuration price than the average price of a system sold by Dell over the telephone. It appears that, as customers, we tend to upsell ourselves naturally when we are serving ourselves. We don't need a salesperson to recommend more memory or a leather carrying case. In fact, many of us are more likely to add on purchases when someone isn't "pressuring" us to buy more.

The Web site does not seem to have reduced the volume of telephone calls to Dell. This is hard to assess, however, since the company has been growing by approximately 40 to 50 percent a year, an increase in overall volume that could cloak a shift from the telephone to the Web.

Patty's Rx for Dell

Competition is breathing hotly down Dell's neck. Compaq Computer has recently revamped its ordering and manufacturing processes so that it will be able to build to order in 1998. Gateway 2000 has long followed the same direct sales model as Dell, and Gateway too offers an easy-to-use Web site that enables customers to configure and purchase their computers online. Compaq is pursuing both the high-end corporate market and the low-end mass consumer market. Dell attempted a foray into consumer retail channels but beat a hasty retreat when the company discovered it could not profitably sustain that business. Yet now with over $2 billion per year coming from customers who buy via the Web, Dell has launched a new product marketing division to focus on consumers.

Dell is definitely on the right track to sustain a highly profitable high-growth business. This is a business that is predicated on knowing who your customers are. So far, Dell leads its competitors in having the most complete customer information base. And unlike many of its competitors, Dell can sell as cost-effectively to small businesses as it can to large corporations.

So how can Dell build on the strong foundation it has in place? The company needs to continue to pursue its relationship management strategy by pushing the Premier Pages concept down from its largest corporate accounts to even the smallest of businesses. Small companies want the same kind of transparency in dealing with Dell that larger corporations do. They may not have the same purchasing clout, and they may not make as large demands on the manufacturer in terms of requests for special software and peripheral configurations. But they have the same needs for a consistent, easy-to-maintain set of computer systems, purchased cost-effectively. Like large corporations, small companies need help managing their computer assets. Keeping track of different models and configurations of computers is not something on which businesspeople want to spend their time. And small businesses are even more likely than larger companies to need exquisite and cost-effective technical support because they are less likely to have in-house technical staffs.

So my prescription for Dell is that the company continue to focus on the business market but extend its reach way down into the smallest companies worldwide. By using its Web channel to market, sell, and support these small-business customers, Dell can build a franchise that will be hard to beat. The technical support function is by far the hardest area to grow and maintain. Putting the infrastructure into place to answer questions and troubleshoot repairs from an end-user base of 10 million and growing is no mean feat. Although the corporate standard is to answer customers' technical support e-mail queries within forty-eight hours, I have personally sent e-mails that have gone unanswered for a much longer period of time. The company clearly has some work to do to shore up its interactive technical support e-mail handling capability. Unlike in a call center, where you can control the volume of calls, you can't control the volume of support e-mails you receive. Dell clearly needs to invest in much better staffing and automated routing and handling of technical support questions.

Moreover, by continuing to build, maintain, and continuously improve its customer profile information, Dell could beat out the competition by knowing exactly who the majority of its 10 million plus customers are. Remember, while Dell sells its computers to the technical staff, the purchasing agent, or the department head, each end user who actually uses the computer is Dell's ultimate customer. By using the Web to advantage, particularly for purchasing, help desk, and support functions, Dell can cement close relationships with the end users of its computers within both large and small companies. Then, when those end customers move on to other companies, they'll sow the seeds of that customer loyalty in their new jobs.

"Take-Aways" from the Dell Computer Story

1. Recognize that having a direct relationship with each of your end customers provides valuable information you can use to better manage your business. By using the Web to support these relationships, you can expand the number of end customers you touch and learn from exponentially.

2. Make sure that your Web site is well integrated into your telephone-based sales, order entry, and service functions. Customers should be able to begin an interaction on the Web and flip over to talk to someone on the phone without starting over again. If a customer places a

sizeable order on the Web, the order should be confirmed both by Web and by phone.

3. Notice that customers will configure and purchase relatively expensive products via the Web if you make it easy enough for them to do.

4. Give customers access to all the same troubleshooting and help information that your own technical support people have. They'll be grateful, and it will save you a lot of customer service time.

5. Give customers easy access to status information about their orders placed and the resolution of their service calls.

6. Design your Web site so that customers can bring portions of it into their own intranets, integrate it into their own internal processes, and tailor it for their own employees to use, the way Dell does with its Premier Pages. Not only will that lower your customers' cost of doing business with you, it will also keep them as loyal customers longer and extend your reach so that you'll begin to build direct relationships with their employees—your real end customers.

LET CUSTOMER HELP THEMSELVES:

iPrint
www.iprint.com

Executive Summary

iPrint is a good example of how a commodity business—printing business cards and small quantities of stationery—can be transformed by focusing on the end consumer's experience. iPrint discovered that people cared a lot about how their business cards and stationery look, but most people aren't trained graphic designers. They needed an easy way to create and preview professional-quality designs before items were printed. By developing a Web-based custom printing service and providing its service and software through a variety of channels, iPrint hopes to become the "CheckFree of the quick-printing business"—the company that handles all the complexity behind the scenes so commercial printers can better serve their end customers.

Critical Success Factors in the iPrint Story	
Target the right customers	✰ Let customers help themselves
Own the customer's total experience	Help customers do their jobs
✓ Streamline business processes that impact the customer	✰ Deliver personalized service
Provide a 360-degree view of the customer relationship	Foster community
✰ = Featured in this discussion	✓ = Touched on in this discussion

iPrint: Letting Businesspeople Create Commercial-Quality Printing

ROYAL P. FARROS is an inveterate entrepreneur with a deep understanding of a specialized niche: preprint processes. In other words, he understands all the steps required for a commercial printer to put words and graphics onto paper. First a word about his background; then we'll talk about how he's using the Internet to create a new business model by making it easy for customers to help themselves.

Farros's first company was T/Maker. It introduced ClickArt (the first electronic clip art), WriteNow, and PFS:First Publisher. Its customers were graphic designers who used computers to create professional-looking documents. When T/Maker was acquired by Deluxe, the fourth largest commercial printer in the United States, Farros created and ran that company's Electronic Direct business. His team designed electronic printing kiosks for Staples, the large discount office supply chain. Here Farros encountered a new set of customers: businesspeople who wanted professional-looking business cards and stationery but who didn't want or need to know about fonts, point sizes, leading, runarounds, and all the other esoterica that make up commercial typography. Not only were these small business customers naive about typography, they also weren't particularly computer-literate. So the kiosk used a touch-screen ATM-like interface. Customers didn't have to figure out drop-down menus or drag-and-drop manipulations. The kiosks were very successful. Before, customers would select the "look" they wanted for their business cards from a book of samples and fill in a form by hand with the information they wanted to appear on the card. There was no way to preview the results. With the kiosk interface, customers could type in their copy, select the look, make adjustments, preview their cards, print out a hard copy, and place the order. The error rate on these specialty print orders dropped from a costly 16 percent to 1 percent! Kiosks were rolled out into 425 stores across the country.

Introducing Self-Service Commercial Printing via the Internet

FARROS LEFT DELUXE in 1995, and with Deluxe's blessing, he assembled a team from the people he'd worked with both at T/Maker and at Deluxe to go the next step: to bring commercial printing to the masses via the Internet. iPrint opened its doors for business in December 1996, billing itself as the first "Discount Printing and CyberStationery Shop of the Future." Farros had inked a deal with Business Cards Tomorrow (BCT), the nation's largest wholesale printer. BCT was one of the first commercial printers to offer courier delivery anywhere in the country. The combination of fast turnaround and wholesale pricing was exactly what Farros was looking for. Later, iPrint added relationships with other commercial printers—for greeting cards, Post-it notes, mugs, T-shirts, and other specialty items.

Designing Commercial Print Jobs

When you log on to iPrint.com, you are entering the iPrint "store." Here you can design, proof, and order a variety of custom-printed products: business cards, stationery, labels, Post-it notes, greeting cards, and so on. You can also design "cyberstationery" for free—business cards you can insert into your e-mail messages, for example. The process of selecting and designing each item is very straightforward. You simply select the type of item you want to create, choose the size, and select from among a series of proposed designs. You then enter the information you want to appear by filling in a form. Within a few seconds, you'll see your "typeset" piece on the screen. You can select different fonts, change font sizes, move items around, and select from a set of graphic clip art or import your own logo, all using a simple push-button interface. You don't have to point, click, and drag items around. Nor do you need to pull down menus and choose options. Nor do you need to know about typography.

Once you like the look of your piece, you can select ink colors and type of paper and complete your order by using a credit card. Your print job will arrive in the time specified (usually within two days, longer if it's a two- or three-color job). iPrint's printing prices are considerably lower than those of most commercial print shops, particularly for low-quantity orders.

What's unusual about iPrint is how deceptively simple it is. As someone who has been involved with commercial-quality typesetting and printing all my life, I can appreciate all of the behind-the-scenes complexity that's required to allow naive customers to produce high-quality printed products they can be proud of.

Customer Service

Farros is rightly proud of the customer service offered at the iPrint site. First, the company has done a good job of providing notification of the status of your print job at each step in the process. You are notified by e-mail both when the order is placed and when it is printed and shipped (and your credit card is billed). At any point, you can go to the Web site and review the status of your order. Once your order is shipped, you can follow its progress to your home or office as UPS moves it across the country. Second, the Web site contains a useful set of frequently asked questions and answers. And, finally, you can ask specific questions by e-mail, phone, or fax.

Your print jobs are maintained on-line for you. So if you want to reorder or make modifications to a previously ordered item, you simply log on, enter the iPrint-supplied ID number for the item in question, and go from there. iPrint keeps your print jobs on-line for a minimum of two years.

Evolving the Technical Infrastructure

There are a number of elements in the technology that iPrint had to develop that are quite complex and therefore will be hard to emulate. First and foremost is the push-button user interface combined with desktop publishing functionality that has evolved over the last five years. iPrint's custom-designed software includes a powerful typesetting and imaging engine that calculates the exact placement of each line of text. The engine creates a foolproof ready-to-print file in portable Encapsulated Postscript format that is then transmitted electronically to the commercial printer.

The second area of complexity was the development of the "shopping cart" functionality. Unlike most on-line ordering or catalog applications, where the customer selects an item which has a fixed price and specifies the color and quantity, in the case of printing jobs, the variables involved are much more complex. For each order, there are many attributes and variables: ink colors, paper weight, quantity discount break points, and so on. Therefore, iPrint had to develop a multivariable, constraint-based ordering application. They did this using a SQL Server database application that can support tens of thousands of pricing tables. This has proved useful as the company inks deals with different channel partners, each of which wants to establish its own pricing and discount structures.

For its secure payment infrastructure, iPrint uses the combination of Netscape's Enterprise Server, CyberCash credit card– processing software, and Wells Fargo's merchant banking capabilities. However, Farros reports that getting this all to work smoothly was not just a matter of plugging everything together. It took about three months to get all the kinks out. Farros says that the saving grace was that his developers had implemented very complete diagnostics, so they were able to track down and fix inconsistencies in the interfaces among the various systems.

For scalability, iPrint began using server clustering of its Windows NT servers in May 1997. This has allowed the company to continue to add additional Web servers to sustain performance as traffic to the site grows. One other tip Farros offers: the company has rewritten its code so that each module remains persistently in memory. One NT server runs all of these persistent modules. You don't want to have to launch a new executable each time a remote user starts to use a new function. That slows things down too much.

iPrint's Business Model

As WITH MANY Web businesses, the iPrint Web site is the tip of the iceberg for Farros's business model. It's a proof of concept. It's where the iPrint software is developed and refined with the toughest customers in the world. But the company also has many other channels through which it distributes its software and services. iPrint plans to leverage the Internet to become the world's leading "neutral" supplier of quick printing. The common denominator for all these channels is that end customers design their own products and the rest of the work is handled behind the scenes. Yet customers always know exactly where their orders stand. Here are some of iPrint's distribution channels:

1. **DIRECT TO CONSUMER.** iPrint is targeting consumers who know how to use a bank ATM machine but don't feel comfortable using today's typical graphical point, click, and drag, pull-down menu, double-click type of interface. The company also welcomes computer-knowledgeable consumers who simply want the fastest, most convenient way to create and order commercially printed items. The company's focus is on personalized and customized products. Today, these are stationery items such as business cards, letterhead, labels, or Post-it notes. Soon they will include business form items such as checks, purchase orders, or invoices, or even advertising specialty items.

2. **DIGITAL PHOTOGRAPHY.** iPrint intends to specialize in giving high-tech end-users an easy way to convert the photos they've taken on their digital cameras into commercially printed items: calendars, T-shirts, mouse pads, mugs, and so on. For example, Intel's digital cameras promote iPrint's services. And iPrint is in discussions with OfficeMax and Office Depot, which sell digital camera packs, to lure customers to the iPrint site for their specialty printing needs.

3. **CORPORATE CUSTOMERS.** But the end-consumer direct market is only one of iPrint's channels. The company is also targeting the corporate market via direct sales. One of iPrint's first large business customers was the Internal Revenue Service. All 2.1 million government employees, including IRS workers, are required to purchase their own business cards. Yet the IRS's cards must conform to the agency's standards in terms of the logo used, the typeface, and the placement of information. So iPrint created a customized Web site for the IRS. Employees can log on, create their own business cards using the IRS-approved template, supply their personal credit card number, and complete the order. Rockwell International is another one of iPrint's early corporate customers. The human resources department at Rockwell wanted to control the process of issuing business cards, so a new em-

ployee or a person who is promoted and given a new title can go on-line and order a new set of business cards.

4. COMMERCIAL PRINTERS. Another major channel that iPrint has been successfully pursuing is commercial printers themselves. Instead of by-passing commercial printers or competing with them, Farros wants to turn them into business partners. For example, a commercial printer who already has close working relationships with several large corporate customers can license iPrint's print shop software to install on each customer's in-house intranet. Company employees would be able to design and order their business cards, stationery, and business forms using that company's standard design and logo, according to a set of business rules that could be maintained by the client company. A typical business rule might be "You can't place a new business card order within three months of your last 500-card order," for example.

5. QUICK PRINTERS. Another category of commercial printers that Farros has wooed as partners is the "quick printers" who serve individuals and businesses across the country. Farros sees this market as an opportunity to revisit the self-service kiosk idea. This time, the kiosks won't be expensive, hard-to-maintain PCs, but low-cost, trouble-free network PCs. Walk-in customers can use the in-store kiosk to design and place their orders. In-house staff can use the same terminal to generate reports and interact with iPrint and to access the rest of the Internet. Customers with Web access from home can design their orders and send them off to the local quick-printing shop. Sir Speedy, the largest chain of custom printers in the world, is an iPrint licensee. CopyMax has an on-line print shop called PrintLink. This is a private-labeled version of the iPrint software.

6. SPECIALTY SERVICES. Farros's imagination knows no bounds. He is wooing Mail Boxes Etc., a chain with 3,400 locations worldwide, to add business card and stationery printing services to its packaging and mailing services. He's talking to a Japanese company about providing custom-printed "kitty phone" cards for teen-age girls who use a "kitty phone"—a very popular cell phone among Japanese girls—so they can pass their phone numbers to each other. The list goes on and on.

iPrint expects to generate 50 percent of its revenues from partnering with commercial printers and quick printers and 50 percent of its revenues from the combination of direct consumer and corporate end-user channels.

Results

THE iPRINT WEB site has won numerous awards for its powerful ease of use. Revenue and site traffic are increasing about 25 percent per month. Although the thirty-person company was not yet profitable in 1997, after twelve months of business, Farros did succeed in raising $3.3 million of first-round funding from Intel, IT Ventures, and a handful of high-profile industry investors. In 1998, iPrint continues to grow its business using the three-pronged strategy that has been working so far: going directly to end consumers via the Internet, signing up corporate customers, and partnering with commercial printers to help them serve their customers better.

Most important, customers love the ease of use and the service they receive from the site. Here are some examples:

Subject: I love iPrint & want to tell the world!!

Hi,

I am a deliriously happy customer. Previously, I would have spent at least $2,000 for design, plus printing costs, plus many hours of my time, to get business cards and stationery of approximately the same quality.

Diane H.

Madam or Sir:

This is an absolutely amazing Web site. I've ordered business cards from local printers for years but have never been satisfied, because I could never quite visualize the final product. I will be placing an order this Wednesday but wanted to know ahead of time whether it was possible for me to ask when making the order if iPrint could determine what the appropriate size of my graphic should be to make the cards look their best? I thank you in advance for your response to this question and for the fantastic service. You can look for my order on Wednesday.

Atty. Rod M., Wisconsin

Follow-up Message

Madam or Sir:

I recently placed the above order for business cards from you. I received them this week. You "knocked my socks off"! The service was prompt and individualized, and the product is first-rate. You'll have me as a steady customer. I will likely be ordering stationery and envelopes in the near future. Please place me on a list to let me know when labels and checks are available. Again, thanks for everything.

Atty. Rod M., Wisconsin

The business cards for Amida Press arrived, and we're very pleased with the result of ordering from iPrint on-line. The cards are far nicer than the computer screen version depicted and are a very high quality. We will be proud to offer this card in the course of doing business. Thank you so much for providing such a valuable service and product to the on-line business community. Your personalized and prompt attention went far beyond what one usually receives in a walk-in print shop . . . and I didn't have to leave the office!

Ann M.

Patty's Rx for iPrint

Farros's new company is off to a great start. iPrint has three important next steps to take. First, the tiny company needs to focus on scalability. Today, the company processes hundreds of orders per day. If Farros's distribution strategies pan out, soon it will be looking at hundreds of thousands of orders per day. The issue is not how to scale the Web site but how to streamline more of the back-end processes of communicating with its wholesale printers. Today, although iPrint immediately acknowledges the customer's order via e-mail and customers can track their UPS shipments, the printers iPrint works with don't automatically notify iPrint by e-mail when the job is put on press and when it's shipped out the door; much of this communication is handled by phone. Tomorrow, iPrint needs to have streamlined workflows from the end customer through the print shop and out through the delivery company. UPS, the shipping company, is developing a business-event-based infrastructure that will allow all its logistics partners to track processes within and across organizations. I think that iPrint might want to piggyback on that effort.

Next, iPrint needs to expand its design libraries. In 1998, the company plans to offer hundreds of personal and business checks, business forms, second sheets, and memo pads. For each type of product it offers, iPrint currently offers two dozen starting designs from which to choose. This is too few. Ideally, the company should commission many more designs from world-class designers. Customers are already asking for many more clip art items from which to choose. Again, it's a simple matter of commissioning artwork. This could be done on a royalty basis. iPrint could pay royalties as the artwork is actually used. Finally, iPrint needs to offer a larger collection of type fonts, including many "name brands."

Finally, iPrint needs to make it easier for customers to give it pre-existing designs they want to reproduce. Of course, most companies already have their own logos, and many have corporate standard designs. Today, it's a relatively easy matter to take any logo you already have in electronic form and place it on the business card or stationery you're designing at the iPrint site. But it isn't as straightforward to re-create, exactly, an entire design you already have (since you begin with one of iPrint's standard design templates). The next step would be to allow customers to send in a printed version of the design they want to re-create. This would require some prepress production work on iPrint's part, but this is something that the company can easily "job out" to a local prepress shop and is a service customers are used to paying for. The benefit to the customer would be the ability for even small businesses to have electronic versions of their corporate designs stored and maintained electronically by iPrint, so they could order new stationery, business cards, forms, and so forth on an as-needed basis.

"Take-Aways" from the iPrint Story

1. Use a single, Web-based infrastructure and a single set of Web-based application services to reach end customers through multiple distribution channels.

2. By targeting naive end users as your customers and using what they need as the design center for your offerings, you will wind up with a capability that is easy for all to use, whether they are experts or beginners. This is a particularly successful approach when your service is something people use infrequently. Since most of us need business cards only once or twice a year, it's unlikely that we'll become expert at creating them.

3. Note that if you are developing an offering in which the ordering process involves a complex set of interlocking constraints, you'll need to design or buy a more elaborate ordering system than the typical "shopping cart" functionality used on most Web sites.

4. If you offer a service that would be of value to businesspeople, consider

whether it makes sense to develop an intranet version of your offering—something that companies could put inside their fire walls to offer their employees. This is what National Semiconductor, iPrint, and Dell Computer have all done.

5. Note that "coopetition" is the name of the game on the Internet. Farros may seem to be competing with your local printer, but he's really wooing that company as a partner.

Let Customers Help Themselves: Lessons Learned

There's no question that today's customers want to be able to help themselves to information, transactions, and status information twenty-four hours a day, 365 days a year. Why are Web-based systems becoming at least as popular as automated phone systems for this purpose? First, Web sites are less inflexible than interactive voice response (IVR) systems. They don't shoehorn you into a single set of options that may or may not meet your needs. Second, Web sites can offer a lot more information to help the customer make a decision or answer a question. The alternative, of course, is to staff a round-the-clock call center with knowledgeable, well-trained people who have at their fingertips all the information about your products and about each customer. This is an expensive option. And most of the companies that have invested in call centers are also investing in Web sites. Why? Because many customers don't want to interact with a person, particularly if they're just looking for information and are not ready to make a purchase yet. The best combination is the one in which customers can help themselves on the Web but get a real person on the phone with the touch of a button. Dell isn't quite there yet, but I expect dell.com to be one of the first Web sites to offer this integrated capability.

End Customers Will Design Their Own Products

NOTE THAT THE two examples featured in this chapter—Dell and iPrint—have both embarked on business models that are predicated on having direct interactions with their end customers. In both cases, end customers design their own custom offerings, and these are "built to order." Moreover, both companies have designed their Web-based offerings in such a way that they can be brought in-house by large corporate customers and tailored with that company's specific set of options. Then the company's employees—the real end customers—can select from the available options, configure their own product, place the order, and accept delivery, while the appropriate corporate account is charged.

Needed: A Configuration Rules Engine

IN ORDER TO support the ability for customers to configure their own computers or design their own business cards, these companies have developed sophisticated configuration engines. As Royal Farros explains, designing a business card may seem like a simple operation, but there are literally thousands of combinations and permutations of ink, paper, and color, each with its own ramifications in terms of turnaround time and price. Configuring computers is also not a simple matter; there are so many options from which to choose. In both cases, a business rules approach is used to constrain the choices the customer has at his disposal. And large databases of choices and rules need to be kept constantly up to date. The benefit of this approach is that customers spend their own time experimenting with configurations. You aren't tying up an expensive sales resource to walk them through options. This is the ideal allocation of resources in many cases. Sure, there are customers who would rather have you tell them what they need (and both companies do this with canned options and special offers), but a large proportion of your customers will *want* to configure their own products.

Payback: Bathe Your Company (and Partners) in Customer Information

DELL IS JUST one of many companies that have discovered and harvested the benefits of dealing directly with end customers. The company uses the information it receives from these customers' "what if" sessions and from the orders they actually place to inform its inventory management and procurement processes. Dell's suppliers know exactly what orders are being placed on a daily basis. They don't have to guess. By keeping its inventory to a minimum and passing customer order data to its suppliers in real time, Dell has the leanest cost structure in its industry.

The other advantage Dell reaps from having a great deal of information about its customers is its ability to segment the market and to focus its product marketing efforts. Two years ago, Dell had no consumer product line. Today, it has a consumer division. Why? Because it noticed that the number of PCs being bought by end consumers from its Web site was on the increase.

Remember, the more you let customers do on their own, the more you're likely to learn about what they want and need from you in the future. Your job is to make it as easy as possible for customers to help themselves and then execute flawlessly. You'll be rewarded with customer loyalty, referrals, and profits.

Help Customers Do Their Jobs

Business-to-business Internet commerce is booming! I predict that revenues of at least $310 billion will be generated in business-to-business electronic commerce on the Internet in 1998. But that's only the orders placed directly on the Web. It doesn't count the $100 billion or so of orders that were researched on the Web before a phone call was made or a purchase order faxed in to close the deal. It also doesn't count the billions of dollars that will be saved by redirecting a percentage of customers' fact-finding away from call centers (at an average cost of $10 per call) to the Web (at an average cost of $.50).

The business-to-business market is the fastest-growing area of electronic commerce today and promises to continue to be so. But how can your company cash in on this bonanza? When your customers are businesspeople who use your product or service in their jobs, you need to do more than just make it easy for them to get information, place orders, check on the status of orders, and get help. Those are all prerequisites. To win over business customers, you need to understand exactly where your product fits within customers' business day (or night!), how they need to use it, and how you can make it easier for them to do so. In the case studies that follow, you'll see how Boeing makes it easy for its commercial airline customers both to manage their spare parts inventories and to procure the parts they need to service their planes. And you'll see how PhotoDisc makes it easy for graphic designers to select and acquire the photos they need for their clients' print and media projects. In both cases, the services offered provide an extension and an enhancement to the way the customer had been doing his job.

Here are some of the key ingredients you'll want to be sure you get right if you have business customers:

- Develop a deep understanding of how your customers do their jobs.
- Continuously refine your business processes to make it easier for your customers to do their jobs.
- Give customers direct access to your inventory.
- Give customers the ammunition and tools they need to make purchasing decisions.
- Prepare bills the way your customers need them.
- Make it easy for your customers to satisfy their customers.

Of course, what you're really trying to do is to make your business a necessary extension of your customers' businesses. The points listed here are really the bare minimum. The companies that will excel in this area over the next five years will become so electronically intertwined with their customers that it will be very difficult to tell where one company stops and the other begins. This borderless business model will become the way most organizations do business in the twenty-first century. If your company isn't well on its way to practicing these principles, you're going to be locked out soon!

Develop a Deep Understanding of How Your Customers Do Their Jobs

ONE OF THE first case studies in this book, the one featuring National Semiconductor, was a great example of learning to understand how customers do their jobs. One of the first steps Phil Gibson's team took was to survey the customers they were targeting. The survey asked customers, step by step, how they decided what chips they were going to procure. They discovered that most designers started by surveying the field—researching the capabilities of the current products on offer. To do this, they relied on the volumes of material they had already been given by each of the major suppliers. Most said they began with the binders of data sheets they had on their shelves. A few used CD-ROM catalogs. Many of them said they'd then check with the vendors' sales reps to make sure they had the latest information, and a few said they would look on the Web for product updates. This information told National Semi where to start: it needed to make it easy for design engineers to get the most current information about its products without worrying about keeping loose-leaf binders up to date or having to pick up the phone to call a sales rep. The fact that a few customers were already looking on the Web pointed them in the right direction.

Next they discovered that when engineers look for a part, they want to be able to search based on the parameters they are seeking: low voltage, a certain price point, a particular function, or a minimum clock speed, for example. Finding something that met all the criteria was time-consuming if a customer had to leaf back and forth through catalogs. So National Semi scoured the countryside for a parametric search engine it could use on its Web site. The company found one, but it had to be rewritten (in Java) to do the job.

Then it learned that once engineers had pinpointed a few products with the right specs, the next things they needed were the information and tools required to evaluate the chips for their project: detailed technical specifications, software simulations they could run against their own data, and samples of the chips they could test in the lab. So National Semi made it easy for engineers to download detailed data sheets, download software simulations, and order sample chips, each with a single click.

Continuously Refine Your Business Processes to Make It Easier for Your Customers to Do Their Jobs

ONCE YOU UNDERSTAND your customers' business processes you have to redesign your processes to fit the way they want to work. As you do so, you'll discover new ways you can save time and money. Boeing redesigned its information systems to give customers access to its spare parts inventory information so they could see what parts were in stock and what each would cost. Customers loved that functionality because it helped them plan ahead. But they needed another piece of information: Where was the part warehoused? This made a difference to customers who had repair facilities and airplanes scattered around the world. So Boeing noted the warehouse location of each part in inventory.

National Semiconductor continues to refine its Web-based systems to cut steps out of the searching and ordering process. When it launched its Web site in 1995, customers typically needed 8 clicks to get onto the site, find what they needed, and get off. By mid-1997, the average was 2.5 clicks. National Semi watches what its customers do on the site and continues to streamline the interaction process to make it easier and faster for them to do their jobs. But it doesn't just offer its Web site to design engineers via the external Internet; it will also deliver its Web site directly into your company. Tektronix, one of National Semi's big customers, liked the site so much it wanted to make the site part of its own internal systems. So

National Semi delivered an intranet version of the site to Tektronix. This site runs within Tektronix's fire walls and is customized to feature the kinds of chips Tektronix needs for the products Tektronix designs and builds.

Give Customers Direct Access to Your Inventory

ONE OF THE most profound changes afoot in electronic commerce is the ability for customers to peer into your inventory electronically. Time-pressed customers aren't satisfied to know about price and capabilities; they want to know what you have on hand and how soon they can have it. We see this trend in both business-to-consumer and business-to-business electronic commerce. And it's becoming a major competitive differentiator. Earlier, we profiled American Airlines and described all the work that had gone into designing its Web site. In January 1997, however, American's competitors began offering a capability that American still didn't have: the ability to pick a seat from a diagram of available seats left on the plane. Then American had to play catch-up. The company knew that customers weren't satisfied just to see fares and schedules and book their tickets electronically; they wanted to pick the seats they'd be sitting in from the available inventory.

As we've already mentioned, the Boeing case study you're about to read deals with this topic. But so, in a very different way, does the PhotoDisc case that follows. PhotoDisc's "inventory" consists of a database of digitized photographs. Unlike airplane spare parts or seats on a plane, this inventory is never depleted. However, in order to select the photograph that best meets their design requirements, customers needed ways to see into that photographic database—to search through it in all the ways they think about photographs (by topic, color, mood, design, and so on).

Here's another analogous example, which again stretches our definition of "inventory" a little. A&a Printers is a small print shop in Palo Alto, California. Back in 1996, A&a developed a quite amazing Web site (www.aaprint.com) for its customers. Customers could use tools on the site to do their jobs: they could get quotes for different-size print runs with different paper stocks or estimate the width of a binding for a 200-page booklet that would be printed on 25-pound stock, so they could typeset the right-size type for the spine. But one of the most popular features of the site was the ability to see the availability of the different types of printing presses the company had. You could look at the big offset press, and you'd see a calendar with the hours colored in green if press time was available and in red if the time was already allocated to another customer. You could plan ahead and schedule when your job needed to arrive at the printer by knowing what press time was available. When I complimented the owner on this feature, he laughed and explained that there was more to the application than met the eye. He said that his customers all had different styles when it came to meeting deadlines. Some would call on Tuesday and say that a job would be ready on Thursday, but it was never actually ready till the following Monday. Others were always accurate in their estimates. So, he explained, each customer who logs in sees a different version of the press availability calendar. The customer whose estimates are accurate will see the real schedule. The customer whose estimates are always off by three days will see a schedule that has been "doctored" to induce them to get their work in sooner!

Give Customers the Ammunition and Tools They Need to Make Purchasing Decisions

THE PHOTODISC CASE study that follows gives an exquisite example of the kinds of tools you may need to provide to customers to make it easy for them to purchase your product. Bill Heston, senior vice president of business development, recognized that the graphic designers who purchased digital photos from his company didn't work in a vacuum. They needed to convince the rest of their design team, and their customer, that the image they'd selected was the right one for the job on hand. So Heston's team came up with a way for a designer to pick out his favorite photos, annotate them, and invite the other members of his design team to comment on his choices, make their own selections, reach a consensus, and then invite the customer onto the PhotoDisc Web site to cast the deciding vote among the front-runners.

As another example, Cisco Systems discovered that customers were having trouble purchasing its products because they were so complex. It was difficult for customers to come up with the configuration they needed in order to get an accurate price quote. So the company invested in a new software application—a configuration engine—and entered all the configuration constraints related to each product (for example, this router must be combined with one of these two network interface boards and this software package). Then it let customers configure their own products right on their Web site. That way, customers could experiment with different configurations and price points, but they would always wind up with a system that would work.

And of course, as we've already mentioned, National Semiconductor lets customers download software simulations, order sample chips, and interact directly with product designers by e-mail to answer any technical questions that aren't answered by the company's technical documentation.

Prepare Bills the Way Your Customers Need Them

FRANKLY, MOST COMPANIES don't think enough about billing when they think about electronic commerce applications. In business-to-consumer electronic commerce, the trend is toward purchasing by credit card, preferably by having your credit card number on file with the merchant. In the world of business-to-business electronic commerce, however, billing looms large in customers' decisions about whom to continue to do business with. If bills aren't accurate or if they can't be configured the way they need to allocate costs, it's just too much work and they're going to take their business elsewhere. Telephone companies have had the biggest challenge dealing with their billing systems. As we saw, in the Bell Atlantic case, that company focused first on its large corporate customers when it redesigned its billing systems. Why? Because those are the customers that need to have their telephone bills customized by geography, by division, by product line, or by department. Every company wants its done a slightly different way.

PhotoDisc discovered that its large corporate customers—advertising agencies with a number of different client projects—needed to have their bills broken down by project. Then the company discovered that one-person design shops had the same need. They might purchase three photos in a single credit card transaction, but they needed to bill these to three separate clients, and they needed their statement to reflect the different project names so they could keep them straight.

Make It Easy for Your Customers to Satisfy Their Customers

AT THE END of the day, you're trying to streamline your customers' jobs so they can meet their own customers' needs as easily as possible. For design engineers, the name of the game is designing innovative new products that are cost-effective to produce faster than someone else can. Therefore the faster a chip designer, such as National Semi, can get advance information to the potential market, the sooner those engineers can design new appliances with those chips. One other way that National Semi speeds up this process is by streamlining the procurement of the sample lots that designers need to make their prototypes for market testing. Typically, they want to procure these small lots of production-quality chips within twenty-four or forty-eight hours so that they can put the prototypes together and get out into the field to get customer feedback. By linking its low-volume catalog suppliers directly into its purchasing resources Web site, National Semi streamlined this market testing phase.

In PhotoDisc's case, every step in the selection process is designed with the end customer in mind: free low-resolution photos that can be used as "comps" to print and show the customer, a "light box" where the end customer can be shown the selected photos, even royalty-free licensing terms, so the customer doesn't have to worry about how many copies he's going to print or whether a brochure is going to be distributed internationally. By licensing a photo from PhotoDisc, he can use it any way he chooses.

Ingram Micro, the world's largest wholesaler of computers, software, and peripherals, invested a huge amount of money in codifying and organizing all the information a purchaser would need to know about each of the 50,000 products it sells. Ingram Micro's partners—the companies that resell computers and software to end customers via stores, catalogs, and systems integrators—can now easily offer their customers customized electronic catalogs on the Web by simply tailoring the information Ingram Micro provides them.

Johnson & Higgins/Marsh & McLennan, the world's largest insurance brokerage for businesses, linked its customers electronically to all the relevant insurance underwriters, who now receive the clients' requests for proposals electronically and can respond electronically, dramatically shortening the time it takes to negotiate these large and complex insurance contracts. By making it much easier for its corporate customers to do their jobs, J&H has ensured its role as the valued middleman in the process.

Now let's take a closer look behind the scenes at what it took for Boeing and PhotoDisc to make it easier for their customers to do their jobs.

Boeing
www.boeing.com

Executive Summary

The customers for Boeing's spare parts are operations managers for the world's largest airlines. They need up-to-the minute information about the availability, location, and current price of the spare parts they need to repair and maintain the airplanes in their care. Boeing designed a Web front end to its preexisting spare parts inventory and EDI system. Within a few months, customers were flocking to the Web site to run queries, get information, and place orders. Call center and fax traffic has remained flat, while traffic and orders on the Web site continue to grow exponentially. This application has been so successful that Boeing is now rolling out more than fifty customer-facing applications in its new Boeing Partners' Network.

Critical Success Factors in the Boeing Story

✓ Target the right customers	☆ Let customers help themselves
✓ Own the customer's total experience	☆ Help customers do their jobs
✓ Streamline business processes that impact the customer	✓ Deliver personalized service
Provide a 360-degree view of the customer relationship	Foster community

☆ = Featured in this discussion   ✓ = Touched on in this discussion

Boeing Lets Customers Order Spare Parts via the Web

THE COMMERCIAL AIRPLANE market is growing by leaps and bounds! Boeing's strategic planners expect world air travel to grow by 70 percent over the next ten years. To meet that demand, commercial airlines are expected to increase their fleet sizes significantly. Within the next twenty years, Boeing expects 12,000 new commercial airplanes to be built worldwide. Approximately $850 billion will be spent on new airplanes to expand existing fleets, and $250 billion will be spent to replace obsolete planes. And of course, Boeing hopes to get its fair share of that market. (The company currently produces more than 60 percent of all commercial jet airplanes in the world.) Boeing's management understands that maintaining market share in a growing industry requires more than ramping up production; it also means keeping existing customers satisfied so they'll keep coming back for more.

What Boeing's management would prefer not to do, however, is to increase its head count proportionately as it takes on this anticipated new business. The company wants to use information technology to keep costs down, while ramping up volume and sustaining and improving quality. So everyone in Boeing's Commercial Airplane Group has been chartered with doing more with the same number of people. Tom DiMarco, senior manager in the customer services division of Boeing's Commercial Airplane Group, took this charter seriously when he embarked on a new initiative in early 1996. Darce Lamb, the vice president of Boeing's Airline Logistics Support organization, wanted to improve the process by which Boeing's customers procure spare parts. Lamb and DiMarco both realized that the larger the fleets grew and the more airplanes Boeing produced, the more spare parts customers were going to need. DiMarco formed a project team including members of the information systems staff, led by Cloyd Summers, and chartered them to come up with new ways of electronically communicating with Boeing's spare parts customers. The team researched several solutions and recommended several feasible options, one of which was the Web. Lamb approved the recommendation, and the project got underway.

Spare Parts: A Mission-Critical Business

THE AIRPLANE SPARE parts business is a mammoth industry in itself. When an airplane sits idle on the ground, it costs the airline between

$5,000 and $7,000 an hour! So maintenance and unscheduled repairs have to be performed as quickly and efficiently as possible. An airline doesn't want to wait unnecessarily for a needed spare part to be flown in from abroad. Therefore, the operations manager has to carefully manage his spare parts inventory to ensure that all the anticipated parts are in the places he's likely to need them when he needs them. When unexpected incidents occur, he counts on his parts supplier (Boeing or a third party) to have that part in inventory in the nearest convenient depot and to get it to him as soon as possible.

Although Boeing has a large share of the spare parts business for its airplanes, there are competitors. Boeing would naturally prefer that its customers buy their spares from Boeing directly, not only for financial reasons but because it can guarantee the quality of its own parts and therefore be confident that the structural integrity of the airplane hasn't been compromised. Thus, there are three reasons why the spare parts business is strategic to the company:

1. Customers need quick and easy access to Boeing's spare parts in order to remain loyal and satisfied. (Customers may order new airplanes once every five years; they order spare parts every week.)
2. The spare parts business provides an important ongoing revenue stream for the company.
3. Boeing would prefer that its customers buy Boeing spare parts to ensure consistent quality and safety.

Of course, not every part that goes into every Boeing airplane is manufactured by Boeing. Engines come from Pratt & Whitney, General Electric, and Rolls-Royce, for example. Boeing has more than 2,000 different parts suppliers. But each part is spec'd by Boeing and given a Boeing part number. Customers may choose to order these parts directly from the original manufacturer, but to do so, they need to be satisfied that they're getting the correct part for their Boeing aircraft. And Boeing maintains electronic linkages with all of its suppliers so that its spare parts inventory is replenished automatically.

Acquiring Spare Parts

IN THE PAST, ordering spare parts from Boeing was a cumbersome process. First, customers had to look up the part number and description they needed in the Boeing-supplied binders (or CD-ROMs) of parts information. Then they would call the company's spare parts call center to ascertain the current price, find out if the part was available, and find out how long it would take to get the part to the repair location. Then they would place the order. They could do this by phone, or often, after getting the information, they'd hang up the phone, fill in the necessary paperwork for a purchase order, and fax in the order. Boeing's spare parts call center operates seven days a week, twenty-four hours a day, with additional overtime coverage during peak travel seasons, such as the Christmas holidays.

Some of Boeing's largest customers (for example, United and Air Nippon) have a different mechanism for actually placing the orders. Once they've ascertained the availability, location, and price of a part they need, they order the part using their electronic data interchange (EDI) linkage to Boeing. However, there's still a glitch with this part of the process: typically the part number and description are typed into the EDI system. Sometimes there are typing or formatting mistakes, which cause the order to be rejected because of errors. And only 70 of Boeing's 700 airline customers have EDI hookups with the company.

The biggest problem with this call center–based arrangement was that, as Boeing's business grew, its call center operations would also have to grow. DiMarco wanted a more scalable approach. Both he and Summers thought that the Internet could play an important role. Although only 10 percent of Boeing's airline customers were currently using electronic linkages to do business with the company, in the near future all of these customers would presumably have Internet connections and access via Web browsers.

Streamlining the Spare Parts Process

WHEN THE PROJECT team met to discuss the requirements for a new streamlined spare parts application, several requirements were identified:

1. Seven-day-a-week, twenty-four-hour-a-day, 365-day-a-year customer service coverage (with no additional head count).
2. Support for all the business processes the call center personnel currently performed. (Verify part number and description; check inventory and location; provide accurate pricing information; take orders; report on the status of orders; and so on.)
3. The ability for customers to perform ad hoc queries for parts pricing and availability.

4. The ability for new customers to help themselves to electronic self-service.

5. The ability to interface with the existing mainframe system without any modifications to the existing applications; in particular, there was to be no impact on the existing mainframe spare parts inventory and EDI system.

6. Last, but not least, security.

Lamb also laid out a vision for the new spare parts application. He said, "Our goal is to respond so fast that customers can regard our inventory as virtually their own."

DiMarco and Summers assumed architectural responsibility for putting together the components and pushed the project through the various internal departments within Boeing. They decided not to interfere with the current back-end spare parts inventory, ordering, and database applications but to give customers access to that information via the Web. The initial project took about nine months.

The original Boeing PART Page Web site went live in October 1996. Boeing's customers could register through the call center hot line, and then, once they received their log-on instructions (this is a secure site, available only to Boeing's registered customers), they could go on-line with their Web browsers to:

- View up-to-date parts information such as prices, availability, location, and interchangeability (which parts can be substituted for others).
- Enter a new purchase order, change an existing purchase order, or check the status of orders, including the ability to view multiple purchase orders at once by entering selection criteria, such as "All open purchase orders".
- Request a price quote or view existing price quotes.
- Get answers to questions using the "Help" and "Frequently Asked Questions" sections.

What amazed DiMarco about the success of the application was its immediate acceptance. Within three months, 125 of Boeing's 700 airline customers were using the Web site on a regular basis, and customers were coming on board at the rate of fifteen per week: "When you compare that adoption rate to the adoption rate of EDI—seventy companies in eighteen years—it's really phenomenal!"

Another initial surprise was the kind of activity the site experienced. On a typical night in early 1997, the site was getting about 800 hits and about 40 orders per night. This ratio of inquiries to orders was much higher than in the call centers. What were these customers doing? "They were doing research," DiMarco explained. "They were looking to see what parts were available and how much they cost." This helps in the inventory-planning process. If customers know Boeing has a particular product in stock, they may choose not to order it right away but to wait until they really need it. Most customers wouldn't think of calling Boeing's call centers to ask about the availability of parts that they weren't planning to order right away. But they would check the Web site.

So it wasn't too surprising that the first thing customers asked to be able to see was *where* parts were warehoused. "If you're in Australia, it's comforting to know that a part you may need soon is in the warehouse in Singapore, rather than Seattle," DiMarco explained. Much to Lamb's delight, customers were beginning to treat Boeing's spare parts inventory as an extension of their own.

Evolving the Technical Infrastructure

The first thing the project team did was to focus on the content for the site. What would be needed to meet Lamb's requirement: to give customers the same functionality they had when they called in by phone? And what additional information could easily be offered in a Web-based environment? The team decided to focus on the same functionality offered with the existing EDI mechanism.

The second architectural exercise the project team undertook was to decide which Web platforms to use. They chose to design for browser independence, to use Secure Socket Layer security on the browser side, to focus on the inventory and ordering applications, to use HTML for their data format and Netscape for their Web server software, and to support both the Internet and the airlines' proprietary leased line network for access.

The Web site design focused on giving customers access to the actual parts inventory information. But first, Boeing needed to worry about security. It couldn't have one airline looking at information that was destined for a competitive airline; for example, TWA has negotiated different terms and conditions than United and the two airlines may not use the same models of planes. So the project team hooked the Web application into a two-step security authentication process. The first level of authentication gives the customer access to Boeing's secure spare parts Web site. The second level gives each customer the correct permissions in the database, which contains the parts pricing and interchangeability information that's appropriate for that company as well as the inventory levels and location of the parts.

The project team wrote their own middleware layer for sending through to Boeing's IBM mainframe–based inventory and order system the information that customers fill in on a Web-based form. In effect, the Web provides a simple forms-based interface (complete with data entry validation and error checking) with Boeing's preexisting EDI systems.

As different groups within Boeing began building other customer-facing applications using the Web, William Barker, the manager of information systems for the customer services division of Boeing's Commercial Airplane Group, has been able to extend the architecture designed for the spare parts application. He expanded it to include the reverse proxy fire wall so that it serves as a single entry point for any customer—commercial, defense, or aerospace—coming into Boeing's systems. Once customers log on to the site, they are given a simple list of all the Web sites and applications they are entitled to access. No further log-ons are required. Barker likes this approach. It's secure and elegant in its simplicity, and the customer doesn't have to remember different log-ons for each application.

Results

BY THE END of 1997, 334 of Boeing's customers had used the Web-based spare parts application and another 50 had just registered. In its first year of operation, Boeing's spare parts Web site serviced companies located in thirty-eight states and forty-one countries and handled 460,000 requests. Equally important, Lamb had been able to hold the line on call center staffing. In fact, during the peak travel seasons in both 1996 and 1997, Boeing avoided overtime in its call center. Customers were very enthusiastic about the ease with which they could now interact with Boeing and get the information they needed to do their inventory planning and to pro-cure spare parts. So by the end of 1997, almost half of Boeing's 700 commercial airline customers were doing business with Boeing over the Web. A large number of suppliers and partners were also using this service. That number meets DiMarco's expectations. "Some of our customers are relatively small companies in underdeveloped countries. It will take a while before they're using the Web routinely for business. But we're ready when they are."

Perhaps even more impressive than the Boeing spare parts application by itself is the catalyst that it became for the way Boeing now does business with its customers. The spare parts application has became the focal point for other customer-facing Web applications. Boeing now has more than ninety-five customer-facing applications planned for its new Web-based Boeing Partners' Network. Ten of these applications were up and running by the end of 1997. Boeing is adding about five new applications a month. They include everything from supplier tool inventory tracking; new product release and update information; a spare parts exchange program that lets customers rent a part and then turn it in and exchange it for a new part; a WindTemps application, which calculates flight times between any two points in the world at selected altitudes; an on-line training program for a consortium of Japanese companies; and so on. The floodgates are now open, and Boeing is in the process of allowing access to an additional 4,000 suppliers in a cost-effective and user-friendly environment on the secure Boeing Partners' Network.

Patty's Rx for Boeing

The next step for Boeing's spare parts Web site is to streamline the process even more. Without requiring its commercial airline customers to invest in EDI technology, Boeing can give each one more EDI-equivalent functionality. For example, customers should be able to establish standing orders for certain parts over the Web, linking in their own parts inventory systems and writing business rules to govern the automatic triggering of business processes. For example, "Whenever we fall below five of these parts, order five more." Given where technology standards are going, it makes the most sense for these interfaces to be written using the Extensible Mark-up Language (XML) and for Boeing to add XML tags to all of the parts descriptions in its database. Boeing can then do an even better job of linking its inventory database with those of its suppliers, so that an order received by Boeing could be drop-shipped from a supplier's site. Once that has been accomplished, the customer will have a transparent, seamless view of the entire value chain.

"Take-Aways" from the Boeing Story

1. Electronic data interchange (EDI) is a high-overhead way of establishing relationships with trading partners and customers. Giving customers the ability to order information using a simple forms-based interface on the Web is a much better way of linking customers to you electronically. In eighteen years, Boeing had succeeded in getting only 70 of its larger customers up on EDI linkages. In twelve months, it had 334 companies ordering from the company electronically via the Web!

2. Customers need a lot more than the ability to order. They need to be able to play "what if" games with your inventory, pricing, and availability in order to optimize their own business processes. You'll need to give customers access to all the information they need to make effective decisions.

3. Each customer's terms and conditions are different. So each customer's view of your inventory information has to reflect that customer's pricing, delivery, and service contracts with your firm. That means that you'll need to use a business rules–based approach and be able to dynamically generate specific views of the data that are relevant for each account.

4. Note that Boeing didn't stop with the spare parts application. Boeing has used the same security and Web infrastructure to welcome all of its customers into its internal systems. And customers only have to remember a single password for all their dealings with Boeing's different applications and departments. Once they've been authenticated, they are shown a dynamically created Web page telling them which applications and information they're entitled to access.

5. Once customers are hooked directly into your inventory systems, you'll need to be sure you can continue that linkage back through to your suppliers. As DiMarco points out, ultimately you may not need to stock supplier inventory at all but simply give your customers the ability to order through you and then have your suppliers ship directly.

HELP CUSTOMERS DO THEIR JOBS:

PhotoDisc
www.photodisc.com

Executive Summary

PhotoDisc's customers are graphic design professionals who need rapid, affordable access to commercial-quality photographs and imagery they can use in their design projects. PhotoDisc pioneered a new business model for making publishing-quality photographs available to the graphic design community: customers pay a low onetime licensing fee that gives them virtually unlimited rights to use the photos. Design professionals from advertising agencies, magazine publishers, and corporate marketing departments search PhotoDisc's digital library, select the photos they want, purchase them, and download them electronically. Perhaps most important, PhotoDisc's Web site supports the way these customers work with their clients—collaboratively, on cross-organizational teams. All of the players working on a project together can use a "light box" at the PhotoDisc site to collaborate on their final selections of images for each project.

Critical Success Factors in the PhotoDisc Story

✓ Target the right customers	✓ Let customers help themselves
✓ Own the customer's total experience	★ Help customers do their jobs
✓ Streamline business processes that impact the customer	✓ Deliver personalized service
Provide a 360-degree view of the customer relationship	Foster community
★ = Featured in this discussion	✓ = Touched on in this discussion

PhotoDisc Helps Its Customers Look Good to Their Customers

Seattle-based PhotoDisc was founded in 1991 with a clear mission: to market and distribute royalty-free digital stock photography. As one of the developers of Muzak—the background music you hear in stores and elevators—CEO Mark Torrance had a great deal of experience in the music industry and in the licensing of intellectual property. Now he wanted to build a company that would specialize in distributing multimedia information directly to personal computers—an industry that was about to take off! However, instead of targeting the mass consumer market, Torrance's colleague Tom Hughes convinced him that professional graphic designers would be an ideal target market.

Hughes had worked in publishing for more than twenty years, in such varied jobs as production manager, photographer, darkroom technician, and publisher for a variety of newspapers and magazines. Hughes realized that one of the most difficult and time-consuming tasks confronting any graphic arts professional was procuring and licensing photographs. Now with the technology available to scan and digitize photographs in the high-resolution formats required for professional publishing and the ability to distribute these digitized images cost-effectively on affordable CD-ROMs, Hughes and Torrance felt that they had the makings of a profitable niche business.

Developing a "Friction-Free" Business

ALTHOUGH THERE WAS a handful of CD-ROMs with clip art and photographs coming onto the market in the early 1990s, these were all targeted for the home or business computer user. What graphic arts professionals needed were high-quality photographs that could be used in magazines, corporate brochures, and advertising. The traditional way of getting such photos was to purchase them from stock photography agencies, which represent the work of professional photographers. They have very stringent licensing requirements: the photographs are typically licensed for onetime use, with the cost ranging from $100 to $10,000 depending on the reputation of the photographer, the desirability of the photo, and the number of impressions that will be made (in the hundreds or in the hundreds of thousand of copies). And the stock agencies have very stringent limitations on photo manipulation. Although you may size the photo, you may not be allowed to crop it, nor would you be allowed to perform any digital manipulations, such as recoloring, highlighting, or removing elements. So Hughes and Torrance decided that they would challenge the entire business model of the stock photography industry. They would license digitally scanned, professional-quality photographs for an affordable price ($20 to $200), permit virtually unlimited use, and have no limitations on digital manipulation. They expected to make up in volume for the difference in the royalties paid to professional photographers.

The other area of friction for graphic designers was simply finding the images they needed. Typically, a designer would call one or more stock photography agencies and describe over the phone, in as much detail as he could specify (topic, color, mood, and so on), the concept of the piece he was looking for. The customer service rep would then pull 35-millimeter slides out of the company's files, arrange them on a light table, and call the customer back, verbally describing the photos. If any of them seemed to meet the customer's needs, he could be sent a color proof or the actual slide on approval by courier or express mail. This process would be repeated as many times as necessary, with as many agencies as necessary, to make a selection. Hughes knew that if customers could search a library of photos electronically, by using the same key words they would use in talking to an agency, they could cut much time and annoyance out of the process.

Launching the First Products

PHOTODISC RELEASED ITS first set of digitized photographs on floppy disks in 1991. The floppies were accompanied by a catalog depicting the images so customers could find what they needed and load the correct floppy. The company released its first CD-ROM in January 1992. It contained 400 professionally scanned and color-corrected photographs and was priced at $300. The CD-ROM was key word–searchable so designers could locate what they were seeking by topic. Innovative graphic designers quickly learned about this new treasure trove of royalty-free, professional-quality digital photographs, and demand for the company's products grew. The new business model worked! Soon, more and more photographers were offering their work to PhotoDisc, intrigued by the business model that let them retain the ownership of and copyright on their photographs while paying them a royalty stream that was prorated based on the number of photos they had on each CD-ROM.

Getting into Customers' Heads

AS A PROFESSIONAL in the publishing field, Tom Hughes, then PhotoDisc's president, knew a lot about what designers needed. But he and his team listened constantly to the questions they were asked and the feedback they received. The company's target customers were graphic design professionals in design firms, advertising agencies, publications, and businesses' marketing and communications departments. First they needed to find images that conveyed a particular message or related to a particular theme. PhotoDisc addressed this need by organizing its images into "collections": business and industry, science and technology, nature, fine art, and so on. Then it made searching easy. Designers could either browse through PhotoDisc's full-color catalogs, or pop a CD-ROM into their computer and search by key words ("man and computer," "woman and baby," and so forth).

But what if the designer didn't yet know which of several images would appeal to his client? The company offered customers and prospects a free "starter kit." This included full-color catalogs containing all the available images, a few free sample high-resolution photographs, and a complete set of free low-resolution images on CD-ROMs that designers could use in their "comps"—the design samples they give to their customers. "Comping" is an important step in the graphic design process. It's very difficult to visualize how everything—pictures, type, layout—will look in its final form without making up a preview. Designers typically produce these comps by hand or use page layout programs and print the pages out on low- or mid-resolution printers. Any designer who had access to a color printer could now print out a low-resolution image of the proposed color photo in situ in his design.

Once the designer (and his in-house or outside customer) selected the particular photograph(s) they wanted to use for a particular printed piece, the designer could call PhotoDisc's toll-free number and have the CD-ROM containing the "high res" image sent by FedEx. PhotoDisc prided itself on being able to accept orders as late as 6 P.M. from the East Coast and still guarantee next-day delivery. Of course, once the designer had received the CD-ROM, he had gotten not just the one photo he needed for that particular job but another two hundred or so high-resolution images he might find useful for the next job, at no extra cost! The onetime license entitles the customer to use a photo anywhere, at any time, and in any medium.

The Web Introduced New Challenges and Opportunities

BY 1994, PHOTODISC was beginning to get a new requirement from its leading-edge customers. Some of them were beginning to get involved with designing home pages on the Web. And they wanted PhotoDisc to "get with it." Their requests ranged from "Why don't you have a Web site and put your catalog on-line?" to "We don't want to have to wait overnight to receive new CD-ROMs; why can't we download digital images directly to our computers via the Internet?" Bill Heston, PhotoDisc's vice president of business development, took these requests seriously. In January 1995, Heston began researching what it would take to interact with customers electronically and to deliver huge digital images over the Internet. He consulted with Clement Mok, a well-known graphic designer who was doing pioneering design work on the Web. Heston learned about the Web and developed a business plan for what it would take to put up a Web site to sell CD-ROMs (his first game plan). He rolled up his sleeves, recruited a fearless young Unix consultant, and began to oversee the design of the company's first Web site. The site went live in June 1995. "It was a pretty good site," Heston modestly reports. "It let people search by category, it contained Postscript Display Format (PDF) versions of the images they could browse on-line, it included discussion forums, and it let you enter a request to have a catalog sent to you."

Heston didn't really know what to expect from the Web site, but he was encouraged by customers' and prospects' responses. Within the first couple of weeks, the company was getting four to five catalog requests per day from the site and was selling at least one CD-ROM per day to someone who had started his research at the Web site. It was time to take the next step: allow customers to purchase and download directly from the Web.

Making It Easy for Customers to Help Themselves via the Web

IN JULY 1995, Heston wrote a specification for what he wanted on his next-generation Web site, and he began shopping for companies that could provide turnkey software PhotoDisc could use. The spec called for the ability for customers to search for images by key words (the same kind of search capabilities that PhotoDisc already offered on its CD-ROMs), view thumbnail-size images, put them into a shopping cart, and, once payment had been received, download the images electronically from the site. Heston also wanted prospects and customers to be able to select and download low-resolution images they could use for comps by registering at the site.

He found two companies that appeared to have the kind of technology platforms that might be able to do the job. One was Informix's Illustra multimedia database. The other was a more complete electronic commerce platform from a company called Connect, Inc. Connect had done a demo site for a music company but hadn't yet built a capability to download large digital files via the Internet.

Heston had planned to spend about $150,000 on the development of this next-generation electronic commerce Web site. And he wanted it up and running by September—in less than three months! Apparently, he was very convincing because he managed to do a very favorable deal with Connect. He convinced Connect's management team that this would be a showcase business-to-business electronic commerce site—and that if they worked really hard, they could debut the site at Seybold Seminars' fall extravaganza for the electronic publishing industry, which would be taking place in San Francisco the third week in September. According to Heston, Connect bought into the idea and "threw a bunch of programmers onto the project." Sure enough, the new "try and buy" version of the Web site was unveiled at the Seybold Seminars meeting in San Francisco in September 1995. This allowed customers to do keyword searching for images, view the thumbnail-size photos, put images into a shopping cart, and either download low-resolution (comp) images for free or, if they had a credit card on file or a corporate account established with PhotoDisc, download the high-resolution images directly.

The new site was a big hit with the publishing community. Traffic to the site picked up considerably. Heston reports that the company learned a sobering lesson that fall. It had a hardware problem over Thanksgiving— one of the disk controllers crashed—and it was off-line for a few days. "Boy, did we hear it from customers," Heston reports. "Until then, we had no idea how mission-critical our Web site had become to customers on tight deadlines."

Selling and Marketing via the Web

FROM SEPTEMBER 1995 on, PhotoDisc was selling and delivering its products via the Web. But it wasn't until February 1996 that it added secure credit card purchasing at the Web site. Before, most customers had called in and set up an account with the company, either arranging to be billed each month (for large corporate accounts) or by providing their credit card numbers to be debited as they ordered. As soon as the credit card purchasing was working well, PhotoDisc launched its first major marketing campaign featuring the Web site. "This was our first companywide focus on the Web from a marketing and merchandising standpoint," Heston reported. "The offer was that customers could come to a special version of our Web site, fill in a questionnaire, select any image they wanted, and download it for free. We used direct mail, print advertising, outbound e-mail, PR—the whole nine yards. For a small company, it worked really well." In fact, it worked so well that the traffic brought PhotoDisc's actual Web site to its knees. The company quickly brought in a new set of servers to handle the additional search traffic.

Profiling Customers

As you may have guessed by now, one of the things Heston's team did right from the outset was to capture information about each prospect who registered and each customer who ordered in a customer database. In addition to retaining the customer's name, address, and credit card or other billing information, this database is used to track each search each customer does and every purchase the customer actually makes. The detailed customer profile information captured on-line may be then converted into a data mart and analyzed, and the results used by two different groups: the content procurement department (it needs to see what customers have been looking for that PhotoDisc doesn't have) and the marketing department (it wants to see which kinds of images are ordered by which kinds of customers).

Heston said that for the first year of operation the company thought it would be able to use the information about the types of images customers bought to customize future offers for them. However, what they hadn't taken into account was the fact that most graphic designers don't work on a single type of project or for a single account. Instead, they jump from project to project, each of which typically calls for different material. For example, a designer at an advertising agency who had been looking for family photos one week might be looking for airplane artwork the next week. On the other hand, because PhotoDisc keeps track of the kinds of images customers have been asking for, it's able to notify customers by e-mail as soon as that category of images becomes available.

Segmenting Customers

However, PhotoDisc has found that there are ways of profiling and segmenting customers that make sense. Corporate accounts—advertising agencies and large corporations' marketing departments—are handled by a small corporate accounts sales team. Account managers call on these customers face-to-face. These accounts want their projects billed to a common corporate account (not a credit card number), and they need to have each project clearly identified by client (for an ad agency) or by department (for a corporate marketing group). PhotoDisc reaches out to the rest of its customer base using e-mail, among other techniques. Different e-mail messages are targeted to different types of customers. According to Heston, "Our customers are very fashion-conscious, and a lot of their work is seasonal in nature. So we promote 'specials' that we think will appeal to certain groups of customers at particular times of year." In addition he points out that customizing e-mails is the most inexpensive form of target marketing. "It doesn't cost you any more to send ten different e-mails to a group of a thousand customers than it does to send one." This form of promotion has proved to be very cost-effective and extremely successful.

Customer Service

PHOTODISC'S CUSTOMERS AREN'T shy about communicating with the company. The Web site receives a large number of daily e-mails. These are typically answered by the department to which they're addressed: sales, tech support, licensing, and so on. The company's goal is to respond to e-mails within twenty-four hours. Customers may call needing help navigating the Web site or downloading images. Or they want to check to make sure they weren't billed twice for an image they had trouble downloading. (Although the PhotoDisc Web site provides very thorough instructions for downloading image files, a lot can go wrong with these very large files, from Internet outages to difficulties getting them through corporate fire walls.) PhotoDisc has had to invest heavily in customer support for its Web activities.

Customized Billing

ONCE PHOTODISC MADE it possible, in the fall of 1996, for customers to order individual images from the Web rather than to buy an entire CD-ROM, customers' billing needs changed dramatically. They needed to be able to bill the cost of the individual images to different clients and projects. As mentioned, corporations were given the opportunity to establish corporate accounts with the company and to receive monthly itemized bills. Yet individual designers and other professionals who paid for their digital photos by credit card also wanted to be able to bill these to specific clients or departments. So PhotoDisc had to change its back-end accounting systems to give customers the reporting flexibility they needed.

Supporting Collaborative Work

PHOTODISC'S CUSTOMERS NEED to confer with one another and with their customers in the selection of the images they plan to use. It's not uncommon for four or five creative people from different cities with the same ad agency or design firm to be searching for the right "look" for a piece. They need to compare notes, confer, and come up with an agreed-upon shortlist that they then share with the client. In 1997, Heston's group launched an innovative new capability to address the needs of its customers to collaborate with others: an electronic light box.

Like a physical light table on which you spread out a series of 35-millimeter slides for others to see, any customer or visitor to the PhotoDisc Web site can create and name his own light box, placing a variety of photographs on it for others to see and comment on. He can then send an e-mail to other team members, giving them a link to the PhotoDisc Web site and the name of the light box. The invited visitor can go to the site, call up the light box, and place his comments next to each proposed picture. This has proved to be an immensely popular feature of the Web site.

Adding Additional Search Functionality

WITH MORE THAN 75,000 photographs in the PhotoDisc collection, you can imagine that searching for what you want can be a daunting task, particularly if you're looking for a particular visual effect rather than a photo of a particular subject matter (dogs, airplanes, and so forth). From the outset, the company offered customers two ways to search: by browsing collections that were organized by photographer or topic or by using keyword searching. Customers quickly told PhotoDisc that they needed other ways of searching, so in 1997 Heston's team made two significant enhancements to the site's search capabilities.

First, they added the ability to search images based on color, composition, structure, and texture. Once you find an illustration that has something of the "look" you want, you could conduct a search through the library based on these attributes until you found what you're seeking.

Second, they added a more refined key-word searching capability. Each of the photographs in the collection is carefully tagged by PhotoDisc's professional staff, with twenty to thirty key words. The new natural language capability lets customers be more verbose in their search specifications to still find the topics they're looking for.

Evolving the Technical Infrastructure

PhotoDisc's Web site still runs on Connect's Connect-One electronic commerce platforms, although the base platform has been continuously modified and refined over time to support PhotoDisc's business. PhotoDisc uses Sun Solaris running on one of Sun's largest Sparc servers (Enterprise 4000) for the core of the Web site. This Unix core functionality is surrounded by NT-based application services that are running on Dell servers. The entire site is mirrored for backup and to handle peak loads.

Heston's technical team (now approximately twenty-three people) has decided that it makes the most sense to hedge their bets with different types of technology platforms to support the same functions. So while there's a Commerce engine still embedded in the Sun Solaris servers, most of the searching now takes place on a group of clustered Windows NT servers. Similarly, although PhotoDisc began by using Oracle databases for its image store, key-word attributes, and customer profile information, the company now also uses Microsoft SQL Server databases for many of those same functions, as well as for the back end of its search process.

PhotoDisc has more than 300 gigabytes of digitized images online. Image files are stored in multiple resolutions, from 150K images (for the comps) to 28MB images for ultra-high-resolution versions. The files are downloaded in compacted versions, and they expand automatically when they reach the customer's system.

For its secure payment infrastructure, PhotoDisc uses Verisign and CyberCash. And it uses TaxWare's software for calculating the appropriate taxes for each state and country in which taxes are due.

PhotoDisc's original key-word search engine was provided by Fulcrum. When search traffic picked up substantially, the technical team decided to move all the searching to multiple clusters of NT servers. There they use Fulcrum for key-word searching and Erli (originally from the French government) for the natural language search capabilities. The visual image analysis and search capabilities provided by Virage are currently being enhanced, and the company plans to offer this type of searching on-line again in 1999. Using Virage, each scanned image is analyzed for color, composition, structure (wire-frame analysis), and texture in a preprocessing pass before it's stored. The results of the analysis are stored along with the key-word attributes associated with each image in an SQL Server database.

One of the biggest technical challenges PhotoDisc faced was rationalizing the two different customer databases it had—one for its CD-ROM–based business and one for the Web. As it became apparent that the same customers would often order CD-ROMs and search the Web for additional images, the two separately developed customer databases had to be merged. Since there was much more detailed customer profile information in the Oracle database used to power the Web site, the CD-ROM customer information has gradually been migrated to that database. Another challenge, which was both business and technical in nature, was the rework of the underlying accounting systems both to accommodate the customized billing requirements described above and to rationalize the pricing for both domestic and international customers. (When PhotoDisc sold only CD-ROMs, the prices were considerably higher outside the United States. But if an image is being downloaded anywhere in the world, whether in Bangkok or Boston, the price should be the same.)

Results

WHEN HESTON WROTE the original specs for his second-generation, transactional Web site, he budgeted $150,000. Two years later, the company had spent well over $2 million on the site and was still investing heavily! Yet Heston is very pleased with the results. PhotoDisc's Web site has more than met his expectations as a new channel for cost-effectively delivering digital media to the PCs of the company's customers around the world. Not only that, but the popularity of the Web site and its ease of use have contributed to sales of the company's CD-ROM–based products.

PhotoDisc's revenues grew from $28 million in 1996 to approximately $42 million in 1997. Through June of 1998 PhotoDisc's total sales were already at $26 million. Direct sales of images via the Web accounted for about 10 percent of revenues in 1996 and 18 percent in 1997. By June 30, 1998, Web sales accounted for approximately 32 percent of PhotoDisc's total sales. Traffic to the Web site continues to grow at 20 percent per month.

Apparently, others were equally impressed. In mid-1997, U.K.-based Getty Communications agreed to purchase PhotoDisc for a generous stock-plus-cash deal. Getty Communications' other holdings include a variety of stock photography agencies (Hulton Getty's archival collection, Tony Stone Images' contemporary stock photography, and Liaison agency's news and photojournalism images), Sports Photography (Allsport), and film stock footage collections (Energy Film Library), as well as a strong international distribution presence. The combined collection includes 25 million images and 9,500 hours of film footage. What Getty lacked, however, was the royalty-free model and the Web-based delivery platform that PhotoDisc offered. The combined companies are known as Getty Images.

Patty's Rx for PhotoDisc

PhotoDisc will be spending most of 1998 and 1999 integrating its operations with those of the various Getty Images companies. I suspect and hope that PhotoDisc will remain the engine of innovation, at least in terms of business models and Web electronic commerce, for the combined organizations. This will be a challenge not only technically but also organizationally. I suspect that part of the rationale behind the acquisition is to help Getty's stock photography businesses digitize their considerable image libraries and make them searchable. It seems unlikely, however, that the entire company will espouse the royalty-free licensing model that PhotoDisc has pioneered. Chances are that the new, combined companies will espouse very different business models: the onetime fee, royalty-free model that PhotoDisc has promulgated and the "pay-per-use" model that the rest of the Getty Images companies currently use.

However, there is a lot more that PhotoDisc brings to the party that can be leveraged by its sister companies. The entire model—how creative designers can use the Web to locate the right image or effect to use in a particular work and then quickly procure that artwork—is definitely replicable. Whether a customer is searching for film footage, classic photographs, or artwork from a specialized collection, the paradigm should be similar.

The next steps for the existing PhotoDisc site are the migration to Microsoft's NT platform, the continuous improvement of the user interface, and the process of downloading multiple large images via the Internet. To date, the company has done a good job of explaining the steps a customer needs to take: how to set up one's browser preferences to download the right file formats directly to disk. But the process is still a daunting one for customers who are not "techies."

"Take-Aways" from the PhotoDisc Story

1. Climb into your customers' heads. Understand how they do their jobs and what their biggest causes of friction are. Eliminate them. PhotoDisc's founders realized that the current licensing practices and pricing for commercial photographs were a major cause of friction for graphic designers. So they came up with a new "friction-free" business model. It worked!

2. Notice that most of the best Web sites offer customers at least three different types of search engines. In PhotoDisc's case, you can, for example, search by topic, color, and shape.

3. Keep track of what customers look for and don't find. With Web site tracking, you can gather exquisite information not just about who your customers are and what they bought but also about what they looked for and didn't find. Then, as soon as you have what they were seeking, you can offer it to them via e-mail.

4. Use electronic mail for targeted marketing. It's the most cost-effective approach you'll find. As long as you offer customers things they've said they're interested in, they won't get annoyed.

5. Listen to what your customers tell you about the information they need to appear on their bills. Most business customers will have to submit your bills for payment or reimbursement. The closer you can match their internal requirements, the happier they'll be.

6. Note that customers don't work in a vacuum. They work with colleagues in other departments or organizations. They have customers, too. How can you design your offerings to make it as easy as possible for

your customer to involve her customer in the use of your product? PhotoDisc did a great job of this with its electronic light box.

Help Customers Do Their Jobs: Lessons Learned

In order to help customers do their jobs, you need to climb into their heads. Don't guess. You have to understand exactly how they do their jobs. Spend time with them. Understand how they operate, what tasks they need to perform, and how they do those tasks within the context of their companies. Then start eliminating every barrier you can find between the job they're trying to do and their ability to get that job done. The products and services you provide obviously need to be part of that streamlining process.

Eliminate All Sources of Friction

BOEING AND PHOTODISC focused on eliminating all the sources of friction in the customer's ability to do his job. What slowed the customer down? How could they make it easier for the customer to reach the end result he needed: a well-maintained airplane, in the case of Boeing's customers; a memorable design, in the case of PhotoDisc's customers? Boeing realized that customers needed to know exactly what parts were available, where they were, and what they cost. Then they needed an easy way to place their orders without extra paperwork. And they had to be able to count on the fact that the part would arrive exactly when it was promised. It turned out that forecasting their needs and planning their inventory requirements was as much a part of the job as maintaining airplanes was. PhotoDisc realized that customers needed a completely different business model in order to procure and use digital photographs and artwork. So it created one.

Make It Easy for Customers to Find What They Need

BOEING, PHOTODISC, AND National Semiconductor (which also does a great job at helping customers do their jobs) have put a lot of effort into the different ways that customers can search for what they need. In Boeing's case, customers can search by part number, part description, or subassembly. PhotoDisc discovered that graphic designers needed to search not only by topic or by photographer but also by shape and color. So they found pattern-matching technology they could use to make it easy for customers to find images that way. National Semiconductor discovered that its customers needed to search by parameters, product category, and design. So it supports all of those search modalities at its Web site.

Customize Information and Processes for Each Company

IN THE BUSINESS-TO-BUSINESS world, customization is probably even more important than it is in the business-to-consumer world. When Boeing's customers search the spare parts database, they'll be shown only the parts that correspond to the planes they actually have. So they don't need to wade through parts that aren't relevant for their company. PhotoDisc's customers made it clear that they needed to be able to customize the billing details for each job by project or client. Both Boeing and PhotoDisc have customers with different terms and conditions. They may have different pricing structures based on the quantity of goods they purchase. Each has a different payment arrangement. These need to be stored along with the customer's profile information. The business processes triggered for each customer will depend on the business rules governing that specific relationship.

Deliver Personalized Service

Personalization, privacy, and profiling are hot topics among Web marketeers. The debate that swirls around personalization has two aspects to it. The first issue is whether it's really necessary to customize the Web experience for each and every returning customer. Technologists worry about guaranteeing fast response times for Web pages that must be dynamically generated for each new customer. Marketing managers wonder if micromarket segmentation isn't at least as useful as targeting markets of one. The second issue revolves around how much to personalize. Do customers want to see only "their" home pages displaying information on the topics they've preselected? What about all the other information they might miss and would have found useful or interesting? If you're making personalized offers to customers based on what you know about their interests, at what point does that practice become invasive?

Privacy is not a topic that's debated by people who run businesses on the Web; it's one that's pretty sacrosanct. Everyone knows how important it is not to violate customers' privacy by divulging information about them or passing their e-mail addresses on to a third party. Of course, there are occasional lapses, such as the compromising situation that arose when an AOL administrator divulged the actual identity of Timothy McVeigh to an officer in the Navy—information that was used to link his AOL profile, identifying him as gay, with his identity and causing him to be discharged from the Navy. But such episodes are the exception, not the norm, on the Internet. The biggest infraction of privacy actually occurs when people post their own e-mail addresses in public places on the Net. This practice allows unscrupulous marketeers to scour discussion groups and directories for customers' e-mail addresses and then to send unsolicited junk e-mail to those addresses. Yet, "Netiquette" is pretty clear on this subject: don't send unsolicited e-mails to people you don't have a relationship with, particularly if you are trying to sell them something. It will simply backfire.

Profiling is still an art and a mystery. Yet profiling is at the core of personalization. You can't personalize a Web site or an offer unless you have built a customer profile. But how should you profile customers' interests? Do you simply infer them from the pages they visit on your site and the information you glean along the way as they transact business with you? Or do you ask prospects and customers to fill in questionnaires? If so, at what point in their visit should you ask them? As you'll see from the discussions that follow, the best approach seems to be to let customers give you the information they want to provide you in exchange for a specific service rendered. The other important corollary is the customers should always be able to see the profiles you have on them and make modifications to them.

Personalization, privacy, and profiling are not unique to the Web. As you'll see from the General Motors example, there are many non-Web situations in which profiles and personalization are appealing to customers as long as they can be sure their privacy is not being violated.

Here are the specific points to bear in mind when your organization is ready to embark on offering high-tech/high-touch personalized service to your customers:

- Develop a warm, personal relationship with each customer.
- Let customers specify and modify their profiles.
- Custom-tailor information presentation and offers based on customers' profiles.
- Provide appropriate service and information based on customers' needs.
- Give customers access to their transaction histories.
- Encourage customers to "leave something of themselves behind."

Develop a Warm, Personal Relationship with Each Customer

CUSTOMERS DON'T RELATE to anonymity on your part or theirs. If you want to differentiate yourself based on personalized service, you need to be prepared to interact with customers—even millions of them—as individuals. That means greeting them by name and giving them yours. Tripod is a company that understands this well. Every e-mail that comes in to its Web site (and there are thousands each day) is responded to by a person who customizes the answer the company's automated systems propose and then signs the e-mail by name.

On the other hand, I feel I have a warm relationship with Virtual Vineyards even though I've seldom interacted with a person at the site. I receive e-mails every month from Peter Granoff, its master sommelier, and that gives me the personal touch. Each time I come back to Amazon.com, I'm welcomed by name and offered some suggested new books I might find interesting based on ones I've ordered in the past. Each time I go to *The Wall Street Journal Interactive Edition*, I see news tailored for me. Today it's possible, and very cost-effective, to create a highly personalized experience for customers without ever having a human being involved. However, you need to be prepared to back up your automated scripts, friendly robots, and dynamically created Web page content with actual people—people who will respond in a warm, helpful manner to a phone call or an e-mail.

Let Customers Specify and Modify Their Profiles

THE APPROPRIATE TIME to ask a customer to fill in or update his profile is after you've built a trusted relationship with him, not before. Once the customer has begun doing business with you, it's okay to ask for more specific information, but always in the context of the service you're providing. For example, Hertz sends you a profile form to fill in once you've asked to become a member of the Hertz #1 Club Gold. The form asks for exactly the kind of information you'd expect: your driver's license number, your credit card number and expiration date, the size of car you prefer, whether you want a smoking or nonsmoking car.

Another way to build a customer profile is the incremental approach. This is the one Microsoft takes. The first time you visit Microsoft's Web site with a specific browser and Internet address, a profile is automatically created for you. Each time you return to the site from the same Internet address, using the same browser, any information you volunteer will be captured in your profile. If you download some software and supply an e-mail address in the process, it will be added to your profile. If you supply your name, title, and company in a feedback form, that information will flow directly into your profile. At any time, you can ask to see your profile, add to it, or modify it. Microsoft has been pleasantly surprised by both the type and quality of information its customers volunteer. What's surprising to me is how many Web sites don't automatically capture the information provided by customers' transacting business with them and place that information directly into a customer profile. Microsoft's approach is the exception, not the rule.

Bell Atlantic combines both explicitly and implicitly offered information in its customer profiles. Along with a residential customer's billing address, phone lines, and services, the company's telesales consultants enter information that the customer volunteers or that they pick up from external cues about the customer's family: Do they have young children, teenagers, or elderly parents living at home? Do they have a home office? This profile information is used to help target marketing campaigns and special offers to groups of customers.

Custom-Tailor Information Presentation and Offers Based on Customers' Profiles

ONCE YOU HAVE the beginnings of a customer profile, what should you do with it? First and foremost, use it to make it easy for the customer to do business with you. Don't ever ask the customer for the same information twice. Yet always show the customer the information you have on file at the relevant point. For example, when a customer places an order at most Web sites, they'll show her the credit card number(s) they have on file for her and ask her to select one. They'll show her the shipping addresses she has used in the past, again asking her to select which one she wants to use for this transaction. Travel-related sites typically keep two sets of preferences attached to her core profile: one for business travel and the other for personal travel.

But the real fun begins when you can be more creative about the offers you make based on the information you have in your customer profiles. Remember our discussion about American Airlines' popular NetSAAver e-mails? By the time you read this, American won't just be sending out information about all discounted fares to its 1 million–plus NetSAAver subscribers. Instead, they'll be receiving tailored offers featuring flights to and from their "home" airports to their preferred weekend destinations. Shortly, you'll be reading about Liberty Financial Services and the fact that it uses the information customers have supplied to avoid showing them irrelevant information. If they don't have children, for example, it won't offer them financial calculators to help them save for a child's college education.

What's the most effective way to offer personalized service to Web users? Use e-mail. While there's a lot of interest in and activity around the idea of creating dynamic Web pages that are personalized for each customer, the fact of the matter is that the majority of successful Web businesses that have been offering personalized service through 1997 have been doing so using e-mails targeted to individuals or small groups of customers. PhotoDisc and Amazon.com, for example, send out e-mails to alert customers to new offerings in areas they've asked to be told about. And as you'll see shortly, *The Wall Street Journal* uses both approaches to personalization. Customers can create a personalized newspaper on-line and specify companies or topics for which, when something important happens, they'll be notified by e-mail.

Provide Appropriate Service and Information Based on Customers' Needs

EVEN IF YOU have a profile of me as a customer, you have no idea what I will want from you the next time we interact. If I'm a GM OnStar subscriber, the chances are that you know who I am, where I live, what car I drive, and what kind of gas credit card I have. But you don't know what I will want from you when I contact you from my cell phone. So it's important to capture as much context with each interaction as possible. GM does this by giving the customer the option of pressing a green button ("Need information") or a red button ("Am in an emergency situation") and by automatically transmitting any relevant data from the car (the air bag just deployed), as well as the geographic coordinates for the customer's current location.

Amazon.com also gives the customer the ability to set a context quickly. It offers a one-click ordering option that defaults to use the credit card number and shipping address a customer used on the last order. So if you want to keep ordering books for yourself, or for your son in Ohio who wants to learn Java, you can do so with a single click. On the other hand, if you are shopping for someone new, you just fill in the shopping basket, check off the credit card you want to use, fill in the shipping address, and select the shipping option you prefer. Or, with American Airlines, if you visit the site directly from a NetSAAver's e-mail, they'll know that you probably want to see which of the discounted flights are still available.

There are a lot of ways of knowing something about the context in which a customer finds him or herself, whether he or she is interacting via the Web, on the phone, or from a kiosk. The trick is to pass that context along with the customer's initial interaction, so the person or application interacting with the customer can make some informed guesses about what the customer might need. The best way to be sure, of course, is to give the customer a way to cue you in, as Amazon.com and GM's OnStar do. Let the customer explicitly tell you what kind of interaction he's about to perform, and make it really easy for him to do so.

Give Customers Access to Their Transaction Histories

THERE'S ONE FORM of personalization that's fairly easy to do and very valuable for the customer. Even if you don't have a customer database with customer profiles, chances are that you do have a history of the orders each customer has placed. Virtual Vineyards and Amazon.com have both discovered that customers love the ability to see the orders they've placed in the past. This helps them keep track of the items they've bought and paid for, and it makes them feel special. They're being treated like a valued individual, not one of a pack. Once these virtual companies set the standard for giving customers access to their past order histories, other companies that were doing business on the Web discovered that their customers expected to have access to their order histories as well. American Airlines quickly discovered that customers didn't just want to make new reservations on the Web; they also wanted to make changes to reservations they had made by phone or through a travel agent.

Encourage Customers to "Leave Something of Themselves Behind"

I HAVE TO attribute this notion of "leaving something of themselves behind" to Bo Peabody, the CEO of Tripod. He's the person who first articulated the phrase. He was describing the feature, at the Tripod Web site, of letting customers create and post their own home pages for free. Peabody was convinced that if he could get customers to invest some of their psyches in his Web site, in the form of personal home pages, they'd keep returning, both to update their home pages and to explore other areas of the site. Peabody was right: 2,500 people build and leave their home pages at his Web every day. And 1 million of them have stuck around, coming back to the Web site at least once a week! All these registered Tripod users feel a personal connection to "their" Web site.

Stein Roe Farnham, Wells Fargo, and Security First Network Bank are three financial services companies that also believe in encouraging customers to leave information behind. Intuit's Quicken.com is another "one-stop-shopping" financial management site. Each offers tools that let you manage your finances or do financial planning. Once you've entered all your bill payment information (in the case of Wells Fargo and Security First) or your entire investment portfolio (in the case of Stein Roe Farnham mutual funds or Quicken.com), you're not likely to want to expend that kind of time and effort in reentering that information somewhere else. As long as you're receiving the promised benefits—the right bills are paid on time, the value of your portfolio is always up to date—you'll happily return to the site. But perhaps more important, you'll feel a strong connection to the service provider because it has made your life easier by offering you this level of personalized service.

Examples: Dow Jones and General Motors

I SELECTED Dow Jones' *Wall Street Journal Interactive Edition* and General Motors' OnStar to profile in this section. *The Wall Street Journal* was the first mass-market on-line newspaper to charge Internet customers a subscription fee and the first to offer a personalized newspaper. General Motors' OnStar service tickles me because it's a wonderful example of using electronic technologies to maintain and nurture an ongoing personal relationship with customers as they go about their daily lives.

DELIVER PERSONALIZED SERVICE:

Dow Jones' *Wall Street Journal*

Interactive Edition
www.wsj.com

Executive Summary

Dow Jones' experience in building a successful, subscription-based electronic version of *The Wall Street Journal* on the Web proves that customers will pay for information of value on the Internet. Dow Jones is using its brand name and its reputation for high-quality analysis to lure a new target market: wired customers who don't have the daily newspaper habit. Most of these customers have renewed after the first year. *The Wall Street Journal Interactive Edition* combines personalized service with convenience and community to attract and retain customers.

Critical Success Factors in the Dow Jones Story	
✓ Target the right customers	✓ Let customers help themselves
Own the customer's total experience	✓ Help customers do their jobs
Streamline business processes that impact the customer	✮ Deliver personalized service
Provide a 360-degree view of the customer relationship	✓ Foster community
✮ = Featured in this discussion	✓ = Touched on in this discussion

Dow Jones' *Wall Street Journal Interactive Edition* Provides Much More Than News

FOR AT LEAST a decade, newspaper publishers have been talking about their vision of a "personalized newspaper" delivered to your doorstep, TV, computer, or fax machine. The concept spurred great debate in the publishing industry: If people received news only on the topics in which they declared an interest, wouldn't they miss knowing what was going on in the world around them? And what about the "serendipity factor"? Often a story piques your interest for no obvious reason. Wouldn't customers miss that? And what would become of the advertising revenues that fueled the newspaper-publishing business? If customers opted not to receive the classified ads or the help-wanted ads, would those revenue streams dry up?

Now, after two years of really solid commercial experience with on-line newspaper publishing on the Web, the answers to those questions are in. Customers seem to want both: they want to see the paper exactly the same way that everyone else sees it, and they want to see a more personalized version as well. Advertisers are happy to pay more for ads that are targeted to people who have expressed an interest in their category of products. And help-wanted ads and classified ads now have a new, more avid audience: customers who are actively seeking jobs or products and who value the interactive matchmaking services that are offered.

Using the Internet as a publishing platform raised a new set of questions for publishers, however: With so much information available for free via the Web, would customers be willing to pay for an on-line newspaper subscription the way they are willing to pay for a paper to be delivered to their door each morning? The majority of the world's newspaper publishers went in search of a different business model. They made their on-line newspapers available on the Internet for free, using advertising revenues to help fund their efforts. Many papers began to position themselves as a community magnet. *The Boston Globe* created Boston.com and invited museum, movie, theater, restaurant, sporting event, and concert listings for the greater New England area. The *San Jose Mercury News* became the magnet for the high-tech community in Silicon Valley. Its mission: to keep up with the rapid pace of events in the high-tech world and create a place for dialogue and discussion among the digirati. Both of these papers give away the bulk of their content on the Internet (although they charge for access to their archives) and get their revenues from advertising.

Dow Jones took a different tack with its *Wall Street Journal Interactive Edition*. The company wanted to charge for subscriptions to its on-line newspaper as well as to sell ads. At the same time, *The Wall Street Journal* hoped it could attract a new and different set of customers by using the Web as a channel.

A Strong History in On-line Information Services

IN THE LATE 1970s, Dow Jones began a successful on-line database publishing business, offering full-text retrieval of news stories for rapid research and analysis. By the early 1990s, before the advent of the World Wide Web, a large percentage of Dow Jones' revenues were derived from electronic news services, including broadcasting. For example:

- Dow Jones provides the worldwide financial services industry—including traders and brokers—with real-time business and financial news, such as Dow Jones News Service, the AP–Dow Jones news wires, and Federal Filings.
- For business analysts, news reporters, and other researchers, Dow Jones offers an on-line research service, Dow Jones News/Interactive, comprising a database of 65 million items, fully indexed and rapidly searchable through an interactive text retrieval engine.
- For businesses interested in providing their employees with a comprehensive electronic news service, Dow Jones distributes DowVision, the exclusive electronic source for the combined current daily editions of *The Wall Street Journal, The New York Times, The*

Washington Post, the *Los Angeles Times,* and the *Financial Times* (London). Companies subscribe to DowVision on a per user basis and then receive continual updates of news stories that meet their interest profiles.

Competition for Business News Forces Dow Jones to Look for New Markets

IN RECENT YEARS, Dow Jones and *The Wall Street Journal* have been facing increased competition in the market for business information, not only from traditional competitors such as Reuters and the *Financial Times* (London) but also from new companies such as Bloomberg's *Business News* and *Investors' Business Daily.* For instance, while readership of the international editions has increased slightly, the paid subscriptions for the domestic *Journal* declined from 1,840,000 in 1993 to 1,796,000 in 1995.

So when the Internet and the Web began to catch on as a platform for disseminating information, Dow Jones' executives were ready. Starting back in 1993, Neil Budde, an editorial director in Dow Jones News/Retrieval, had been experimenting with early prototypes for an interactive *Journal.* These early prototypes were programmed in Visual Basic. When the Web began to build momentum, Budde and Tom Baker, director of business development for Dow Jones Interactive Publishing, approached management with a new business proposition. Since our traditional domestic market is waning, they said, let's use the Web to target the next generation of customers, younger people who are interested in business and investing but who don't have the daily newspaper habit. Budde and Baker proposed to make the on-line version of the paper an extension of the current daily *Wall Street Journal* but to add two dimensions the paper product couldn't offer: interactivity and personalization. Baker also suggested that the brand name and editorial quality of the *Journal* should allow the company to charge for subscriptions—not as much as it charged for home delivery of the printed paper but perhaps one third to one half the price of a print subscription.

Developing, Piloting, and Launching the *Interactive Edition*

AFTER GAINING APPROVAL from the board, Budde and Baker created a separate business unit for *The Wall Street Journal Interactive Edition* in the spring of 1994. The new organization was structured into three interrelated teams. One, led by Budde, focused on editorial content, another, led by Susan Cayne, focused on the information technology, and the third, led by Baker, on business development. This new management team made three key decisions during the initial design phase:

1. **COMMERCIALLY AVAILABLE PRODUCTS.** They decided to use commercially available products and technologies whenever possible, rather than doing a lot of in-house development.
2. **RECRUITING.** They decided to recruit technical talent from both inside and outside the existing Dow Jones information systems organizations. The new venture needed engineers and programmers who were familiar with the rapidly developing Web and Internet technologies.
3. **EDITORIAL CONTENT.** They wanted to use the editorial content of the *Journal* and other existing Dow Jones publications. However, they expected to add their own editorial staff as the popularity of the site grew and to produce additional content areas tailored to the sensibilities of *Interactive Edition* subscribers.

Budde and his team spent the first year building the business and technical infrastructure. They focused on creating a prototype version for the Web site that would allow them to test and refine the Web site design and test marketing strategies. They launched the prototype for the *Interactive Edition* in July 1995, offering the "Money and Investing Update" section of the daily newspaper free to Internet users willing to register and provide information about their backgrounds and interests. Baker began to compile a subscriber database for market research.

The prototype Web site was much more successful than originally anticipated. More than 340,000 people registered and used the site at least once during the six-month trial period. Follow-up e-mail surveys conducted to supplement the registration information showed that these prospects were a serious and affluent business audience. They were slightly younger than the regular newspaper readers, with a median age of 42, compared to 54 for the print edition. They were also active personal investors. But best of all, 60 percent of them were not regular readers of the *Journal*. This is exactly the profile that Baker and his team were hoping for.

With this corroboration in hand, Baker's team continued with its plan to launch the full on-line version of the newspaper. The *Interactive Edition* went live on April 29, 1996. It was offered for free to all of the current subscribers to the "Money and Investing Update" prototype and to any others for a three-month trial period. During those first three months, a total of

650,000 people registered to use the *Interactive Edition*. After the trial period, about 34,000 people signed up for a year's subscription on the Web. A year later, there were 100,000 paid subscribers. The subscription price for the on-line edition was $49 per year for new subscribers or $29 per year for customers who already subscribed to the printed *Journal*, *Barron's*, or *Smart Money Magazine*. This price compared to $175 for an annual subscription to the print version of the *Journal*. Baker reported that about 65 percent of their initial on-line customers were not subscribers to the print edition.

Developing Interactive, Personalized Content

WHEN YOU MOVE a hard-copy published product onto the Web, there are a lot of design trade-offs to be made. You can't simply replicate the "look" of the front page and each section of the paper. But you do want readers to feel comfortable that they're accessing the same branded, trusted information they're familiar with on paper. So the *Interactive Edition* was designed to look a lot like the print newspaper in terms of the typefaces used and the use of a newspaper column layout. But the information was arranged differently. There are more brief summaries. To read an actual story, you click on the summary. One thing that Baker's team had learned from the pilot stage was that customers didn't want to see their "personal page" first. They wanted to see an overview of all the important business news of the day, organized based on the priorities the *Journal's* editorial staff determined. That's what they felt they were paying for: trenchant analysis and editorial judgment. So over time, the *Interactive Edition* evolved to include:

* A front page highlighting "What's News" in business and finance, worldwide news headlines, and brief summaries of key stories in major news areas such as "technology," "media and marketing," and "the law."
* Links to individual topical sections such as "marketplace," "money," "sports," "Europe," "Asia," and "the economy."
* Direct access to the "Personal Journal" section, where subscribers receive a customized selection of news and feature articles that correspond to the interests in their personal profiles and stock portfolios.

Each clickable headline and brief summary is immediately linked to the complete article. Subscribers can quickly scan the contents of individual sections and then go to the items of interest. And the *Interactive Edition* contains much more information than the print newspaper that would be delivered to your home or office. It includes the U.S. edition, *The Wall Street Journal Europe*, and *The Asian Wall Street Journal* as well as stories from the Dow Jones news wire. In addition, subscribers to the *Interactive Edition* can get immediate access to a number of related Dow Jones sites directly from the *Interactive Edition*'s home page, using their own user names and passwords for single, seamless log-ons. These related sites include *Barron's Online*, *SmartMoney Interactive*, The Dow Jones Publications Library, and Careers.wsj.com. The last is a modern-day, free, interactive help-wanted service. It has a database of more than 12,000 jobs from twenty-eight participating companies, as well as helpful information about job hunting advice, résumé writing, succeeding at work, working globally, starting your own business, and many other topics of interest to both job seekers and human resource professionals.

Dow Jones Interactive Publishing has steadily improved the personalization capabilities of the *Interactive Edition*. Initially, readers could select from a fixed list of relatively limited categories or use free-text phrases to create a single profile. This was an awkward process that did not always produce the desired results: The predefined categories did not consistently capture readers' interests, and often readers were interested in tracking a number of different trends. It was easy to create a profile to track particular companies or industries, for example (up to the twenty-five permitted). But it was difficult to track concepts like "Internet banking" or "telecommunications deregulation."

The second version of the "Personal Journal," introduced in the spring of 1997, addressed these issues. It let customers create up to five different personal profiles and track five separate stock portfolios—putting all the information related to particular topics into specific folders. So, for example, I have one folder that tracks customer care–related stories and another that tracks Internet and electronic commerce topics. Subscribers can enter both fixed categories and free-text words and phrases to locate timely collections of articles that match their particular areas of interest. And they can add information about their portfolio holdings to calculate their current values. In addition, they can specify which sections—Walter Mossberg's technology column, technology coverage from Europe or Asia—they want to track. Through trial and error, Baker's team had discovered how to get customers to "leave something of themselves behind" and to keep coming back day in and day out to see how business events were affecting their personal view of the world.

If you think about it, you'll realize that there's a lot more than good search technology that enables a useful personalization capability. In the *Interactive Edition*'s case, the utility of its search engine is enhanced by the human knowledge management that goes into the assignment of key words for each story. For example, there is a subject matter expert on the editorial staff assigned to each core concept. That is the person who decides whether a story is really about the Internet or not, for example.

The original content that makes up *The Wall Street Journal*'s various editions and its sister on-line services is heavily tagged by authors and editors as part of the editorial process. Then the copy flows through a series of automated processes to convert it into on-line-publishable form. *Interactive Edition* staff members review the results of these automated processes and add more tags. They've found that they need to enhance the granularity of the document-tagging rules and criteria to improve the effectiveness of the automated information flows. Specific categories and tags that are appropriate for print publications are insufficient for interactive information access. These *Interactive Edition* editors also write appropriate summaries before publishing the new information on the Web site.

Personalization is one dimension of interactivity, but the *Interactive Edition* actually offers several other dimensions that are equally important to customers and that keep them coming back for more. For example, any article that mentions a publicly held company links to a Company Briefing Book, a compilation of business information about that company. Each Briefing Book provides a brief overview of the company—including a financial overview, recent stock performance, company news, and recent press releases—from information collected by Dow Jones. Thus, readers reading about a company on-line can immediately "drill down" to find relevant background information selected from Dow Jones and other sources and then (if desired) link to the company's Web site or to other comprehensive company-specific news services (from Hoover) or to peruse recent SEC filings (from Edgar). I've found this briefing book capability to be an invaluable adjunct to the news.

Another aspect of the *Interactive Edition* is its timeliness. Unlike the print versions of the paper, the *Interactive Edition* is revised twenty-four hours a day. So you can always find updates of late-breaking stories— updates that are prepared with the same analytical spin you'd expect from the *Journal*. As you can imagine, all of this customization and updating takes extra manpower. In addition to relying heavily on *The Wall Street Journal*'s editorial staff and the various Dow Jones news feeds, the *Interac-*

tive Edition has its own staff of journalists who report to its editor in chief, Neil Budde.

Evolving the Technical Infrastructure

At an architectural level, the *Interactive Edition* is made up of a series of systems that perform specific business functions: coupling the back-end news reporting, analyses, and editorial processes with the front-end publication activities on the Web. The overall environment is based on a modular and extensible architecture, enabling an ongoing series of technical enhancements to the core information repository.

The Web site is hosted on multiple Sun Solaris systems—mostly ES 3000s and ES 4500s—located in South Brunswick, New Jersey. New servers are routinely added as traffic increases. The site itself is partitioned between two data centers and accesses the Internet through two T-3 connections, one from MCI and the other through UUNET Technologies. The site is designed as a fail-safe environment where one part can function independently of the other if necessary.

Dow Jones has invested heavily in the design and development of the *Interactive Edition* Web site, integrating components from multiple vendors. The *Interactive Edition* is based on the capabilities of the Netscape Publishing System for hosting content and distributing it through the Internet. The Netscape System provides the key link for user name/password authorizations and access to the site. User background, billing, and subscription data are stored in an Oracle7 database that is also integrated with the Netscape Publishing System. The Netscape system also includes Verity's Topic text retrieval engine together with basic tools for managing Web-based content. All of the content is fully indexed, and the indices and associated stories are then stored as a series of flat files on the site. Since the access procedures and content management requirements are fairly predictable, developers have decided not to absorb the overhead associated with a database repository.

Individual back-end news systems aggregate content for the *Interactive Edition* and prepare it for on-line publication by (1) interpreting the structured tags attached to individual news stories and assigning these articles to the appropriate Web pages and search categories and (2) scanning the article contents for company names and inserting links to the Company Briefing Books. Cayne's group selected OmniMark, a document-oriented scripting environment, to automate some of these linkages.

Baker and his team decided to outsource key functions of the business: advertising and support for on-line discussions. After initially trying to manage its own advertising inventories and the administrative chores of reporting results to advertisers, they decided to use the capabilities of DoubleClick as a remote service bureau. DoubleClick automatically serves the ads that appear on the *Interactive Edition* pages and then counts both the impressions and click-throughs. Discussion group services are run by *Interactive Edition* staff but maintained at a remote, third-party site, hosted by the Well Engaged (www.wellengaged.com), a spin-off from The Well, one of the pioneering venues for computer-based conferencing.

Supporting Communities of Interest

RIGHT FROM THE start, the *Interactive Edition* has attracted a high proportion of small business owners and readers involved in technology-based businesses. So the *Interactive Edition* managers have expanded the coverage in these interest areas and created discussion forums specific to them.

1. SMALL BUSINESS SUITE. This is a separate section on the site, accessible by a single click on the home page, designed to provide timely features on issues that matter most to small-business owners, entrepreneurs, and others looking to start or grow a business. It includes coverage of small office/home office (SOHO) issues from the *Journal,* on-line discussion groups, a searchable archive of small-business news, and a collection of links to additional Web-based small-business resources.

2. THE CENTER. The Tech Center, also accessible from the home page, summarizes all of the daily news of interest on a single page and offers one-click access to the in-depth articles and background information. It contains news and information not only from the print edition of

the *Journal* and other Dow Jones news services but also from an expanded *Interactive Edition* news staff based in New York and San Francisco. In addition to tracking breaking stories, alliances, and the converging worlds of telecommunications, media, and computing, it offers a growing library of issue-oriented briefings, in-depth background information, and moderated readers' forums.

3. SPORTS. Working with Total Sports, an independent publisher of sports information and statistics, the *Interactive Edition* now publishes an expanded sports section. Subscribers can now receive continuously updated coverage of major professional and college sports events.

4. TOPICAL ON-LINE DISCUSSION FORUMS. In addition to these ongoing communities of interest, different news events spawn reader interaction and discussions. These "hot topics" come and go in the discussion forums section of the site. What distinguishes them from other on-line forums you'll find elsewhere on the Web, however, is the caliber of people who participate. *The Wall Street Journal Interactive Edition* tends to attract many of the leading thinkers in their fields. So it's not uncommon to see world-famous economists or CEOs of major companies commenting on recent events.

For all of these discussion forums, *Interactive Edition* staff vet the individual contributions before posting them for subscribers.

Results

THE *Interactive Edition* has grown into a substantial publishing enterprise. It is staffed by more than 110 full-time employees, including approximately 55 writers and editors dedicated to content creation. It has an operational staff responsible for ensuring around-the-clock operations, seven days a week. Baker's team has succeeded in offering customers an experience that provides them both business and personal benefits. By combining personalized information services with a branded experience and a sense of community, *The Wall Street Journal Interactive Edition* has become one of the premier business destinations on the Web.

As of April 1998, the *Interactive Edition* had roughly 200,000 paying subscribers. Subscriptions have been growing steadily at around 2,000 readers per week. More telling is the number of renewals: 85 percent of the subscribers have signed up for a second year and give every indication of becoming loyal and continual customers. Only one third of the subscribers also receive the print edition. By venturing into cyberspace, *The Wall Street Journal* has been able to reach an untapped audience. This on-line audience is younger than the readers of the print publication and also slightly less affluent—in part because of their age. Although Baker has no proof that there's a direct correlation between the growth of on-line subscriptions and the growth in print subscriptions, it is interesting to note that in 1996, the first year of the on-line service, domestic subscriptions to the print *Journal* rose to 1,841,188 from 1,796,000 in 1995. Certainly, there's no obvious cannibalization going on. Print subscribers do not appear to be canceling their print subscriptions in favor of the less expensive on-line service.

The Web site continues to sustain a high level of interest that has been steadily increasing. In October 1997, the site generated 35.3 million page views, up from 18 million page views in October 1996. By August 1998, about 70,000 people were accessing the site each business day, approximately 30 percent of subscribers.

These demographics and the ever-increasing number of subscribers are one set of indicators for the business proposition. The ever-expanding base of advertisers is another. The *Interactive Edition* can now command premium prices for its advertising inventory, with a base rate of roughly $65 per thousand impressions—and with higher-rate cards for specific, targeted pages.

At the start of the effort, senior managers and editors assumed that it would take roughly four to five years for the site to become profitable. Over the years, this has been the average amount of time that Dow Jones has needed for a new publication to become profitable. *The Wall Street Journal Interactive Edition* appears to fit that model. Based on the experience over the past eighteen months, it appears likely that *Interactive Edition* will begin to turn a profit within the next year or two.

Patty's Rx for *The Wall Street Journal Interactive Edition*

Tom Baker's next push will be into international markets. An international audience represents a major growth area. Without any advertising or special efforts, currently about 10 percent of the *Interactive Edition*'s subscribers have overseas addresses. Many more should be interested, particularly given the fact that readership of the English-language European and Asian print editions and that of the Spanish-language Latin American print *Journal* have been growing faster than the domestic readership. However, in order to provide a sustainable on-line version of the *Journal* that truly meets the needs of businesspeople in other parts of the world, the *Journal* would need to invest heavily in round-the-clock coverage of local business news.

On the other hand, the on-line discussion forums are a great way to add local content and to keep up with the pulse of the changing business climate in different parts of the world. By fostering high-level dialogue and discussion on topics of both local and international interest, such as the devaluation of currencies in Asia, the bailout of Japanese banks, or the United Kingdom's reluctance to support the EMU, the *Interactive Edition* could become the "in" destination for anyone interested in the global business and economic climate. I would therefore recommend that the *Journal* invest in hiring astute local columnists in various parts of the world, not just to contribute news analysis and reporting of local business events but also to lead thoughtful discussions on-line.

As for the personalized services offered by the *Interactive Edition*, as a subscriber, I'd like to see even more e-mail "push." Today, I receive at the most a couple of alerts per week from the *Journal* on topics of interest to me. Yet each day my personal folders are brimming with new information. I'd like to receive e-mails summarizing the contents of the top three items in each of my personal folders each day. That way, I'd know whether or not I needed to log on to the site. Dow Jones has been experimenting with the use of a variety of "push" technologies to meet this requirement. It has tried BackWeb, Microsoft's Internet Explorer channels, and Pointcast. So far, e-mail appears to be the most prevalent platform and the easiest way to reach subscribers. Therefore, I would like to see the *Journal* do a lot more with its personalized outbound e-mail. However, it must be possible for each subscriber to easily change his e-mail threshold, so that nobody gets overwhelmed by news-related e-mails.

"Take-Aways" from the Dow Jones Story

1. Customers don't want personalized information services to the exclusion of seeing the whole picture. They do value personalization *in addition* to having access to all the information everyone else has.

2. By seducing customers into "leaving something of themselves behind"—the topics and companies they want to follow, their favorite sections of the paper, their stock portfolios, the parts of the world they're interested in tracking—*The Wall Street Journal Interactive Edi-*

tion has succeeded in creating customer loyalty. More than 85 percent of its subscribers renewed after their first year.

3. The ability to drill down to get more and more detailed information about a topic that interests them is also critical to customers' satisfaction.

4. Customers expect on-line information services to be continuously updated, twenty-four hours a day.

5. Customers will pay for information services on the Web as long as they get what they are paying for: a branded, consistent, high-quality set of information, judgment, insights, and analysis.

6. Once you succeed in giving customers an easy-to-use, essential tool that enhances their personal and business lives, they'll remain with you as loyal customers.

7. Fostering community is an important adjunct to personalization. The *Interactive Edition* creates and sustains communities of interest by hosting discussion forums on hot topics.

8. A trio of competencies is required for any serious Web endeavor: business development/marketing, editorial oversight, and technical vision and oversight.

DELIVER PERSONALIZED SERVICE:

General Motors
www.onstar.com

Executive Summary

All car manufacturers want "customers for life." In the past, they've strived to meet this goal by designing more appealing cars each year and encouraging their dealers to offer good customer service. General Motors has embarked on a new approach, which, if it takes off, will revolutionize the automotive industry. For its new OnStar service, GM is moving from the sale of physical goods to the sale of subscription-based personalized services. If the company is successful, it will have customers for life.

Critical Success Factors in the General Motors Story	
✓ Target the right customers	Let customers help themselves
✽ Own the customer's total experience	✓ Help customers do their jobs by enhancing the mobile environment
✓ Streamline business processes that impact the customer	✽ Deliver personalized service
Provide a 360-degree view of the customer relationship	✽ Foster community
✽ = Featured in this discussion	✓ = Touched on in this discussion

General Motors' OnStar Provides Personalized Safety and Convenience

GENERAL MOTORS' CUSTOMER research revealed that customers had a set of common concerns: they feared for their lives and for the security and safety of their families on the road. They didn't just want safer cars; they wanted safer roads. They wanted to be safe from carjackers. They worried about having an accident on a deserted road: how long would it take for someone to notice and come to their rescue? These customer concerns converged with a set of new mobile technologies that GM executives found promising. What if GM could offer its customers peace of mind—the knowledge that no matter where they were in their car, someone would be there with them, able to summon assistance or give directions? Thus the concept of GM's OnStar service was born.

OnStar is an optional service you can purchase for many current GM cars and light-duty trucks. It consists of a built-in cell phone, global positioning system (GPS) satellite technology, and an electronic linkage to a round-the-clock customer support center that locates your car as soon as you call for assistance (or when your air bag deploys in an accident or your car's theft alarm goes off). The OnStar adviser knows who and where you are, quickly determines what you need, and summons help or gives detailed directions. If you've been in an accident, the OnStar adviser summons the closest emergency help. If your car is stolen, OnStar will track the vehicle and notify police of its location until it is recovered. If you're locked out of your car, the adviser can open it remotely. If you're out of gas, the adviser can arrange for gas to be delivered to your car. If you just need directions to the nearest cash machine or fast-food restaurant, the adviser has all that information at her fingertips. If you need a recommendation for a good restaurant in the area along with reservations, the adviser can handle that as well. Or if you'd like even more personal service, a concierge can get you tickets to a "sold-out" sports event or a table at a restaurant you'd normally have to book months in advance, or track down that hard-to-find gift for your wife—all while you're driving to work.

Using Electronic Technologies to Deliver Personalized Service Remotely

GM's ONSTAR SERVICE is about as personalized as service can get. Let's see how GM got into the business of offering in-car service to customers.

Beginning the early 1990s, several times a year, the technology strategists from Hughes and Electronic Data Systems (EDS), would make presentations to GM's management about emerging technologies that might affect GM's future. Harry Pearce, vice chairman of GM, who had organizational responsibility for Hughes and EDS at GM, began to notice a set of new technologies that looked really interesting for a company in the transportation business. These technologies were GPS; voice recognition technology; a nationwide, ubiquitous cellular communications infrastructure; and sophisticated, digitally controlled, in-vehicle electrical systems. As these technologies matured, Pearce, along with the engineers at GM North American Operations (NAO), and colleagues at Hughes and EDS became more and more excited about the possibilities this convergence of technologies implied. There was obviously a whole new class of services that would be enabled by knowing exactly where a vehicle is, being able to communicate with the driver via cell phone, and being able to control many of the car's electrical functions remotely (for example, unlock the car's doors).

By early 1995, GM management gave the go ahead to launch a new service business—a business designed to provide service to people while they're in their cars. They tapped Chester A. "Chet" Huber, a twenty-three-year veteran of GM's locomotive business. The new business needed to pull together resources from GM's car and truck divisions, Hughes, and EDS (which is now an independent company). "I was the right man for the job, because I hadn't worked for any of them. I was a neutral third party," Huber explained.

In June 1995, Chet Huber became general manager of the OnStar division. He was given an open mandate to develop a business chartered to "deliver great service to people while they're on the road." Huber sees his challenge as that of growing a new business revenue stream for GM—creating a business that's related to GM's core business but very different in its business model and value proposition. Instead of selling a physical good once, collecting the money at the time of sale, and hoping to sell to the same customer again in a few years, the OnStar business is a subscription business. The customer buys the option, has it installed in her car, and then pays a service fee each month. "Our job is to create relationships for life with our customers," said Huber.

Huber's biggest challenge was to design an entrepreneurial, fast-moving business that could thrive within GM's $100 billion bureaucracy. He did this in part by bringing many people in from outside of GM and by relying on a number of outside consultants. Currently about 50 percent of the employees in the OnStar division have a telecommunications or high-tech background, while the other 50 percent come from the auto industry. "We had to have a deep understanding of our dealer channel," Huber explained, as well as an intimate knowledge of in-car electrical and mechanical systems.

Developing and Launching the Initial Service

IN THE FALL of 1995, GM decided that OnStar would be a separate division of GM's North American Operations and would report to Ronald D. Zarrella, vice president and group executive of the NAO Vehicle Sales, Service, and Marketing Group. The new division would deliver its first product and service to the market in twelve months—fall 1996 for the 1997 Cadillac. It had targeted the Cadillac audience for the initial service launch. Cadillac owners are GM's most upscale market, and Huber's team knew it needed to price the OnStar option competitively at about $1,000. But most important, the Cadillac's electrical architecture was the "most hospitable one"—the one that would be easiest to integrate the option into.

When Huber's group met with the Cadillac team, the Cadillac folks were somewhat incredulous. "Normally, if you want to be involved in a car program, you need to appear two to four years before the launch date of the new car, with validated components," Huber explained. His team had the audacity to show up less than twelve months before the car launch date with parts that had never before been integrated into a Cadillac!

But the Cadillac folks were game. They liked the OnStar vision. And they always like to be first to the market with a new capability. They agreed to go forward with the project on an accelerated time schedule as long as the OnStar team could meet its obligations and deadlines. There was a clear understanding on both sides that the project would be aborted if they couldn't meet their objectives.

In order to complete the design and development of the OnStar service, Huber's group of about forty people (plus project teams from Hughes and EDS) had several parallel efforts to undertake. They had to design, test, and integrate the physical components into the Cadillac. They had to develop the systems and databases that would interact with the in-car hardware. They had to test the communications capabilities in different parts of the country. And they had to design, staff, and train a round-the-clock call center operation.

Evolving the Technical Infrastructure

What gets installed in the car if you purchase the OnStar service? There are two boxes, each crammed with technology. The first is the Vehicle Integration Unit (VIU). It talks to the car's computers, which can communicate the state of many of the in-car systems— *The air bag just deployed*—and can control functions—*Unlock the doors*. The VIU also contains the GPS unit, which tracks and communicates the car's position. The second box is the Vehicle Communications Unit (VCU). This contains the voice recognition system and the built-in cell phone. The voice recognition system was named Veronica by the engineers. It talks to you and prompts you. It also "learns" and then recognizes the numbers and commands you program into it. So you can store up to twenty different numbers associated with voice commands ("Call Fred." "Call home." "Call the office."). When you initiate a call (by lifting a lever on the steering wheel column and either giving the number to Veronica or using a voice tag), your CD or radio will mute and the incoming call will be routed through the high-fidelity speakers associated with the in-car stereo system. Your voice will be picked up by a built-in high-fidelity microphone located in the ceiling just above the steering wheel.

One of the biggest challenges in designing the infrastructure, Managing Director Chet Huber reports, was dealing with all of the different cellular networks that cover the country. Even though OnStar had initially chosen to deploy using analog cellular services in the United States (since there is no nationwide digital coverage), there were a lot of challenges. There are many different vintages of cellular systems, each with different capabilities. The data collected by the GPS system and the in-car computers go through a software modem over the wireless network. The OnStar design team had to be absolutely certain about the integrity of the signals being transmitted on each network. If an air bag is deploying in your car, for example, that signal has to reach the OnStar call center quickly and accurately. Some of the other issues the OnStar team dealt with included:

- How to deal with the fact that some cellular systems required dialing a "1" before the ten-digit phone number for long distance dialing and others didn't.
- How to handle roaming situations if a cell phone is a "nonrecognized roamer" in a particular territory.
- What to do about the fact that different cellular systems require different power levels.
- How to teach the system a personal identification number (PIN) and how the cell phone will know when the PIN is required.
- Ensuring that the GPS positioning data that were being transmitted along with the call could be accurately received by the OnStar system.

To resolve these and other technical issues, the cellular communications team worked very closely with the Cellular Telecommunications Industry Association (CTIA). In fact, that organization was impressed with the breakthroughs OnStar made in solving many of these technical problems as well as with the way the OnStar system transmits the caller's location using GPS data. As a result, the CTIA gave its coveted Future Vision award to OnStar in June 1996, a few months before the actual launch of the OnStar service.

The system used to support the OnStar call center operations was custom-developed by EDS for GM's OnStar division. It includes a basic customer profile database for all OnStar customers that contains demographic information about the primary driver of the car and information about the subscriber's car: make, model, appearance, and options. There is also a mammoth geographic information system with all of the geocoded street maps for the entire United States. And there's a database filled with a list of hotels, restaurants, ATM machines, gas stations, and so on, each geocoded so it will appear in the correct location on the map. Finally, there's a knowledge base with information procured from a variety of third parties—restaurant ratings, travel guides, and so on. The OnStar application has been undergoing iterative enhancements. Within the first year and a half, there were several releases of the software. Huber expects that continuous improvement to continue with a new software release every quarter that incorporates customers' requests and priorities.

The OnStar service was launched on schedule in the fall of 1996 for 1997 Cadillacs. By 1998, nearly two million GM cars and trucks were OnStar-capable, including all Buicks and selected minivans, sport utilities, full-size trucks, premium cars (Oldsmobile and Pontiac), and midsize vehicles (Chevrolet Monte Carlo and Lumina models). The cost for the service was $895 plus dealer installation for the OnStar options package and $22.50 per month for the ongoing service. What seems right about that pricing model is that it's analogous to how cellular phone services are priced. While OnStar is more expensive than a basic cellular service, you're also getting a lot more than dial tone; you're getting highly personalized service. Your car has now become a "smart car." It knows where you are and can help you get where you need to go.

Providing Personalized Service

WHAT HAPPENS WHEN a call comes into an OnStar call center? The adviser sees a map on the computer screen in front of him with the car positioned on the map. Another window appears with the subscriber's information and the vehicle information. At the top of the screen the adviser sees what kind of call this is—air bag deployed, theft deterrent system invoked, red emergency button pressed, green "information/assistance" button pressed. Another window provides him with information about who the 911 emergency service provider is for this particular location (sometimes it's the local police, sometimes the state police). The initial window with the customer's name and the reason for the call appears immediately. It takes about twenty seconds for the map and the correct emergency contact information to display on the screen. So by the time the adviser has introduced himself and greeted the subscriber ("Hello, this is Patrick————, how can I help you?"), he has everything he needs to assist the customer. The call center personnel are recent college graduates and are highly trained. They really like their jobs because they're helping people who really need their assistance every day, sometimes in life-threatening situations.

By the fall of 1997, OnStar advisers had dealt with dozens of accidents in which air bags had deployed, two carjackings, and countless other requests, from "Where's the nearest ATM?" to "Can you get me season tickets for the Green Bay Packers?" Take the example of OnStar subscriber Jim Dickey from Pendleton, Oregon. Returning home from dinner with some business colleagues at a restaurant that had been recommended by an OnStar adviser, Dickey took the scenic route. A deer bolted across the road and ran into the front of his Cadillac. The air bags deployed, sending an emergency notification to OnStar. "My car hadn't even come to a stop, and my phone was already ringing," says Dickey. "I was impressed. An adviser was immediately on the line, checking to see if I was all right." Within minutes, OnStar sent local police to the scene. Another subscriber was held up at gunpoint at a highway rest area and told to get out of his car. He did so, but as he did, he pressed the red emergency button, alerting the OnStar staff. Within minutes, one policeman had rushed to the scene, picked up the customer, and calmed him down, getting a detailed account of the incident, while a second patrol car was on the trail of the stolen car, being directed by the OnStar adviser. Within an hour the stolen car was captured and the arrest made.

On a lighter note, one subscriber came out of a shopping mall with his granddaughter and couldn't remember where he'd parked his car. "Watch," he told her as he dialed the OnStar toll-free number on his cell phone. "Grandpa's going to ask an angel to flash the car's lights and beep its horn."

Of course, there are some things the OnStar system won't do for you. If you call the OnStar number and ask, "My wife has been out for a while with the car. Can you tell me where she is?" you'll get a polite refusal. OnStar's policy is to divulge the location of a car only to the nearest law enforcement authorities in the case of an actual emergency.

Growing OnStar Partnerships

ONE OF THE key assets of the OnStar service is its ever-growing database of hotels, restaurants, and other destinations. By the end of 1997, there were more than 3.9 million listings in the OnStar database, in categories ranging from video stores to copy shops. If you need to find the nearest post office that's open after 5 P.M., or a hospital, notary public, or car wash, it's likely to be in the database and an adviser can find it for you.

Many of these destinations and resources have become "OnStar partners," ensuring a level of personalized service designed to carry the OnStar experience over into the rest of your day. So, for example, OnStar has Hilton Hotels, Embassy Suites, Days Inn, Best Western, and many more hotel and resort chains as partners. These are organizations with which OnStar has made special arrangements that give you preferential treatment. Other partners include American Floral Service—so it's easy and quick for you to order flowers for delivery anywhere in the country—and Mobil. The *Mobil Travel Guide* is available on-line to the advisers, to help them make restaurant recommendations and reservations for you.

Next Steps

MOST OF THE changes that are being continuously made to the OnStar application are the result of direct customer feedback. For example, the OnStar team soon learned that organizing the database listings into ATMs and gas stations wasn't good enough. Customers wanted to know where the nearest Amoco gas station was, or the nearest Wells Fargo cash machine. OnStar needed to keep more customer profile information on record and use that profile to retrieve or highlight the most relevant information for each customer.

All of these customer requests and refinements are noted and prioritized. Of course, OnStar advisers keep track of what customers ask for that they can't deliver or that take too long to access. In addition, Huber explains that all of the company's employees are required and given incentives to spend one hour per month sitting next to an adviser to gain firsthand experience with customer interactions. Huber set this up as a team incentive. If a single employee misses his hour in any month, the entire team loses its bonus for the year.

One of the areas of feedback that surprised Huber was the fact that customers began asking for remote diagnostics of their cars' mechanical systems. Huber and the other marketing executives had thought that customers didn't want to know about the inner workings of their cars' engines and hydraulic systems, so they hadn't planned to perform remote diagnostics. But what customers said was, "I want you to do triage on my car for me. If it starts acting up, or if the "Check engine" light goes on, I want to be told if this is something serious that I need to have looked at right away or something I can put off for a while."

In addition to remote diagnostics, there are several other areas of enhancement planned. First, Huber wants to expand the customer profile information that's kept in the database. Right now, the database contains basic information about the subscriber and the car. GM would like the customer to be able to add more information he'd like the OnStar folks to know: other family members who typically drive (or ride in) the car, as well as preferences for gas companies, restaurant chains, banks, and so on that would help an adviser quickly find a preferred resource. Huber plans to maintain these profiles in two ways: by sending them out by mail and by encouraging customers to go to the OnStar Web site to modify or extend their profiles at any time. Second, he wants to extend the customer contact information to track each interaction with each customer. For example, he said, "If the last three interactions the customer had were very positive ones with Bill, Judy, and Anne, if any of those advisers is available the next time he calls in, I'd like to route his call to one of the people he's already got a good rapport with."

Huber wants to do more with inbound call routing as well. For example, "If we have someone who grew up in a particular geographic area and a customer is calling from that area, we should put the person with local knowledge on the phone." Eventually, he explained, specific advisers could be trained to be experts in specific metropolitan regions, and calls from those areas could be routed directly to them.

In terms of expansion, OnStar is already available in the United States and Canada. Next, Huber plans to expand the service to Europe. That will take a lot of doing, because the cellular infrastructure is different, the emergency communications networks are different, and, of course, there are a number of different countries, languages, and cultures. However, Huber expects to roll out OnStar service in Europe by 1999.

Results

BY THE END of 1997—OnStar's first year of operation—there were approximately 20,000 OnStar customers. And the system had been thoroughly tested and debugged. Now that OnStar is considered ready for prime time, GM is ramping up advertising and sales for the service. Those first 20,000 customers constitute about 1 percent of the current potential market for the service: the 2,000,000 new-model GM cars and trucks that are now OnStar-capable. By the time OnStar reaches 10 percent of its potential market in a couple of years (my estimate, not GM's), the service should be profitable. Perhaps more important is the customer loyalty that GM will be experiencing as OnStar customers continue to opt for GM cars.

After the first year, GM's dealers were also becoming more enthusiastic about promoting the service for two reasons. First, many of them had had an opportunity to use the service on the demo car at their dealership, so they had firsthand experience with the service. Second, they had discovered the benefits of the "halo effect" the OnStar option conferred upon their dealership. GM customers are routinely surveyed after the purchase of their cars and after they've had them for a while. They are asked about the experience of buying the car and about the quality of ongoing service they've received from the dealership. OnStar customers always rate the dealer higher than do non-OnStar customers in all of the areas measured.

Just about the time other competitors begin to offer comparable services, OnStar will no doubt be ready to up the ante by making deals with car rental companies and with other car manufacturers. Sure, GM will then no longer be able to use OnStar to differentiate its cars from those of competitors, but, in the meantime, the company will have built a successful service business that is tightly linked to its actual end customers and their households—a very valuable franchise.

Patty's Rx for GM's OnStar

In addition to extending the service internationally, I'd like to see OnStar do a lot more with its Web site. Today, the site is very informative about the service itself, and it contains a frequently asked questions section for OnStar subscribers. But there's nothing else that is designed for current customers. As of early 1998, OnStar was still at phase 1 with its Web site: brochureware, albeit quite elegant brochureware.

As an OnStar subscriber, I'd expect to see lively discussions among other users about innovative uses they'd made of the service—ways it helped them in their lives—that would give others good ideas. I'd also want to be able to see and modify my profile. I'd want to add the names and pertinent information about other family members who might be driving my car (or riding in it) and need assistance. I'd want to find a lot of information on-line that would help me plan my trips. For example, I'd want access to the same on-line knowledge bases of information about restaurants and hotels that the advisers have at their fingertips. I'd like to be able to reserve a hotel room via the Web site and get the OnStar preferential treatment. And I'd like to be able to avail myself of other OnStar partners' services.

As a rental car user, I'd like to see the OnStar service made available to one or more rental car companies. So if I was an OnStar subscriber and I needed to rent a car, I could rent one that was OnStar-capable. Or if I wasn't an OnStar subscriber but I wanted to try out the service, I'd like to be able to do so as an option.

"Take-Aways" from the General Motors Story

1. Today's electronic technologies can be used to improve the quality of life for customers. Use your imagination. General Motors did.
2. GPS systems and cellular communication provide a viable infrastructure for services that can be delivered to customers no matter where they are, at any time of the day or night.
3. Customers are eager for services that offer them security, safety, and convenience.
4. GM has added an entirely new business model to its portfolio: a subscription-based service. This will allow the company to build ongoing relationships with its end customers.
5. In order to keep customers for life, you need to do more than offer good products and service. You need to give customers something they really value—in GM's case, peace of mind. OnStar is much more than an insurance policy. It's a guarantee that someone will be there for you when you need them. In addition to safety and security, you get to enjoy a level of convenience every day that you'll soon come to rely on.
6. An entrepreneurial, fast-moving business can grow within a huge organization. GM's OnStar division moved from concept to delivery in a little over a year.
7. OnStar designed its function starting with the end customer. Then it put into place the infrastructure, business processes, applications, and trained personnel that would be required to deliver that function.
8. The new OnStar modules had to integrate tightly with the existing in-car systems. GM didn't have the luxury of changing the design of its

cars to accommodate these new customer-facing systems. This is yet another form of "system integration" of the kind that you may need to do.

9. If you want to deliver truly personalized service, you'll need to supplement basic customer information with detailed customer profiles and then use those profiles to customize the information that's presented to each customer.

> ### Deliver Personalized Service:
> ### Lessons Learned

It's interesting to note that both the examples I selected to illustrate the delivery of personalized service involve subscription services. Of course, personalized service can be delivered in many other ways. The beauty of a subscription offering is that it usually means that you are in front of the customer every day (or once a week or once a month) for a year. With today's interactive technologies, being in front of customers means a lot more than just sending them a magazine or newspaper in the mail each month. As you can see from the *Wall Street Journal* example, a personalized subscription service means alerting the customer whenever something important happens. And as you can see from both cases, it means being there for the customer around the clock.

Customer Profiles Are Key

OBVIOUSLY YOU CAN'T deliver personalized service without knowing a lot about each customer. Both companies gather their initial customer information at the time a subscriber signs up for the service. In Dow Jones's case, customers then continuously refine their profiles on the Web site. This is done by creating folders with key words associated with them— topics or companies a customer wishes to follow. Or a customer can create a portfolio of companies whose stock and financial information he or she wants to track. In GM's case, the advisers are able to elicit additional profile information as they interact with customers in much the same way Bell Atlantic does. The OnStar database system needs to be extended, however, so that this valuable profile information has someplace to go other than a "notes" field. Customer profiles need to be stored in databases. The entries need to be converted into fields of data that a business rule or a program can act upon. For example, in the case of *The Wall Street Journal Interactive Edition*, the fact that I have selected "Internet" as one of my key words means that every article that the editor in charge of Internet stories deems relevant will turn up in my Internet folder.

Customers Make an Investment of Their Time and Energy

The reason personalized services are so seductive and "sticky" is that once customers have invested their time in creating and/or updating their profile information, it's unlikely they'll go somewhere else to do the same thing. It's very important that customers see a rapid and direct return on the investment of their time. In *The Wall Street Journal Interactive Edition*'s case, the feedback is immediate. A customer enters his or her profile information, and, voilà, new information appears on his or her personal home page. This immediate gratification is really important. The customer wants to see the results of having given you new profile information right away, not the next time he interacts with you.

Personalization Is an Adjunct, Not an End in Itself

Customers may not value personalization per se. As Dow Jones discovered, customers won't sign up just to have personalized service. They have to value the unique brand of information and analysis provided by *The Wall Street Journal*. In the case of OnStar, customers sign up for security and peace of mind. The personalization features of both services cement and deepen the relationship with the customer. By personalizing the delivery of your service, you can continuously delight your customers as long as they remain involved. If a customer becomes disaffected or distracted and doesn't bother to update his profile, he'll probably be annoyed that you keep offering him things he's not interested in. So personalization can backfire. It can seem too intrusive (How did you know that my wife likes Italian food?) or unresponsive (I don't care about the Internet anymore; that's passé; why do I keep seeing this stuff?). Your goal, therefore, is first to ensure that there's enough value in your basic offering to keep the customer satisfied and coming back for more. Next, you want to make it as easy as possible for the customer to see and change his profile at any time. And you want him to be aware that the quality of the personalized services you can provide him as an option is dependent on the quality of the information he's willing to give you about his preferences and interests.

Personalized Service May Lead to a Need for Community

I'M NOT EXACTLY sure why this is the case, but every time I find a good example of personalized service, I'm apt to find a corollary need for a community of interest. Notice that *The Wall Street Journal Interactive Edition* has an active set of discussion forums. One of my prescriptions for OnStar was that it needed to get on the stick to offer an on-line forum for OnStar subscribers. I think the reason that these two opposites go hand in hand is that once you've built a trusted relationship with a company and value the service it's providing you, you're more likely to trust others who have the same kind of relationship. And of course, you have at least one thing in common: you're both customers of the same company, subscribers to the same service, members of the same club.

Other electronic commerce practitioners seem to be having similar experiences. When we last talked, Wells Fargo's Dudley Nigg was in the process of building community into Wells Fargo's Web site. He began this work after two years of providing highly personalized service on the site. So begin with a valuable basic service, increase that value by personalizing your offerings for customers, and then see where it takes you. It may lead to community.

Foster Community

The Internet is a natural venue for building and sustaining community. Here's an example: People who care for relatives with Alzheimer's disease have a very difficult time. It's a thankless, relentless, and despair-producing activity. Realizing this, an Alzheimer's clinic in Cleveland, Ohio, formed a computer support network for families of people with Alzheimer's. They purchased computers for families who didn't have them, set them up in their homes, and showed them how to access the Internet. They formed an on-line discussion group and an on-line resource library. And they made sure that one of their staff was monitoring the discussions, in the same way they made sure that there was always someone available at the end of a phone line. Any time of the day or night, a despairing person could log on, look at the suggestions others had offered for situations they were facing, and pose their own questions ("He keeps asking for the car keys; what should I do?"). The "hottest" time for activity turned out to be in the wee hours of the morning. When their charges had finally gone to sleep, these beleaguered caretakers would log on to the network and gain a few moments of solace in the company of others facing the same rough road.

Communities are often built around common interests, such as raising roses, tasting fine wines, or listening to folk music, or practices: Java programmers, landscape architects, and tax accountants are all people who belong to common communities of practice no matter where they happen to reside. If you have a customer base that shares a common interest or practice, you have it made. You can create a community to keep customers coming back for more. And by eavesdropping electronically on customers' public communications with one another, you'll learn what's on their mind, what they value, and what they care about. Back in the early 1990s, I created a community among Lotus Notes users who gathered around our Notes-based information service. These customers would ask and answer one another's questions not only about Notes-related issues but also about many other initiatives they were involved with in their companies. I showed these discussions to a visiting marketing executive. He took one look and said, "My God, this is primary research—you have your hand on these people's pulses. Most companies would kill for this kind of information. And you say your customers are paying you for this privilege?"

A New Business Model: Building Communities of Communities

THE INTERNET CULTURE has raised people's awareness of the importance of community. Long before the advent of the World Wide Web, people were drawn to the Internet because it was a community of communities. That's one of the things that makes it so fascinating. There are tens of thousands, if not hundreds of thousands, of very interest-specific or practice-specific communities. On the Internet, people can find and communicate with others, anywhere in the world, who share their interests. No matter how esoteric their interest or how small their field—I once met a mathematician who told me that there were only three other people in the world who understood the work she was doing—they'll find people with common interests.

Steve Case, the founder of America Online, has always had a profound appreciation for the importance of communities of communities in building his on-line business. AOL's initial sales and marketing strategy was based on this model. Case started by approaching every preexisting community organization he could find—airline pilots, gardeners, retired people in the San Francisco Bay area—and making them the same offer: Why not give your members a place to "hang out" electronically? It was a brilliant strategy. And it worked.

From the beginning, AOL was conceived as a place where nontechnical people could find kindred souls with whom they could connect. Does that sound "airy-fairy" to you? Well, it's obviously a good business strategy. AOL quickly became and remains the world's leading on-line service provider, despite stiff competition from Microsoft and others. What Case understood that Bill Gates missed is that community, not channels of entertainment, is what draws people to an on-line service. Gates has been struggling to turn the Internet into interactive TV, while Case has captured the essence of the soul of the Internet and blown right by him.

Shortly, you'll be reading about Tripod, a young company that hopes to emulate AOL's success by using the "community of communities" business model.

How to Build Community

So BEING A member of one or more communities makes customers feel special and helps them take care of one another, while giving you an unparalleled opportunity to learn much more about what they want and need. Once you've decided you want to foster a community, how can you build one? A number of key steps are required. They are:

• Seduce customers into the fold.
• Introduce customers to others with common interests.
• Introduce and reinforce common terminology and values.
• Let customers "strut their stuff."
• Encourage customers to become part of the "in crowd."

Let's take a closer look.

Seduce Customers into the Fold

THE FIRST TRICK in building community is letting customers know that there is one and that there's something there for them. For mass-market or consumer-based initiatives, it turns out that a sense of community is key to attracting customers and keeping them. Walt Disney, AOL, Microsoft, and others have discovered this. They've subdivided their Web sites into separate areas, each designed to appeal to people with different backgrounds or interests.

For business-to-business initiatives, the best way to attract customers is in the customer support area. This is what Cisco Systems discovered. Customers are often happy to help one another solve problems, resolve issues, and share tips and techniques. Why are people willing to spend their own valuable time helping others? It appears to be part of the human experience. We're wired that way. We like to offer a helping hand if we think we can be of assistance and we know it's safe to do so.

Introduce Customers to Others with Common Interests

GIVE CUSTOMERS A set of topics or interest areas from which they can choose. Perhaps they're interested in gardening. Maybe they're about to get married. Maybe they need help with a specific technical problem. There's no limit to the types of interests people have. You want to find the interests that the most people have in common. Here's where profiles help. Once customers begin to declare their interests, you can begin to see the common threads and create "infospaces" where people who have these interests in common can congregate. Tripod calls these "pods." Microsoft creates sections at its Web site based on customers' jobs (CIO, developer, and so on). These are essentially communities of practice.

By organizing your Web site to pull together people who share common interests and practices, and by creating an easy way for them to interact with one another, you've done the cyberequivalent of throwing a party.

Introduce and Reinforce Common Terminology and Values

COMMUNITIES OF PRACTICE, in particular, share common vocabularies. But that's also true of communities of interest, age groups, or people who live in the same region. Sixty-year-olds often don't understand what eighteen-year-olds are saying. Mac users speak to one another using a different vocabulary than PC users do. Network administrators use very different jargon than procurement officers do. So for each group of customers you have, you'll need to create a "safe space" in which they can communicate the way they're used to communicating. That way they won't be shocked, offended, or confused by strange terms.

Values are important too. Tripod has done a good job of reinforcing a common set of values at its site. Moderators set the tone in each different community of interest. Members are gently reminded not to use pornographic terms, say things that may be offensive to others, or violate others' copyright or privacy.

Let Customers "Strut Their Stuff"

THIS MAY BE one of the most surprising aspects of community building. You need to find ways to get customers to show off to one another. At Cisco's Web site, customers who offer technical advice to others are helping them, but they're also showing how smart they are. At Tripod, when someone takes the time to develop and publish a Web site that is targeted at a specific community of interest, he's making an offering to the group as a whole. What happens is that as the more outgoing customers begin to make contributions, other, shyer members gain courage and tender their own advice or offerings. The number of members who are engaged and making offers to others is the true sign of a community's vitality.

Encourage Customers to Become Part of the "In Crowd"

TRIPOD'S BO PEABODY describes the "in crowd" phenomenon well. It's like becoming one of the town's old-timers—the people whose opinions really count. People who have been part of a community for a while develop expectations about what they'll find each time they reconnect. They get upset if the community begins to change in ways they don't approve of. So it's important for community members to feel a real sense of ownership for the community. They can do this by becoming "premium members," like Platinum frequent flyers. They can do this by participating in surveys and voicing their opinions about directions or policies that affect the community they've come to be part of. As you'll see shortly, Tripod has done a great job in making its customers feel they're really part of the "in crowd."

Community Is Good for Business

AS YOU'LL SEE in both these case studies, fostering community can be very good for your business. Cisco's success as the leading Internet commerce player is built on its success in reaching out to its customers and building a community of customers helping customers. Tripod's community of communities is one of the fastest-growing Web sites on the planet and one that has advertisers salivating.

FOSTER COMMUNITY:

Cisco Systems
www.cisco.com

E x e c u t i v e   S u m m a r y

Cisco Systems is the world's leader in electronic commerce, with close to $5 billion per year in sales coming from its Web site. The company has also saved more than $550 million per year in customer support costs by letting customers help themselves to technical support information and order status information via the Web. Cisco's success in electronic commerce has been built on a strong foundation of community among its customers. Cisco's customers answer one another's technical questions and help one another out on the company's Web site. This customer support community was the first and most successful step Cisco took in electronic commerce. Then the company was able to branch out to streamline most of the business processes that impact its customers and channel partners.

Critical Success Factors in the Cisco Story

✓ Target the right customers	✓ Let customers help themselves
Own the customer's total experience	✓ Help customers do their jobs
✕ Streamline business processes that impact the customer	Deliver personalized service
✓ Provide a 360-degree view of the customer relationship	✕ Foster community

✕ = Featured in this discussion   ✓ = Touched on in this discussion

Cisco Systems Helps Customers Support Other Customers

NO BOOK OF electronic commerce success stories would be complete without a mention of Cisco Systems. This supplier of networking gear maintains close to an 80 percent share of the fast-growing market for the routers and switches that keep the Internet humming and power the local-area networks within most large corporations. Within a period of sixteen months, the percentage of sales Cisco receives via the Web has increased to more than 62 percent of its total revenues. By July 1998, the company expected to reach $5 billion in annual sales coming in from its Web channel, or 50 percent of its annual revenues. So Cisco is probably the leading practitioner of electronic commerce on the planet. How did it get there?

Much of Cisco's success in doing business over the Internet stems from a set of decisions made back in 1993 and 1994, when Doug Allred was the company's vice president for customer advocacy. Allred had seen how fast sales of internetworking routers were increasing. He was concerned about the company's ability to provide adequate technical support for all these new customers. As he plotted the run rate for the company's sales and then calculated the number of technical support engineers he'd need to service all those customers, he realized he was in trouble. He'd need to grow from the few hundred support engineers he had to an army of close to 10,000—that's every engineer west of the Mississippi!

It also hadn't escaped Allred's notice that the Internet itself was becoming a useful tool for customer support. Since 1989, Cisco customers had been downloading software from the company's Internet site. By 1990, customers could also access Cisco's bug report database via the Internet. So they could quickly find out whether the problem they were having was a known bug or something that needed to be reported. And Cisco made other technical support tools available to customers via the Internet—tools such as a software upgrade planner that would let them prepare their systems to receive upgrades—as long as the customer knew where to look to find them.

Building the Foundation: Community-based Customer Support

IN 1993, ALLRED put a call-tracking system into place so that the company could monitor each technical support call that came in, find an answer to the customer's problem in a database of known problems and solutions, and track that call to completion. What was unusual about the approach Allred's team took, however, was the fact that they designed this system to run both as a telephone-based call center and as a virtual call center via the Web. Of course, the Web was in its infancy in 1993, but as one of the pioneering suppliers of Internet technologies, Cisco was plugged into the action.

This virtual call center application started out as a typical help desk service for Cisco's "enterprise customers." These were the large multinationals that were deploying global networks in very complex environments. They'd often encounter new combinations of hardware and software that nobody at Cisco had ever seen before. A customer would visit the Web site with a question or a problem, search the database to see what similar situations had been encountered in the past, and see how they had been resolved. Then, if he couldn't find an answer to his particular question, he would post the question.

Here's where things got really interesting: Cisco's technical support staff would begin to work on finding the answer to the customer's question, but, miraculously, so would other Cisco customers! Whoever came up with the answer first posted it. Often there were several helpful suggestions and workarounds proposed. As soon as any answers begin flowing into the database, an e-mail was triggered and sent out to the customer, alerting him that answers awaited him at the Web site.

Allred had found a solution to the technical support engineer gap—let customers, all of whom had been trained and certified by Cisco, help one another out. Cisco calls this customer support Web site Cisco Connection Online (CCO), and it's an absolutely vital resource for the company, its customers, and its channel partners. In 1997, an average of 4,500 technical questions were answered each week in CCO's Open Forum. And each week those Q&As are polished and added to the company's growing technical knowledge base.

What happened to the call center traffic? Two things: As Cisco's business grew by leaps and bounds, the call center didn't have to expand proportionately. Customers were happy to go help themselves on the Web site first. Second, the calls that did come in were for much more difficult questions than the call center had received in the past. If the problem was fairly simple, customers could find their own answers. As the complexity grew, that's when they wanted to talk the problem through with an engineer.

Most important, Cisco had succeeded in creating an environment of trust—the most important ingredient for fostering community.

The Evolution of Cisco's Web Business

How DID Cisco evolve its customer support site into the world's largest business-to-business site? Was it based on a grand strategic plan? "No," says Mark Tonnesen, Cisco's director of customer advocacy. "As we built our Web site, we surveyed customers constantly and asked them what they needed. They said, 'I can't find out the status of the order I placed.' 'Your price lists are out-of-date and useless.' 'No one can figure out how to configure your products.' 'Your ordering process is horrendous.' So we addressed each of these issues one by one." Basically, what customers were complaining about were the things that annoyed them and wasted their time. So Cisco tackled each of these annoying time wasters.

Streamlining Customer-Facing Business Processes

First, the CCO team gave customers access to the status of their pending orders via the Web. Almost immediately, 70 percent of the 7,000 inquiries per week Cisco had been receiving moved from the call center to the Web. Customers obviously found that it saved them both time and frustration to log on to the Web to get their order status directly rather than to having call, wait for a rep, ask the question, and wait for a response.

Next, Cisco posted the standard price lists on the Web and kept them up to date, denominated in the currencies of all countries in which the company does business. Although most of Cisco's larger customers receive negotiated prices when they actually place their orders, they wanted to know what the list price was so they knew what ballpark they were in before they began speccing a system. Having the list prices on-line saved them from having to make a phone call.

Configuration was next. This was more of a challenge. The CCO team knew that the in-house configuration system was not something customers would be willing to put up with. Tonnesen described this system as a "bump-and-steer" approach, akin to parking in a tight space. You had to specify all the components you wanted, and only then would the system tell you if you had gotten something wrong. Then you would try again, and again, until you had, at last, configured a valid and manufacturable system, pretty much by trial and error.

So to make it easy for customers to configure their own products, Cisco purchased a new constraint-based configuration engine from Calico and populated it with all of the company's products as well as the rules involved in putting together a manufacturable bill of materials. Again, Cisco hit a home run with customers. "This was a huge success. Customers loved it!" reported Tonnesen. For the first time, customers had a handy way of configuring their own products without having to spend hours on the phone with a sales rep answering questions and making choices.

Cisco's Commerce Agents

All of these on-line business processes are grouped together on the Web site as a suite of "commerce agents" that Cisco's customers and partners can use to do business electronically. The Lead Time Agent gives customers and partners the current lead times for Cisco products. The Invoice Agent lets you view your invoices on-line. The Service Order Agent lets you access information on service orders. The Contract Agent gives you information about your service contracts. The Upgrade Agent lets you request software or hardware upgrades or documentation. The Notification Agent lets you specify criteria that will result in your automatically being sent e-mails about changes in order status or pricing. The Configuration Agent lets you search for Cisco products that are configurable, choose a particular model, and create an on-line configuration. And the Marketplace is where you can configure, price, and submit your orders.

The next step Cisco is taking with these commerce agents is making them easy for customers and partners to integrate them directly into their internal operational systems. For example, companies using line-of-business software from SAP, Oracle, and PeopleSoft can integrate their systems directly into Cisco's inventory and sales automation systems. So, for example, a company such as Sprint, which purchases forty Cisco routers per week for its end customers, estimates it will be able to save $200,000 per year in procurement labor costs by plugging directly into Cisco's systems.

Result: Customer Satisfaction and Cost Savings

How does Cisco know it's on the right track? Customers are very vocal in letting the company know what works for them. And Cisco carefully monitors customers' interactions on the site to determine where they run into problems. Cisco currently receives and processes between 350,000 and 400,000 transactions a month on its Web site. That represents an amazing number of phone calls that no longer have to be made by customers and handled in real time by staff members. And all this is the result of focusing on saving customers time, getting rid of annoyances, and building a community of Cisco users who can help one another out.

The Extended Cisco Community

MORE THAN 70 percent of Cisco's business is handled by third parties, resellers, and systems integrators. Cisco Connect Online is the way most of these partners now place and track their orders. Of course, Cisco's channel partners also have access to the company's entire knowledge base of technical and troubleshooting information, but they also have their own private community sections of the Web site where they can find information targeted directly at them and enter into dialogue with Cisco management and one another.

How is Cisco continuing to use the notion of community to evolve its business model? Tonnesen explains, "In 1995 and 1996, we began to notice that our business was changing. We now have a number of different groups of customers and partners, each with very different needs. For example, we have resellers who cater to the small and medium-sized business; we have Internet service providers and telcos as customers. There's a big difference between the needs of a small business and that of an Internet utility. So we've reorganized our Web site to serve these different groups." Cisco is now beginning to profile its customers by industry, by line of business, and by role within an organization. "What a procurement manager needs is very different from what a network designer needs," Tonnesen explains. In order to offer more targeted features to different communities of practice, Cisco first has to refine its customer profiling and then let customers explicitly choose the kinds of information they need, the products they want to track, and the services they want to access. As customers volunteer more information about themselves, their jobs, their industries, and the products and services they value, they'll segment themselves into natural communities of practice and interest. Then Cisco will be able to continue to refine its offerings to appeal to each of these more targeted communities.

One of the challenges the customer advocacy group tackled in late 1997 was that of helping customers and partners configure not a single product, such as a network router (which is complicated enough with all the options available), but an entire network of routers and hubs. This presales network design step is usually done by expensive network design engineers who work directly for Cisco or for any of a variety of third parties. Let's say a customer in the United Kingdom wants to wire a campus with four buildings. Today, Cisco's technical support group will pull together the appropriate resources from its own staff as well as from training partners and third-party network design engineers to run an audio and video design session across the Internet. The customer and the consulting engineers draw diagrams on an electronic whiteboard, talk about them, annotate them, and confer. When they're satisfied with the whiteboard design, the customer presses a button and gets a list of all the products that will be required for the entire network! Electronically supported collaboration shaves weeks, if not months, off the complex design cycle.

Evolving the Technical Infrastructure

Up through the end of 1997, Cisco's Web site ran on large Sun Solaris Enterprise servers at eight sites around the world. Cisco uses Oracle databases for everything from products to customer data to pricing and downloadable software. The customer profile information includes everything that Cisco has learned about each customer over time: what industry he's in or what industries he sells to (in the case of a partner) and how he has used the Web site in the past. The next step will be to use that profile information to alert customers to information they may find of interest based on what they've looked at in the past (for example, a customer who has devoted a lot of attention to tools to support voice over the Net will be kept apprised of new developments in that area).

Cisco's customer support knowledge base is handled using Documentum's document management software. As of the end of 1997, Cisco had more than 85,000 current documents in that system.

Cisco's order-to-build automated software process links the company's Oracle-based order management system to its scheduling system. The scheduling system looks at product available and product promised data to determine a first available time slot for each order. The component data are then translated into parts orders for Cisco's subcontractors (such as Jabil Circuit) and distributors (such as Avnet), which, in turn, have direct links into Cisco's enterprise resource planning (ERP) systems. So these contractors and distributors act as extensions to Cisco's own internal systems. They can forecast demand and react very quickly.

The next steps for Cisco in 1998 included a major redesign of the underlying architecture of the transactional side of the CCO Web site. Although it offers state-of-the-art functionality today, the site is brittle. It's been continuously improved over the last three years with no real architectural planning. Cisco has hired Alta Software to help it shift over from a site developed using CGI, Perl, and C to one designed using Java, object request broker middleware, and intelligent agents. In the process of rearchitecting its site, Cisco plans to change from reliance on a few large Sun Solaris boxes to an architecture that includes lots of Microsoft NT servers, in order to enhance reliability and scalability.

Results

MARC TONNESEN REPORTS that CCO is saving Cisco $550 million per year. That breaks down into the following categories: $175 million per year on support costs; $8.4 million in hiring costs to fill those support positions the company no longer needs; $250 million on software the company no longer has to send out to customers, since they now download it themselves; and $40 million due to the paperless nature of the documentation Cisco now provides through its Web site. Since CCO went live, Cisco has saved $837 million.

On the revenue side, Cisco is moving from 32 percent of its sales over the Internet in 1997 to an estimated 60-plus percent in fiscal 1998. It looks to me as though fostering community has paid off!

Patty's Rx for Cisco Systems

It's hard to come up with things that Cisco hasn't already thought of doing. The most important investment the company needs to make at this point (and it's doing so) is rearchitecting its industry-leading Web site. CCO has grown like Topsy over the past several years. It's fast. And it lets customers do virtually everything they need to do to transact business with Cisco. However, as is the case with most of today's Web sites, if you look behind the scenes, you'll see that a lot of technical streamlining can be done. For example, today it takes a long time for Cisco to replicate its distributed Web sites around the world. So keeping them all in sync is a time-consuming task.

And many of the interfaces that Cisco and its contractors have built to Cisco's internal systems are ready to be redesigned in a more flexible, extensible manner. As CEO John Chambers continues to push Cisco's business partners to "Webify" their supply chains, quick, painless integration into other companies' operational systems (for customers, channel partners, and suppliers) will be the name of the game.

From a technical standpoint, what I'm really looking forward to, in Cisco's case, will be the company's aggressive use of Java for its next-generation Web-based applications. Cisco's routers and switches are all evolving to support Java, so it makes sense that the company's Web site be designed to take advantage of Java as well. Just as Cisco has led the industry in becoming and remaining the top electronic commerce site in the world, it is likely to lead again in its practical yet innovative use of highly distributed, component-based architectures, leveraging Java. And since Cisco has both a commitment to Java and a commitment to Microsoft NT platforms, the company will be doing the industry a favor by developing and deploying commercial-quality Java applications on distributed Microsoft NT boxes.

From a business standpoint, I'm betting that Cisco will exceed its goal of getting to the point where 60 percent of its revenues are generated via the Web. (A bet I've already won, since the company was already generating 62 percent of revenues on the Internet by August 1998!) By the year 2000, Cisco could well be doing 80 percent of its sales and close to 100 percent of its business overall (customer support, procurement, administration, and so on) via the Web.

"Take-Aways" from the Cisco Story

1. The most cost-effective way to support highly technical and complex products is to let customers act as an adjunct to your own technical support staff. Let customers help other customers solve their problems.

2. One of Cisco's most popular and cost-effective applications is the ability of customers to check the status of their orders via the Web.

3. Customers requested, and received, applications that made it easy for them to access standard price lists, configure their own products, and place orders on-line. Between 60 percent and 65 percent of all the orders Cisco receives now arrive via the Web. Why? Because Cisco has done a great job of streamlining all the business processes that make it easy for customers to do business with it.

4. Cisco helps its large customers link their procurement systems directly into Cisco's ordering and accounting systems.

5. Cisco began by streamlining customer support for its large enterprise customers. Then the company found that smaller customers could use the same functions to place orders, check on orders, and resolve problems. Cisco's distributors and dealers use the Web site in much the same way that the company's large accounts do. They can check pricing and availability, configure systems, place orders, check on delivery status, and get technical support—all via the Web site.

6. Cisco maintains customer profiles, including tracking what each customer did on the site and adding that information to his profile. Next

the company plans to use these profiles as a way to target different communities of practice: network designers, procurement managers, network administrators, and so on.

7. After two years of topsy-turvy growth and evolution, Cisco is rearchitecting its massive Web site to provide a more robust, flexible, and extensible environment. As you evolve the functionality of your site, you'll want to revisit your architecture. You want to be able to add and replace application services in a modular fashion.

8. Once you have an Internet infrastructure that connects your company to its customers and to all of the partners and experts who sell related products and services, you can easily pull together ad hoc groups of experts to collaborate on solving customers' problems. Cisco does this by convening a collaborative design session across the Internet.

FOSTER COMMUNITY:

Tripod
www.tripod.com

E x e c u t i v e   S u m m a r y

In a little over two years, Tripod created a vibrant Web-based community of more than 1 million members, most in the eighteen-to-thirty-four-year-old age range. Members typically visit the Web site several times a week to update their own Web sites and to check out the action on the site. This makes Tripod a very valuable property for advertisers, who value the ability to address a consistent, predictable audience over time. In fact, Tripod's business became so valuable that in early 1998 it was acquired by Lycos for $58 million. Lycos and Tripod seek to emulate America Online's success. They want to be the major "destination site" on the Web—a service that people belong to, embark from, and come back to, over and over again.

Critical Success Factors in the Tripod Story	
✓ Target the right customers	Let customers help themselves
✓ Own the customer's total experience	Help customers do their jobs
Streamline business processes that impact the customer	★ Deliver personalized service
Provide a 360-degree view of the customer relationship	★ Foster community
★ = Featured in this discussion	✓ = Touched on in this discussion

Tripod: Making Community a Business

IN EARLY 1998, a little-known two-year-old company, staffed by twenty-somethings fresh out of college, made headlines when it was acquired by the Internet search company Lycos for $58 million. What value had Tripod created in twenty-seven months that made it worth more than $1 million per employee? Simple: Tripod had created an on-line community of 1 million people, most of them in the highly desirable eighteen- to thirty-four-year-old age bracket. Not only did Tripod have a highly desirable clientele for advertisers eager to sell their wares to upwardly mobile Gen Xers, it also had a business model to die for. To wit, you lure customers to your site and then get them to come back several times a week. And you don't need to spend a penny creating or buying content; the customers themselves create the content that other customers value. You create the "safe space" that allows customers to entertain and inform one another. Sound simple? Well, it's not.

Creating and sustaining a vibrant on-line community is one of the most difficult challenges of electronic commerce. In founding and leading Tripod, twenty-six-year-old Bo Peabody proved he's a master in this very difficult game. Steve Case of America Online is another past master. Peabody's goal, with the help of new parent company Lycos, is to give Mr. Case a run for his money.

The seeds of Tripod germinated in 1990, when Peabody was a freshman at Williams College in Williamstown, Massachusetts. It dawned on him that while a college education prepared a student to enter the working world, there were still a lot of mysteries facing young adults that nobody taught about at college. So when he graduated, Peabody founded Tripod with his classmate Brett Hershey and Dick Sabot, their economics professor, to provide eighteen- to thirty-four-year-olds with practical knowledge, or "tools for life," about subjects not taught in college classrooms.

Tripod was launched in October 1995 with private backers—Peabody's and Sabot's friends. Soon the young entrepreneur had landed $2 million of seed funding from a combination of private investors and venture capital sources. The company's goal was to create a Web site, a magazine, and other multimedia properties all targeted at a specific demographic group: young adults who were getting started in their first jobs, finding mates, buying their first houses, paying taxes, buying insurance, and saving for their future. From the outset, Peabody's vision was that this group of people would be extremely valuable to businesses—banks, insurance companies, car manufacturers, employers of all kinds. He wanted to create a community and then deliver it to advertisers. But Tripod was more than an on-line magazine. From the outset, Tripod.com had the feeling of a destination, a community. The tone of the Tripod site was hip, upbeat, and slightly irreverent, but intellectually honest and probing. Once customers discover it, they keep coming back for more. And that's the real secret of Peabody's success.

Creating Community: Build on the Small-Town Metaphor

PEABODY DESCRIBED HIS modus operandi to me in the spring of 1996. He first explained that he had grown up in a small town in New Hampshire and that he was modeling the Tripod Web site on that experience. "When someone new moves into town, what do you do? You bake them a cake. Then you take it over to welcome them. That's what we do at Tripod. When you come to the site for the first time, we entice you with sweets for the mind." He was referring to the catchy, irreverent teasers that greet first-time visitors and entice them in. "What's the next thing you do for the new person in town? You invite them to a party and introduce them to your friends." At Tripod, you're invited to get to know people by browsing their home pages, declaring your interests, joining discussion groups, and creating your own home page. It's hard to remain lonely on the site. There are lots of friendly chats, discussions, and invitations to play. "Then, after you've lived in town for a while, you get to be one of the 'old-timers.' You go to the general store every morning and swap stories about local affairs." At Tripod, the longer you've been around, the more involved you're likely to feel, because Tripod's members get to influence the policy and directions of "their" Web site.

How did Peabody attract new visitors to the Tripod site? Mostly by word of mouth and by offering enticing freebies: registered members could create their own home pages and post them on the Tripod site for free. The site also boasted a useful résumé builder. Once they got there, they found many useful bits of information on everything from advice on how to get a job to how to build a nest egg quickly to when you should move in with your "significant other."

Soon young people were flocking to Tripod.com. In its first six months of operation, Tripod grew to 25,000 registered members, most of whom return to the site two to three times per week. Membership at Tripod is free. But there are advantages to registering. The most important incentive is the ability to create and post your own home page. In September 1996, Tripod launched a 1 million circulation magazine that was distributed free to college students across the nation's campuses. The purpose of the magazine was to draw more students to the site.

Building Trust

How does Tripod cement its relationships with its members? First, there's the "stickiness" factor. Because members post their profiles, résumés, and home pages on the site, they return often to update them and to see if anyone has commented on their offerings.

Second, Peabody is fanatical about customer service. Every visitor who comes to the site is a customer, and it's important that each one be made comfortable as soon as possible. "We have a ridiculous commitment to customer service," says Peabody. "Our goal is to become the Nordstrom or L. L. Bean of the Internet." One way that Tripod provides superior customer service is by answering 90 percent of customers' e-mails within twenty-four hours. To keep up with this commitment, Tripod has a staff of four full-time customer service people who handle e-mails. Since the company receives more than 1,000 e-mails a day, a lot of the process is automated. Intelligent agents scan the subject and content of each incoming e-mail and automatically generate answers from the company's frequently asked questions (FAQ) knowledge base. However, these automatically generated e-mails then go to one of the customer service reps, who personalizes the response.

The company also goes to great lengths to answer every question to the best of its ability. For example, when one Tripod user wanted to know how much take-home pay he would receive from a $2,000-a-month salary, the question was routed to Tripod's comptroller, who spent a half hour calculating the inquirer's taxes and composing a return memo.

Third, Tripod gets its members involved in all the decisions facing the company and the Web site. Here's a case in point. When Tripod was about a year old, the number of home pages being hosted on the site had grown to staggering proportions. Peabody realized that it was getting expensive to maintain all that disk space. So Tripod asked its members what they'd like to do. Did they want to pay to host their home pages, or would they accept advertising on their personal pages? Eighty percent of the members said they'd be happy to have ads on their pages as long as they could keep using the free service (many members actually like the fact that name-brand companies such as Northwest Airlines, the Calvert Group, or Duracell "sponsor" their home pages). Ten percent of the members said they'd rather pay. As a result, Tripod continued to offer the free home page service but switched to the advertising model. Members who preferred to pay could do so.

Fourth, Tripod keeps members involved by inviting them to serve on rotating research panels (this is like being one of the "old-timers" who hang out at the general store) and by conducting on-line surveys. Instead of resenting the surveys, Tripod members typically respond, "Thanks for asking."

Evolving the Content

As you'll recall, Tripod began as "tools for life" with lots of "how-to" sections for young people on topics ranging from how to get a job to managing one's finances to managing one's love life. However, what happened over the first two years of its existence was that its members began to get more and more involved in the content of the site. How? First, the number of members' pages mushroomed. Yet, many of these weren't pages describing a person looking for a job; they were idiosyncratic and delightfully interesting travel journals, treatises on a variety of topics, and multimedia essays. Many of these member pages were much more interesting than the content Tripod itself was providing. Second, the discussions and interactions on the Tripod site had taken on a life of their own. Numerous members came back several times a week because there was a lively discussion taking place on something they cared about. Members became more active in declaring topic areas and hosting them.

At the same time that the content of the Tripod site was evolving naturally, many other competitors were offering "channels" of information: finance, news, sports, entertainment, travel. Peabody realized that "at the end of the day, when we looked at the categories we were trying to cover, they weren't that different from the channels others were trying to cover. At the beginning, we had to pursue a diversified portfolio." The résumé builder, the travel planner, and the on-line car care reminder were useful gimmicks to get people to come and stick around. But once Tripod had 400,000 members who wanted to engage in dialogue around topics of their own choosing, Tripod realized that *that* was what members were returning for; it was time to create neighborhoods.

So in the summer of 1997, Tripod began featuring "pods." These are moderated topic areas arranged around communities of interest. In each one, there are lively and provocative discussions led by a "poderator," who is a member, not a Tripod employee. There may also be real-time chats scheduled for specific times of the week, many of them with invited guest experts. And there is typically a list of related resources—other places within Tripod and on the Web where you can find related information.

Anyone can participate in the discussions by pressing the "Add me to this pod" button. When you do, you can choose whether or not you want your home page linked to the pod, so that you can easily "meet" other pod members. And you can choose whether or not you want to have your pod memberships listed on your profile. Some examples of pods that were active in early 1998 were alternative health, small business, music, activism, freebies, home page design, and so on. It's an eclectic set of topics. And it's constantly changing as members' interests change.

The most amazing thing about each pod is the amount of "formal" contributed material created by other members interested in the same topic area. Registered members can also choose to become "pod publishers." They create a home page related to the Pod topic and submit it to the poderator for inclusion. The poderator also gives out "best of pod" awards each week. Naturally, pod publishers vie for this honor.

By early 1998, there were thirty-four pods in all, with more being launched each week. Peabody explains how Tripod decides which pods to launch: "We get lots of requests each day for starting new pods. As each group reaches critical mass, we evaluate the pod ideas based on three criteria:

1. Does it work for the business? Will it attract advertisers?
2. Does it fit our brand image?
3. Are enough members interested in the topic?"

Evolving the Business Model

PEABODY HAD ALWAYS planned for Tripod to make most of its money through advertising. His goal was to create a community that was so valuable, it would attract advertisers. And advertising is still the company's largest revenue stream. What Peabody didn't know at the outset was where the content around which the communities would form would come from. The company began with its "tools for life" theme and a set of topics that was created and maintained by Tripod employees (with input from members), and has evolved to content that is largely based on contributions by members.

By contrast, Bill Gates and his Microsoft Network, ZDNet, CNN, and others have been sinking millions of dollars into creating content and channels of news, entertainment, sports, finance, and so on that would attract people to their Web sites. Yet Peabody's Tripod has many of its members paying for the opportunity to create and publish their own content! Peabody had tapped into a very important reality of Internet culture: people come to the Web not just to find things but to show off, to strut their stuff, and to interact with other interesting and bright people.

Peabody's original goal had been to create not just a Web site aimed at a particular demographic community but an entire multimedia empire for that crowd: books, magazines, videos, movies. What happened to that goal? The magazine served its purpose in the formative days, Peabody reports, but it's no longer needed. Now Peabody's goal is to focus on the Web. But he's not content to run a successful and profitable Web site. He wants to run the next AOL! He wants to be an on-line service provider: a community of communities.

Peabody has learned a lot from being a Web entrepreneur. In particular, he's watched the big boys. Here's what he's noticed: There are a number of high-traffic Web sites. These are the ones that attract the most advertising. Many of these are search sites, like Lycos, Excite, Yahoo!, and Infoseek. These are what Peabody calls "pass-through" sites. Lots of people come through them to find what they're looking for on the Web, but they don't stick around. Then there are destination sites such as Microsoft's, Netscape's, and Disney's. These are places you go to when you're looking for a certain class of information. But the most valuable sites to advertisers, according to Peabody, are sites that are both destinations and home bases. AOL, Geocities, and Tripod fit this description. These are destinations because they're where the action is, where people go to "hang out" on-line. And they are home bases because in each case, members create their own home pages and publish their profiles. They "leave something of themselves behind." This gives these sites the kind of "stickiness" advertisers are seeking, according to Peabody.

And advertising revenues on the Web are increasing. Commerce on the Web is beginning to take off. So companies are increasing their advertising spending. Tripod's advertising revenues doubled each month in the last four months of 1997, and they show no sign of slowing down. "Advertisers no longer think twice about giving me $100,000 to be on our site," Peabody says, "And the big distribution deals are following." Once you can convince a major player that you have traffic and that people come back several times a week, according to Peabody, they're going to be willing to ink million-dollar deals. Think of the possibilities, he says: "Amazon.com has hundreds of thousands of affiliates selling books on their sites. Tripod has 2,500 people a day building their own home pages. [Most of these pages support advertising.] We're creating affiliates really fast."

Results

AS OF JANUARY 1998, Tripod had over 1 million registered members and 1.9 million member-created home pages (some members create more than one). Seventy percent of those members fall within the eighteen- to thirty-four-year-old range to which the site is targeted. (Many of the others are people under eighteen who are attracted by the free home page offer and tools.) Sixty percent of Tripod's members are male, 40 percent female. Membership is growing at a rate of 6,000 new members per day; premium membership is growing at the rate of 50 to 100 new premium members per day.

Premium members are registered members who pay $36 per year to receive some additional services, such as the ability to host a personal chat room, the ability to have a Tripod.net e-mail forwarding address (so that different e-mail accounts all feed into one single mailbox maintained by Tripod), and the ability to store a lot more information on the site (premium members get 22 MB of disk space for their home pages). They also receive a premium members–only newsletter and plenty of special offers and goodies. Members who want to keep advertising off their home pages pay $72 per year and automatically become premium members.

Tripod ranks in the top twenty-five Web sites based on traffic to its site, according to PC Meter. By the end of 1997, Tripod was serving 100 million page views per month; that number was increasing 20 percent per month. PC Meter ranks Tripod as the fifth-fastest growing site on the Web after Bluemountainarts (a Web greeting card company), Geocities (Tripod's closest competitor), Amazon, and Hotmail.

Peabody's vision of becoming the next AOL by converting a "pass-through" search site, such as Lycos, to a destination site, such as Tripod, obviously struck a responsive chord with the Lycos management team. Lycos acquired Tripod in February 1998. Stay tuned. And keep Bo Peabody on your radar. He's probably got a few more tricks up his sleeve.

Patty's Rx for Tripod

What I love about watching Tripod is watching Bo Peabody's business model evolve. He's probably one of the first true Netpreneurs, since he grew up with the Internet and his very first business was a cyberbusiness. Notice that he's been pretty flexible in rolling with the tide. He has remained true to his vision and his understanding about the importance of community. Yet he has evolved his thinking about how to leverage that understanding into a profitable business. I suspect that we haven't seen the last of Tripod's transmogrifications. Peabody has two goals: to head where his customers want him to go and to keep his advertisers happy. Luckily, as long as Peabody continues to deliver fanatically loyal customers to his advertisers, they'll remain loyal too.

What would I suggest to Bo? His closest competition seems to be Geocities.com, in which Yahoo! holds a minority interest. Like Tripod, Geocities gives away free home pages, has a lot of member-intensive discussion groups, and is a community of communities. Geocities had about 200,000 more members than Tripod when I checked in early 1998. So the two are running neck and neck. But Geocities is bland. The tone of the site is much more "middle America." Tripod has a hip feel to it that makes it more appealing to the Gen X crowd, yet still quite seductive to those of us over 34. The Lycos/Tripod partnership will go head-to-head with Yahoo!/Geocities, both trying to replicate the success of America Online. Interestingly enough, the financial backers behind both teams are the same. Geocities is nearly half owned by CMG Information Services, an investment firm that also owns half of Lycos.

I would encourage Bo to stay the course and keep listening to his customers, going where they take him, and staying nimble. Frankly, Peabody's instincts about how to succeed on the Net are much better than mine!

"Take-Aways" from the Tripod Story

1. People are eager for community. They want to share their thoughts, their offerings, and their concerns with other, like-minded people. You can build an entire business on this premise. Tripod has.

2. In order to foster community, you first have to create a trusted relationship with each individual. Tripod does this in two ways: by supporting customers with rapid personalized e-mail responses to their queries and by respecting individuals' wishes (letting each person decide what he or she wants others to know).

3. Next you need to let the community govern your direction. Tripod takes the pulse of its community members constantly, through advisory panels and on-line surveys, and by reading the e-mails and submissions by members. Then it reports back to the community what the consensus has been. The best example was members' decision to accept advertising on their free home pages in order to keep them free but to let people pay for the privilege of not hosting ads.

4. Advertisers want more than a certain number of "eyeballs" on today's Web sites. They want to know a lot about the audience they're serving, and they want to know that these same people will be consistently coming back. They're looking to target a community of interest, not a random set of ever-changing individuals.

5. Tripod discovered that the real value of the business model it had created was the fact that its Web site, Tripod.com, functioned as both a destination and a starting point, not just as a way station in cyberspace. Once your site has become a magnet, once it becomes the place customers go first and come back to often, you have achieved stardom in the Internet world. If you can sustain that sense of community and belonging, you have created lasting value.

Foster Community: Lessons Learned

Cisco and Tripod are very different companies with very different business models. One is a manufacturer that sells to and services many of its customers via the Internet. The other is a Web-based club that appeals to a particular group of Internet denizens. What they both have in common is the fact that their customers are Internet-friendly. Their customers did not have to be lured onto the Internet; they were, for the most part, already there. These two companies were early promulgators of community on the Internet. And their customers are clearly early adopters of Internet technology. Yet we can learn a lot from watching early adopters.

The notion of fostering community is not new to business. For years there have been industry associations, trade groups, and special interest groups representing every conceivable interest. People join these groups, attend conferences, read the same journals, and often swap e-mails. Also for years, companies have used the notion of "membership" to make customers feel special and build customer loyalty. Frequent flyer clubs, buyers' clubs, gold and platinum cards—all are attempts to help customers feel special by inviting them into an "in crowd."

From the very beginnings of the Internet as a vehicle for researchers to share ideas and communicate with one another, it has been used to foster lively, and often somewhat unruly, dialogues among people who share similar interests and passions. As I've said before, the Internet is, above all, a community of communities. The reason I stress this is that if you're going to do business on the Internet, you need to understand that there is an Internet culture, a way of doing things, and a history that needs to be honored. The notion of community is an intrinsic part of the Internet.

What the Internet brought to the concept of community in business was the ability to create safe spaces where community members can interact with one another, in addition to any face-to-face encounters they may have. If you are building a business-to-business or business-to-consumer channel using the Internet, fostering community should be part of your long-term game plan.

Customers Like to Help One Another

CISCO AND TRIPOD both discovered that customers enjoy "hanging out" with one another. But they don't do it just to hang out; they form a community around a common purpose or interest. In Cisco's case, customers visiting the Web site to answer a question or to solve a problem would stumble upon other customers' questions. If they knew the answer, they'd take the time to volunteer what they knew. At Tripod.com, customers welcome one another into discussions around topics of interest. They solicit contributions, and they answer questions. It's a way to make others who are just joining the special interest community feel welcome. At Tripod, when a pod member has a question or a concern, it's almost always addressed by other members of the pod within a day. If not, the poderator—a customer who has taken ownership of this particular special-interest group—will respond.

Community Members Like to Show Off

PART OF BEING a member of an on-line community is letting others know who you are and what you bring to the party. Some community members are lurkers. They just read others' entries; they never contribute. But in any vital community, there are enough extroverts to make things lively and interesting. In Cisco's case, part of helping other customers with their technical problems is showing off your expertise. Sure, there's a feeling of altruism involved as well. But among techies there's also a sense of pride in knowing how to solve hard problems. The fact that customers are proud of what they've learned and figured out is one reason why Cisco's Open Forum works as well as it does. Obviously, if the answers customers gave one another were mostly wrong, the forum would be of little value. But the fact of the matter is that many of these customers have encountered and solved problems Cisco's own technical team hasn't run into yet.

In Tripod's case, the members who choose to moderate a pod and who design Web pages with content that will be of interest to members of a pod are clearly showing off. Again, they're sharing their knowledge, expertise, and interests with others. They enjoy the opportunity to contribute something that others find valuable or interesting.

Customers Want to Be Consulted About the Community

BO PEABODY, CEO of Tripod, has demonstrated a very clear appreciation for the role customers want to play in setting the guidelines and standards for their on-line communities. At Tripod, community members have been consulted at every step in the evolution of the Web site and its business model. Once you build a community, you have to nurture it, or it can easily turn on you or dissolve. Once customers participate in a community, they will feel a sense of ownership. You have, in effect, turned that aspect of your site over to them. You can still set the tone, reinforce a set of values, and even have rules—such as Tripod's rule that management gets to decide when it's time to create a new pod and what pod topics will be most successful. But once you've created a community, the members of the community will want to steer its course. Remember, a community is considered to be a safe space. If you make what feel to members like arbitrary decisions, it's no longer safe, and members will defect.

Communities Create Value

THE TRIPOD STORY is the clearest example of the value the market places on a community of 1 million people. Tripod couldn't have sold a mailing list of 1 million people for $58 million. But the company could sell an ongoing, vibrant on-line community of 1 million people—along with the infrastructure to support it—for that price.

What value did Cisco's community provide? First, it dramatically lowered Cisco's cost of providing technical support. Second, it allowed Cisco to grow exponentially because customers were willing to help themselves and one another via the Web. Finally, Cisco's community of savvy customers acted as a magnet to draw more customers. Prospects for Cisco's technology could quickly see who else was a customer and what their experiences had been in using Cisco's systems. The ability for prospects to be invited on-line to see into the customer community and to eavesdrop on customers' interactions with one another was and remains a powerful selling tool.

Synthesis of Best Practices; Next Steps

At this point your head is probably swimming! How do you take what you've learned from these sixteen best-practice examples and apply it to your organization? Let me try to help.

First, start by focusing on your most profitable set of end customers (not your most profitable channel partners!). I suspect you know who these folks are and a lot about what makes them tick. What if you're just starting out and you have no customers? That's easy; target the ones you think will be the most profitable market segment for you. If you're a nonprofit or a government organization, you may want to pick the most influential group of end customers—for governments, that's probably business customers; for nonprofits, they're the people who use your services the most.

Second, look to see how much information you have about these people and how it's organized. If it's already consolidated into a single customer database, you have a great starting point. If not, that's where to start. Whether you build a new customer information repository, as Bell Atlantic did, or simply pull customer information together on the fly so you can see it all in one place, as Wells Fargo did, is immaterial, though I favor the customer information system approach. The key is to know who your target customers are and to have all the basic information about their dealings with you at your fingertips.

Next, pick their brains. Visit them. Learn how they do their jobs or, if they're consumers, what they care about and value—in other words, do basic market research. But remember, you want to talk to real people. This is not the kind of research you can do at arm's length by hiring a market research firm to survey your customers. As you saw in the examples of Hertz, PhotoDisc, and Boeing, you need to get into your customers' heads.

Your goal is to find out what makes it hard for customers to do business with you and then to eliminate each of these barriers as you redesign your customer-facing business processes. Remember, you may find that the barriers aren't within your business. As the National Science Foundation found out, many of the obstacles to streamlining may have to do with how your customers' organizations do things. As PhotoDisc discovered, it may start with an industrywide business practice that needs to be challenged. Or, as Hertz found, it may be that you're making assumptions about your own industry requirements—customers have to sign a legal form in order to rent a car—that you need to question.

Have you noticed that we're pretty far along in this requirements-gathering process and we've barely touched on electronic commerce technologies? Where's the Web site? Hang on, it's coming! But first you want to map out a streamlined set of business processes. Don't make this a big deal; you can do it in an afternoon. But *do* invite some of your customers to join you in this process. They'll have fun, you'll have fun, and you'll both learn a lot in the process. Don't get bogged down in how it's done today. Just get them to describe their ideal process of buying a car, getting health care, paying their taxes—whatever product or service you provide.

Once you have their ideal scenarios down, you can map out the business process by describing the key business events that took place in the process they described. Capture these. That's what Hertz did when it mapped out the ideal car rental process from the customer's point of view (reserve the car by specifying date, time, and location; arrive at the airport; board the bus; go to the car; drive away). That's what Amazon.com did when it looked at how people want to buy books (search for books by known elements or browse; read description or reviews; see availability and price; purchase with a single click; receive notification when the book has shipped; check what I've ordered in the past). What's hidden in these process/business events descriptions, of course, is the customer profile! In order to actually execute each of these steps, your back-end systems need to have a lot of information available about each customer—more than you may already have.

Now it's time to think about your customer profiles and what kind of information you'll want to elicit from your customers. At the same time, ask your customers how and when they'd like to provide that information. In Hertz's case, customers provide it at least annually, each time they renew their #1 Club Gold membership. In Amazon.com's case, they provide it as they're placing their first order. In Bell Atlantic and GM's cases, they provide it as they interact with the company over the course of time. However you do it, you need to be very up front about it. There is nothing today's customers resent more than having you collect information about them without their consent or knowledge! For every piece of information you elicit, the customer needs to see a direct benefit. And that benefit should

accord with the customer's perception of his ideal scenario of doing business with you. If you're just collecting demographic and marketing information, you're being nosy. If you're helping me do business with you in a
more and more streamlined fashion because you "remember" what I've
told you in the past, and I know that information is on file and can be updated easily, I'll be content. The best ammunition is to give your customers
easy access to their growing profiles and encourage them to change them.
The easiest way may be to periodically fax or mail them the information
you have on file. Hertz does this each time you make a change. It's reassuring to see a copy of your updated profile information each time you've
made a change.

What if your customers, or many of them, don't want to be bothered
with maintaining or checking the profile information you've gathered
about them? What if some of that information is conflicting or confusing?
Now you need to get proactive. This is why you need to have someone
who "owns" each customer. This is the step that Babson College is still
missing. For example, at American Airlines, the AAdvantage program
manager cares a lot about whether my AAdvantage profile is up to date.
He doesn't want me to be given a window seat when I prefer an aisle, to
have the wrong kind of meal served to me, or to have me bumped off an
overbooked plane by mistake. So, the AAdvantage program manager
"owns" me. Now, with 32 million of us, chances are we're segmented in
some way, ideally, by household and travel frequency and/or geography.
The customer profile owner needs to devise ways to interact with recalci-
trant customers to ensure that their profile information is as accurate as
possible (or to delete them from the database or give them a default profile,
if the customer truly prefers to be anonymous!).

Now you have some basic business processes, with business events, and
you have customer information along with customer-profiling requirements. At this point you want to create your first-pass business object
model. Just lay all these concepts out and identify their interrelationships.
Start getting specific about the behaviors of different objects in different
circumstances (if a book is out of stock, alert the customer; if a customer
prefers a subcompact car but none is available, offer a compact at the same
price). Now you're capturing the business rules. Your information technology architects should have been involved all the way through the process
we've described so far. But this is where they will be able to begin to take
action. They can design an architecture from what you've created so far.
Remember, what you want is not an architecture for a Web site, although
that's certainly one of the things you're seeking; what you want is an archi-

tecture that will streamline customers' processes of doing business with you no matter what channel they choose to use to interact with your firm. The technical folks will love this challenge and this approach. It's so much more satisfying to them to have a big picture to start with and then break it down into manageable chunks than it is to constantly have to redo everything because no one took the time to think through the ramifications!

By now you've prioritized your actual technology initiatives. You probably started with the customer information system (a good idea, because that may take the longest to do, as we saw in Bell Atlantic's case). Then, no doubt, you have a game plan in mind, based on the areas of greatest pain or greatest opportunity, as to which interactive channel you're going to tackle first. Notice that both Bell Atlantic and Wells Fargo began with their call center operations. This enabled them to pull the customer information together, link in and/or redesign the necessary back-end systems, and evolve from the kind of user interface that only a trained customer service agent could deal with to one that an end customer could use. On the other hand, there's a lot to be said for starting with the Web. You can iterate quickly. And you can get very rapid feedback from customers. Amazon.com, the National Science Foundation, Tripod, and Cisco are the only examples I've covered here in detail that started on the Web. National Semiconductor already had a sales opportunity management system with a customer database as its starting point. So National Semi's Web efforts quickly converged with its sales systems and processes. Cisco, Dell, and the National Science Foundation had a lot of preexisting systems they had to integrate, as did PhotoDisc, from its CD-ROM business.

Don't forget that you need to build metrics into this process. You'll want to start with as much customer profitability and loyalty information as you can muster and set some realistic goals about what you're hoping to achieve. Don't expect instant success. Do expect to invest a fair amount of money and effort for two years before you reap the rewards. As you've seen from all these examples, getting e-business right is not just putting a pretty Web face onto a set of existing systems and processes. It involves rewiring most of your enterprise to support streamlined, customer-facing business processes!

What will the rewards be? If you do this right (and, remember, it's an iterative learning process), you should see payoffs pretty quickly in terms of reduced costs to serve a larger number of customers. Like Wells Fargo, each time you add more functionality, your costs per customer will go down. Like Dow Jones, National Semiconductor, and American Airlines, you should also begin to be able to target customers with offers or information about specific items they've asked to see. Your payoffs from customer retention, cross-selling, and upselling should be tangible within twenty-four to thirty-six months.

When should you start building community? You can plan your community initiatives at the outset, but you won't be ready to really foster community among your customers until you've built a high level of trust with each of them individually. That trust will come from paying attention to what they say and do and continuously improving their experience of doing business with you.

If you're ready to take action, come to our Web site (www.customers.com) and get your free *Customers.com Guidebook*. There you'll find a checklist for the business executive, a checklist for the technologist, and a description of a workshop you can run to jump-start the process of making it easier for customers to do business with you.

If I can help you on your journey, don't hesitate to contact me. My e-address is pseybold@customers.com.

Index

ABOUT THE AUTHOR

PATRICIA B. SEYBOLD is the founder and CEO of the Boston-based Patricia Seybold Group, a worldwide business and technology consulting firm. Its clients include Ameritech, Arthur Andersen, Clorox, Hewlett Packard, the International Monetary Fund, Microsoft, State Street Bank, and Warburg Pincus.